Best Bicycle Park & Rail Trails in Ontario

60 More*

Volume 2

OBT

*the rest of them

First Edition, 2023

paperback ISBN: 978-1-9991353-7-9
PDF file ISBN 978-1-9991353-8-6

No government funding was provided for this project.

All photos taken by Dan Roitner, unless otherwise noted
Extra photos courtesy of - Paulo LaBerge

Cartography map making & styling by Dan Roitner
*Basemap data credited to © OpenStreetMap contributors licensed as CC BY-SA and information licensed under the Open Government Licence Ontario.

Terms of Use

We hope you enjoy using this guide and have a great bike ride.
By using this guidebook, you agree to take on all risks and responsibilities.

This book is for informational purposes only. The author takes no responsibility for, nor guarantees the accuracy of, the content of this book. Efforts were made to be up-to-date, but trails and conditions do change frequently, so do not assume the information and maps to be accurate.

By using this published information, you agree we cannot be held liable for any injury, inconvenience, or financial loss that may occur while visiting any area mentioned or when dealing with any club, organization, or business listed in this book or on the OBT website.

Ride safely, and within your own skill level.
Always wear a helmet, be sure you can be seen,
and have lights at night.

Bike riding can be dangerous,
so
RIDE AT YOUR OWN RISK
but have
FUN, too!

Table of Contents

Ontario Reference Map

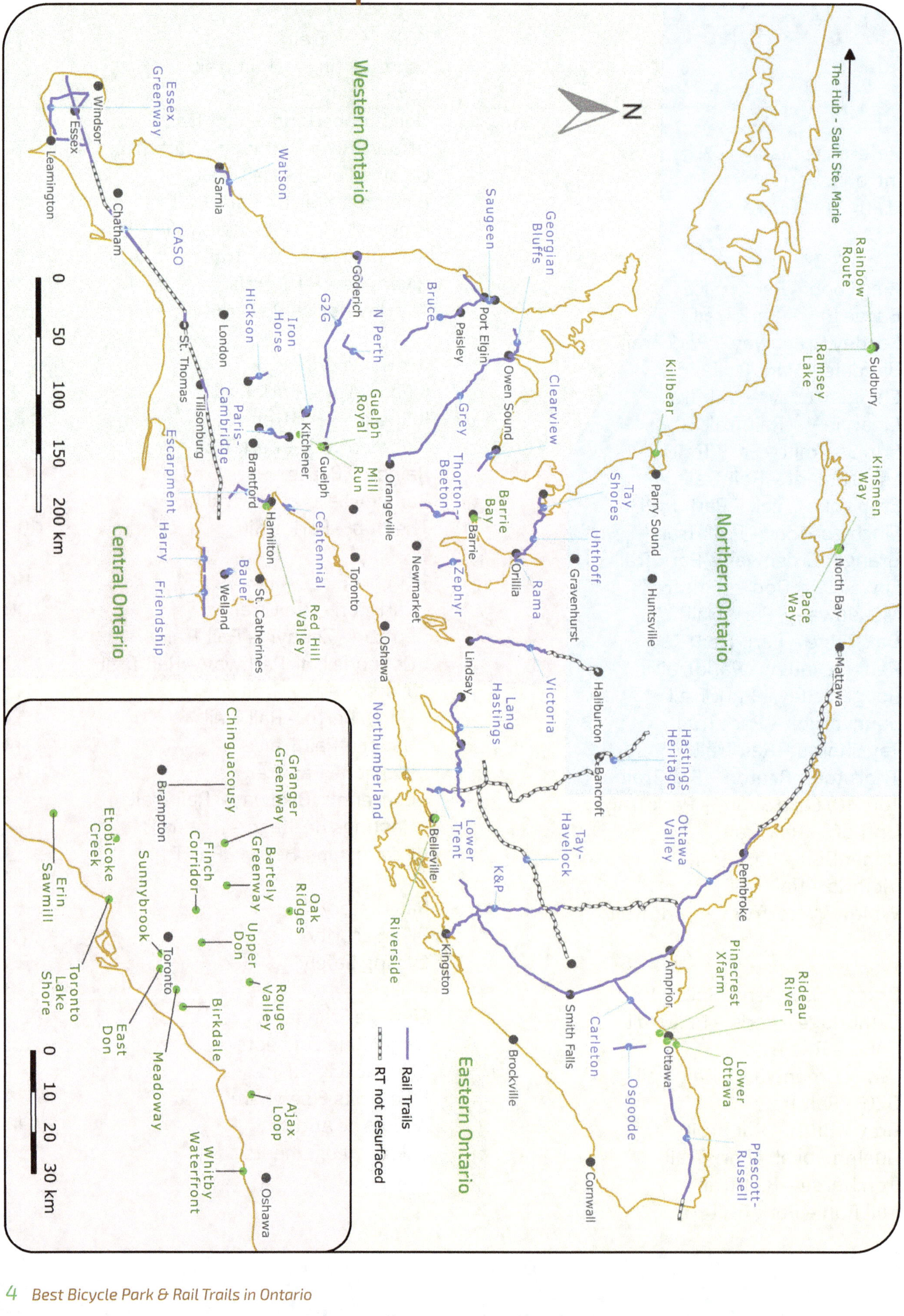

N

The Hub - Sault Ste. Marie

Western Ontario

Central Ontario

Northern Ontario

Eastern Ontario

Essex Greenway
Windsor
Essex
Leamington
Watson
Sarnia
Chatham
CASO
St. Thomas
Hickson
London
Tillsonburg
Iron Horse
G2G
Goderich
N Perth
Paris-Cambridge
Brantford
Kitchener
Guelph
Guelph Royal
Escarpment Harry Friendship
Hamilton
Bauer
St. Catherines
Welland
Centennial
Red Hill Valley
Saugeen
Georgian Bluffs
Paisley
Bruce
Port Elgin
Grey
Owen Sound
Clearview
Thorton
Beeton
Zephyr
Mill Run
Orangeville
Toronto
Newmarket
Oshawa
Northumberland
Killbear
Tay Shores
Parry Sound
Barrie Bay
Barrie
Orillia
Rama
Uhthoff
Gravenhurst
Huntsville
Victoria
Lindsay
Lang Hastings
Haliburton
Hastings Heritage
Bancroft
Ottawa Valley
Tay-Havelock
K&P
Belleville
Lower Trent
Riverside
Kingston
Brockville
Smith Falls
Cornwall
Rainbow Route
Ramsey Lake
Sudbury
Kinsmen Way
North Bay
Pace Way
Mattawa
Pembroke
Pinecrest Xfarm
Amprior
Carleton
Osgoode
Ottawa
Lower Ottawa
Rideau River
Prescott-Russell

Central Ontario (inset)

Chinguacousy
Granger Greenway
Brampton
Bartely Greenway
Finch Corridor
Upper Don
Oak Ridges
Etobicoke Creek
Erin Sawmill
Sunnybrook
Toronto
Toronto Lake Shore
East Don
Meadoway
Birkdale
Rouge Valley
Ajax Loop
Whitby Waterfront
Oshawa

0 10 20 30 km

0 50 100 150 200 km

— Rail Trails
RT not resurfaced

Introduction

Welcome to Volume 2 of Best Bicycle Park & Rail Trails in Ontario

Welcome to **Volume 2** of **Best Bicycle Park & Rail Trails in Ontario**, featuring more great bike rides for you to enjoy. Since **Volume 1** came out, I have searched province-wide to bring you these **60 exciting trails**. It's a collection of existing rides I've recently sampled and some **brand-new routes** ready for you to explore (some are still being extended and enhanced as of June 2023). And in many of these trail reviews, I've **added extra bonus routes.**

This **quick read** has all the essential details you need to find your next great riding adventure. I did the research so **you can spend more time in the saddle!**

After my first book, I realized that many would-be cyclists are reluctant to get on their bikes because **road traffic makes them nervous.** Well, you're in good hands with this book, as I have chosen routes that **avoid these hazards** as much as possible (cars, buses, trucks, ATVs). I've tried to minimize your chances of even seeing or hearing traffic.

You'll find a combination of **easy-going public park paths** and **more demanding long-distance rail trails**. All have trail signage so you can relax, follow the signs, and **seldom have to refer to a map.**

It's Gotta Be Fun on Two Wheels

My criteria for including a trail in my books are as follows:

1. Each bike path/trail needs to be at least **80% off the road** and a safe route.
2. Each route offers at least **a few hours of cycling enjoyment** and some sights to see.
3. Each trail is **self-directed, requiring minimal map use** (if any) because directional signage along the route will show you the way.

Now, with that said, a few worthy trails in interesting places like **Guelph, Hamilton, Sudbury,** and **Sault Ste. Marie**—do require a **little road riding,** due to geography and suburb development. I've included them anyway since they are great fun to ride, and often there are **bike lanes** to accommodate these gaps.

I do not list directions **every step of the way,** since there is **signage in place on every trail**. This is not that kind of cycling guide. I will help you with directions on any known gaps that are missing signs.

Phone map apps that use **GPS** are useful, but for most of these rides, you'll **only need GPS as a backup**—or a way to find where the closest patio is afterwards. I have thought of selling my GPS tracks as an additional aid for my book. If I find a way to tie that in with a phone app, I'll let you know on my website.

Each review has a **checkbox** so you can keep track of which ones you've done. I've heard of cyclists who have challenged themselves to ride them all. Sounds like a fun goal and a great way to get exercise and see Ontario. Maybe there should be T-shirts.

Every trail in this book is free to ride, and most of the parking lots I suggest are free, too. (It doesn't hurt to be thrifty.)

Did you know that 15% of the bike rides I scout you never hear about? No need for you to read about the duds.

You can refer to my website **ontariobiketrails.com** for any current changes or other **official trail, tourism, and weather websites** to plan your outings.

Covid was Good for Cycling

Strange as that sounds, the past pandemic (that we want to forget) had positive outcomes for cycling. Our sport got an unexpected **boost in ridership** for two summers. Suddenly the trails were full of traffic, both longtime cyclists and new riders, all looking for ways to get out of the house and safely get some exercise/ see the sky again. Even lonely Rail trails had riders on them.

All levels of government took note of the numbers and began putting plans and money forward to i**mprove and expand trail networks.** The Ontario bike scene has changed dramatically since. There has been an increasing flurry of building activity, and I hope it continues. (To be fair, some of these are old initiatives that have finally been funded.)

Here in **Toronto**, where I live, new bike lanes have appeared on city roads (after much hesitation) and it's happening in **Ottawa, Guelph, Kitchener** … even **Sudbury** is waking up. Street **bike lanes** are not what I cover, but their presence is a good indication of attitudes **shifting away from a car-only mentality.** I think these are encouraging developments for the world of cycling. My trip last year in **Holland, Denmark,** and **Scandinavia** showed me **how far behind we are and how good it can get.**

Trail Construction Process

When **recreational trails** are on public land, and various levels of **government move slowly** to complete projects, **it can take years for a usable path to be built.**

First, both **cycling activists** and the **government** must think **the concept is of value** to the voting public. Ideally, **local business interests** will also be on board. (Not a bad thing, just saying there are many motives at play.)

If all in are agreement, you would think this could be a very simple thing to implement. However, usually, it's not. Meetings will be held and studies will be made to assess and debate every aspect of a proposed trail: **zoning, access, land ownership, environmental issues, economic development forecasts, etc.**

Money has to be allocated and is rarely available immediately. It can take a few more years to find funds in the budget and begin spending on construction. This is why long trails, or those with bridges, are often **built in smaller segments over many years.**

There also needs to be a **future yearly maintenance plan/budget.** Brush and tree limbs need periodic trimming, while fallen trees and river washouts will need immediate attention. Heavy rain and use can create, over time, uneven terrain that requires grading. Potholes and puddles necessitate filling, as does asphalt which can crack, bulge, and heave from frost.

In researching trails for this book, I noticed that **many official** websites are slow to post their good deeds. The lack of **accurate, current info** is common. This made it aggravating for me to complete the book—yet it's just **another reason why this book is needed.**

Volume 2 -
More Trails to Keep You Moving

There is **not an infinite amount** of trails in Ontario. Between my first volume and this one, **I've covered most**, if not all, of the existing ones that are worth doing. That said, new trails and paths are always being planned, and there will be more built in the future.

A few of the trails in this book—**East Don River, Meadoway**, and **Bartley Greenway**—are so new they still have a year or two until completion. Other existing trails, like **Etobicoke Creek, Granger Greenway,** and **Oak Ridge**, are getting expanded in length and improved. And even more abandoned **Rail Trails are being transformed** into friendly bikeways, including **Ottawa Valley, Thornton-Beeton, Bruce-Saugeen, Grey, and CASO.**

The pandemic **limited my ability to scout trails** for a few years, and I had some bad weather days. So, as much as I was proud to state in the last two books that **I had ridden all the trails**, there are a few exceptions in this one. There are good rides in **North Bay and Windsor** that I have not fully experienced, but I wanted to "put them on the map" and **encourage you to visit.**

The solution was to interview some nice local cyclists for their impressions and get them to take a few photos.

Producing this Book

My last book was met with much interest, and I always planned to do this follow-up to make the set complete. I am now retired and at the beginning of the year ,I eased into production mode with some trepidation, knowing **it was a HUGE project.** As **a self-publisher**, I do just about everything to produce my books. I took a few bike-riding breaks, but nearly **every day for six months** was devoted to this project. (And that's after I saved a month of rendering time configuring my mapping program with a spatial database.)

It has all been written by me, the long, human, natural way. And done **without the help of AI bots**, although as a **slow typer**, I had some success with voice typing (dictation) to move things along, and I do benefit from spell-checking tools for sure. **Jen, my book editor**, has been wonderful to work with, as before.

There is a grin I wear when I think of all my English teachers who thought **I was hopeless.** How'd I do? **Let me know your thoughts** on this book, or cycling in general, at staff@ontariobiketrails.com

I should add that **my opinions are not swayed.** I am **not sponsored or supported by anyone**. Not that I wouldn't mind a **book grant** to help fund my time, but alas, this category of informational nonfiction does not qualify for arts funding. You would think because I do so much **free promotion** for Ontario tourism and the welfare of its people, someone might reach out—not yet.

I truly hope you **enjoy my efforts** (and pay for them). It's been another labour of love and I've **enjoyed the journey**, for the most part, from scouting trails on my bicycle to the long hours hammering out copy.

May these rides bring you, in turn, **many hours of pleasure on the byways of Ontario.** Between the two Park & Rail volumes and my MTB book, that's **180 trail destinations** to pick from! Plenty to keep you interested, healthy, and happy.

Lube that chain and start crankin'!

Dan Roitner - senior cycling statesman

*...and **leave your own bike ride** review on my site. We all want to know how it went.*

Using This Guide

Definition of Trail Listings

Reading these comments will aid you in understanding the format of my reviews

Trail Names: If the name of a trail has been established, is commonly known, and encompasses the length of the ride I am suggesting for the review, **then I'll use it**. More often than I would wish, picking a trail name for one of my rides **gets problematic.**

In our world of change and expansion, a smaller trail may get extended and called a new name. Many times it may be given **multiple names** if it goes through more than one neighbourhood, township, or county. This gets confusing. Which name should I use for my review (if any)? Other times there is more than one name for the same trail or nothing imaginative, just a default plain, generic one. ("Centennial" is so overused!)

In the end, **my trail names are a compromise**: I try to give names that encompass the trail's entire length and are **short and easy to remember**. Some routes are of my own making, and I've chosen a name for them. **There is a checkbox by the name to use when you complete the trail ride.**

Length: Trail length is **one way only**, rounded up in **kilometres**, and based on estimation, as the earth is round, maps are flat, and hilly terrain can add more length, all complicating the total. And it seems every source posts a **different number,** which does not help.

My **percentages reflect what I think are the portions of the trail** on different terrain and any time spent crossing roads, following detours, and riding side streets to make a connection back onto paths.

Elevation: Routes along waterways are going to have a gradual incline. Along bodies of water, they tend to be flat. This book has a few more hills to the rides to give you some exercise, but **nothing overwhelming.**

Rail trails inherit old rail beds that were **kept as level as possible**, with wide turns. This design kept trains from slowing down too often.

Terrain: Singletrack is a hiking path defined as a soil path the width of one person. **Doubletrack** is a soil

path the width of a pickup truck, as the wear in the path comes from two wheel ruts in the ground.

A **Park trail or path** (I use both words for pretty much the same thing) is around **two metres wide** to allow traffic both ways. Park paths in the city are certain to be **paved almost all the time**, but occasionally have a **crushed stone base in sections.**

Rail trails may be **paved** with asphalt when going through a community, but will most often feature a **finely crushed stone base.** I may also describe this base as **limestone screening** or **crushed gravel**; it's all the same material texture used to resurface these paths.

Skill : A basic **rating on how much cycle skill and experience you should have** to ride the route. **It is not based on the endurance** you need to ride the full distance. Most reviews are rated as "**Easy beginner,**" meaning anyone who can stay balanced on a bike can manage the path. Factoring in the trail terrain, elevation changes, and lack of good signage may bump up the rating to **Intermediate** or an **Advanced** ride.

Maps: All the trails I've reviewed have some signage, but the **amount and clarity** to keep you on track varies. Most have a **map board at the trailhead**, to give you an overall sense of the route, and other signs placed along the way. I will mention how well the directional signs work and if you need to use your own map for reference.

No one gives out paper maps at the gate anymore. I am ok with you making a paper photocopy of my maps for your personal use on the trail. There are many **map phone apps** you can use to **track your progress** and find your position. **GPS is a free (weak) satellite signal** that needs a **clear line of sight** to the sky to work. If unsure how well your **phone data signal** is out in the country, **download your basemaps before leaving home.**

Traffic: These are **clues as to what kind of other typical users you will encounter** on the trail. Besides cyclists, city paths have lots of joggers, walkers/hikers, their dogs and kids in tow, and sometimes rollerbladers. Give them a wide berth. Some pay little attention to cyclists, so calling out or sounding your bell helps.

Country Rail trails will have less traffic, and nearly none on the remote sections, but there is the added chance of crossing paths with an **ATV, dirt biker, or horse.** Pulling over and letting them pass works for me. A **deer, moose, or bear encounter** in the wilds of Ontario is rare but possible if they don't hear you coming. Otherwise, a **bear bell** or chatter will alert them to move on.

And if you are hardy enough to **ride in the winter**, meeting a Nordic skier, snowshoer, or snowmobile is possible. Checking the trail entrance signage will tell you who is permitted to use the route. This can change at various sections on a long trail.

Also, keep in mind that **every path in this book is bi-directional, so pay attention.**

Facilities:
To help you plan your day, I list the **extra amenities** and **comforts available** on the trail or nearby, such as parking choices, availability of toilets/ outhouses, picnic benches, playgrounds, rain shelters, water fountains, bike repair stations, and places to eat, lodge, and camp. There are blue markers **on my maps** to point you in the general direction.

If you are heading out **leading a group or with your kids**, it's good to know exactly where these things are before the ride.

Highlights:
Here I list what **interesting sights** you could see on the route and **tourist attractions** you could do during the ride or after.

Trail Fee
- With the **exception** of a day pass to enter **Killbear Provincial Park**, all trails in this book are **free.** So I have omitted this heading for this volume.

Phone:
If there is a phone number listed it is likely a **general inquiry line** to tourism services, city hall, or a parks or conservation regional office.

Website:
I list the **name of the website** for you to **do a search**. Not the actual website addresses, which can be long and have been known to change over time.

Similar Trails:
For **comparison's sake,** I list a few similar bike rides near the one being reviewed. This may help you judge if you'll like this one and/or **help you find others to try.**

Local Clubs:
If there are any bicycle clubs in the area, I list them, since they often have good intel on what you can ride in the area. Clubs tend to be **road-focused,** but often try to **incorporate any off-road trails** in their routes. And it's a great way to **meet like-minded cyclists, make new friends,** and **get inspired** to get out more often and **challenge yourself.**

Access:
All the trails can have **many possible start points.** A linear path will have a ⊕ symbol for an **address at the end of the trail.** On a loop you can start anywhere, so there are no beginning or end points.

I have listed parking lot addresses that **Google Maps** gave ; **if you search that address,** it should show you where they are. A bold capital **P** and a number list locations that are a good starting point. Most are **public and free** lots to park your car. Some may have **closing hours** and a parking fee.

Unfortunately, not all trail builders have supplied places to park. At times you will need to find **street parking.** This has never been a problem for me, but **choose wisely.** A quiet side street or shoulder on a side road away from traffic is best. A **public community centre or arena** can be another good choice. A mall parking lot is a little risky.

If you **hide your valuables and lock up,** all should be fine when you return. I have yet to encounter issues.

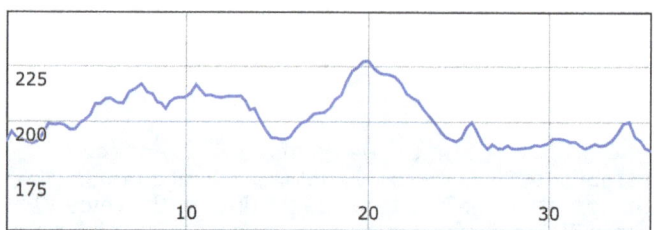

Elevation Graphs:
These are a snapshot of the rise and fall of each trail shown within a **metre range in elevation,** over the **distance in kilometres.**

Routes on the graph run from **left to right** in a **west-to-east** or **south-to-north** for **vertical routes** to sync with the maps. A **loop** will mention a starting point for the **left side of the graph.**

Keep in mind the **length of the trail when comparing.** A Rail trail can slope up over a distance of 20 km and look like the Alps when in actual fact **it will be very gradual.**

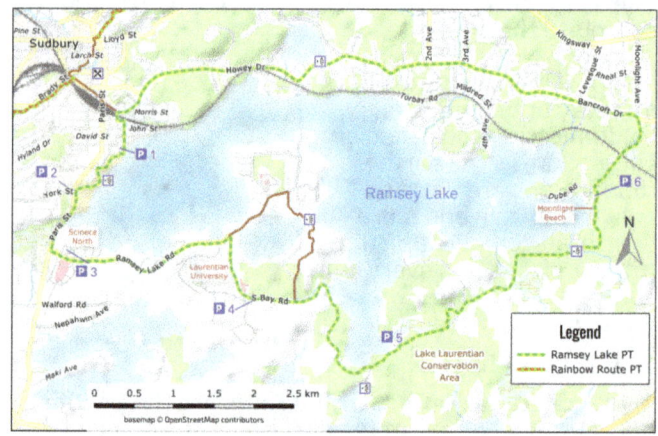

Route Maps:
This gives a wide perspective of the whole trail. Map making is a compromise to fit the whole route in with **enough details,** yet not clutter. An **interactive map on your screen** where you can zoom in & out will reveal a lot more detail.

You can do this on my **OBT website** - ontariobiketrails.com or use other **mapping services** to study the areas. **Aerial and Streetview photos** are a good resource, but check when the photo was taken, as some are **several years old.**

I have switched from showing road names to using road signs with highway numbers. A bonus for you is that I've **added other bike trails from my first book** to

N

the maps. This can help you see how close other trails are. Some trails are so new that I show sections still **under construction** or being resurfaced (as of 2023).

The north arrow icon on the map points to **true north,** not magnetic north. The distance **scale bar is divided into kilometres.**

I made these maps with the utmost care, yet they may have errors and should **not be used as your sole means of navigation. Don't bet your life on them!**

Reviews: Over the years I have gotten better at covering all the important points riders care about. This text should give you an all-around feel as to the **quality and characteristics** of each trail and how the ride experience panned out for me.

I start each trail ride I scout with an open mind and have **no expectations**. I take in the journey and try to **evaluate it as how an average weekend Park cyclist** might experience it.

In some locations I have little to say, while in others I could write pages. I always try to mention any interesting tourist sights. Extra side trails you could add to your day/ride are **brown text.**

As tempting as it is to add **specific names** of recommended places to eat or stay at, this gets complicated and too involved this time around. **But I'd love to hear of any that work out for you.**

Train History: I think a little history about the rail lines you ride on will **help colour your imagination as you pedal. Think of the hardships** to cut a path through the wilderness and lay track.

All the **noisy, busy trains** that moved along these trails before you are now ghosts in the past as you take in the sunshine. The iron rails are gone, but some buildings and bridges remain. **Can you spot them?**

I have included for the book a short summary of what I could dig up on each line. Sometimes it was just a **simple connection to other places,** while other routes had plenty of history and the text flowed on past the page to the back of the book. It's all part of a **fascinating bygone era.**

Photos: I took **most of the photos** that are used. I feel you need to have a cyclist in most of them to give **interest and scale to an image.** Readers need to be able to **see themselves riding** those bikeways. I have gotten good at taking them on the go and pulling a few still frames from my GoPro videos.

As you may guess, many of the subjects in the pix are friends, my son Trevor, and my wife Teresa, who have learned to be patient. The **weather does not always cooperate** by giving me blue sky days like in travel brochures. A few photos were added by others to replace my bad-weather pix (credit noted where used).

There is a **limit in page space**, and I seem to write more than I used to, lol. **Visit my website to see more pictures.** As much as I try to encapsulate what it is like to be there, photos have their limitations. **You just have to be there to get the ambience.**

All of these **strands of information** should lead you to weave an **overall impression** so you have a good chance to discern whether what I am recommending is what you are looking to ride. **Enjoy the outings!** I am glad to share them, knowing others will enjoy these routes as I did.

Start making plans today!

Legend

residential	industrial
Retail	hospital
Industrial	retail, food
Commercial	Lodging
grassland	transport
meadow	parking
farmland	⊢—⊣ railway track
orchard	Freeway
cemetery	ramp
quarry	HWY
landfill	arterial
pitch	collector
recreation ground	local street
school, education	local strata
woodlot, forest	Alleyway
park	P Parking
reservoir, pool	⚻ Toilets
heath, scrub	⊠ Eats
buildings	◁ Views

P Locations of suggested public parking (often free)

⚻ Location of toilets or outhouses on the route

⊠ Location of nearby food stores and restaurants (which have toilets, so I do not mention this twice)

◁ Location of a place of interest, significant feature or lookout

Ajax Loop – Park Trail

Ajax

Length - 15 km (loop)

80% park path

20% roadways & crossings

Elevation - Small rises and dips to keep it interesting, one large hill

Terrain - Wide, paved path; small bridges

Skill - Easy

Maps - No map boards. Not a lot of trail markers; could use more.

Traffic - Cyclists, walkers, joggers, dogs, kids

Facilities - Parking lot, toilets, benches, picnic tables, fitness stations

Highlights - It's a loop! Wetlands, open spaces, quiet, eateries close by

Phone - 905 683 4550

Website - Town of Ajax

Similar Trails - Rouge Valley, Upper Etobicoke, Nokiidaa

Local Clubs - Toronto Bicycle Network - TBN

Access - It's a loop, so you can start anywhere. Any quiet side street should be fine to park on. I only found 2 parking lots by the trail. These are good starting points.

P1 Millers Creek Park - the lot off 275 Westney Rd N, Ajax
P2 McLean Com. Centre, 95 Magill Dr, Ajax

Graph starts at P1 on the map

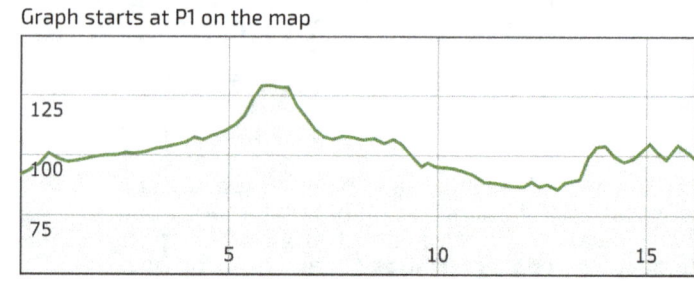

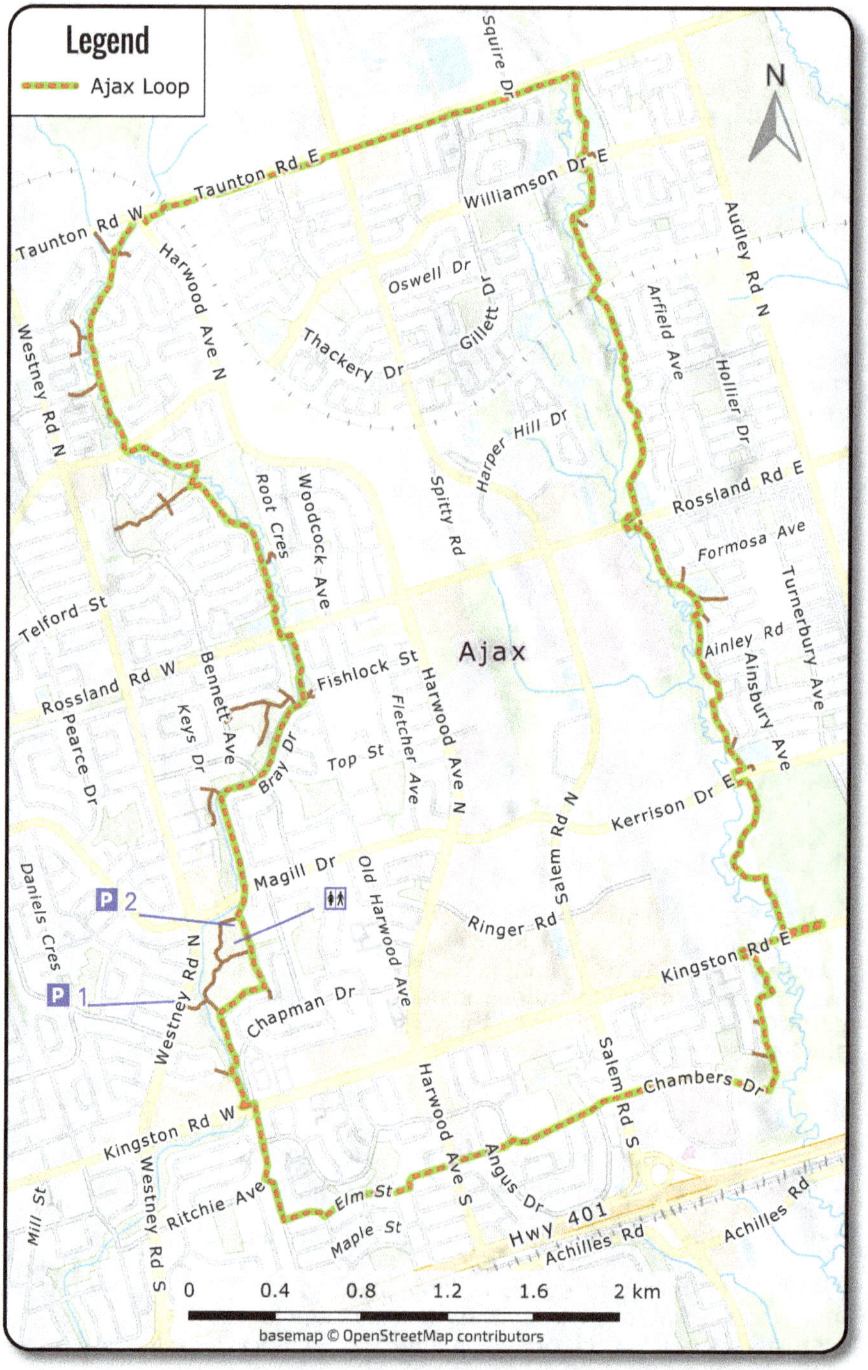

Review:

Out in the suburbs of **Ajax**, there is a **15 km** bicycle loop that's perfect for a **leisurely cruise**. This path winds along small creeks behind neighbourhood backyards and through quiet city parkland. It's a joy for all to cycle with friends on a lazy afternoon.

I first rode this area when it was **undeveloped** and not too pretty. Over the years **vegetation has filled in**, a few signs have been erected, and paths got paved. Fifteen years later, it's grown in and ready to ride, so read on.

Much of the path is in the open, making this a **sunny ride** with not many shady trees, so get out the sunscreen. But there is plenty to see as you coast.

Fields of tall grasses and shrubs give you **views of shallow valleys** where a paved path winds across the creek, back and forth over bridges. The route meanders enough to keep it fun and interesting.

Everyone loves a bike loop, so I actually combined two creek bike paths to create a loop for you (though you could also just do one creek and double back). A separate bike path along **Taunton Rd E** at the north end connects the two park trails.

There are not a lot of parking lots to start from on this ride. You can find street parking or take your chances and park at a mall. I started at **Millers Creek Park** and headed north, then east over to **Carruthers Creek** and back down.

Once you reach **Kingston Rd,** there's a bike lane going west to get you back to **Chapman Dr,** but why would you take it? The traffic is thick, right beside you and you can do without the car noise.

Consider crossing over the road and following the creek a little further south to where it ends at **Chambers Dr.**

Here you will **head west**, then jog north for **about 3 km** through **quiet side streets** to complete the loop. This will require referring to a map as there are a **lot of ways to get to Ritchie Ave**, whereupon you **head north** to cross **Kingston Rd** again to pick up the park trail.

(From Chambers Dr, I continued on to Mandrake St, then left on Doric St, which turns into Ontario St and then becomes Windsor Ave. Then west on Elm St, another right on Beatty Rd, and then north on Knapton Ave.)

See, **you need a map**, and the rest of the route in the park isn't that well signed. But cycling intuition will tell you to keep to the creek path and not take any side connector trails up into neighbourhoods.

This loop offers many spots to stop, sit, and ponder life or spot wildlife. There are also many food outlets nearby to pick from—and patios to enjoy after your ride.

(In the last few years there has been sometimes flooding behind the ***Ajax casino/race track**, likely from a beaver dam. I am told that there will be a permanent fix in 2023 and no more detours.)*

Barrie Bay – Park Trail

Barrie

Length - 9.4 = 6.4 +3 km (one way)

85% park path
5% hiking trail
10% road riding, detours

Elevation - Flat along water's edge; short, easy climbs

Terrain - Paved path, RT is crushed stone, bridges, (wet) dirt path on extension

Skill - Easy

Maps - Map boards, trail markers, painted centre line

Traffic - Cyclists, rollerbladers, walkers (have separate paths half the time)

Facilities - Parking lot, toilets, benches, picnic tables, rain shelter, food & lodging nearby

Highlights - Views across the water, city vibe, downtown, beaches, train station

Phone - 705 726 4242

Website - City of Barrie, Barrie by Bike

Similar Trails - Orillia waterfront (part of the Uhthoff RT),   Ajax Waterfront Hamilton Beach

Local Clubs - Barrie Cycling Club

Access - The good news is there is plenty of parking around the bay. The bad part is most of it is $10 an hour. The north end has a few lots that are cheaper. For free parking, your best strategy is to park away on a side street and ride to the waterfront.

⊕**P1** 79 Lennox Park - Widgeon St
P2 Minet's Point Park - 10 Lismer Blvd
P3 Southshore Centre - 205 Lakeshore Dr
P4 Centennial Beach - Victoria & Lakeshore
P5 Heritage Park - 5 Simcoe St
P6 Johnson Beach - 6 Johnson St
⊕Penetanguishene Rd

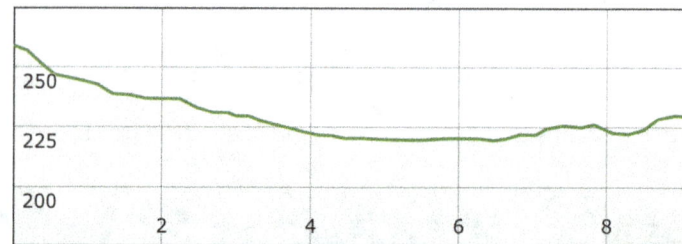

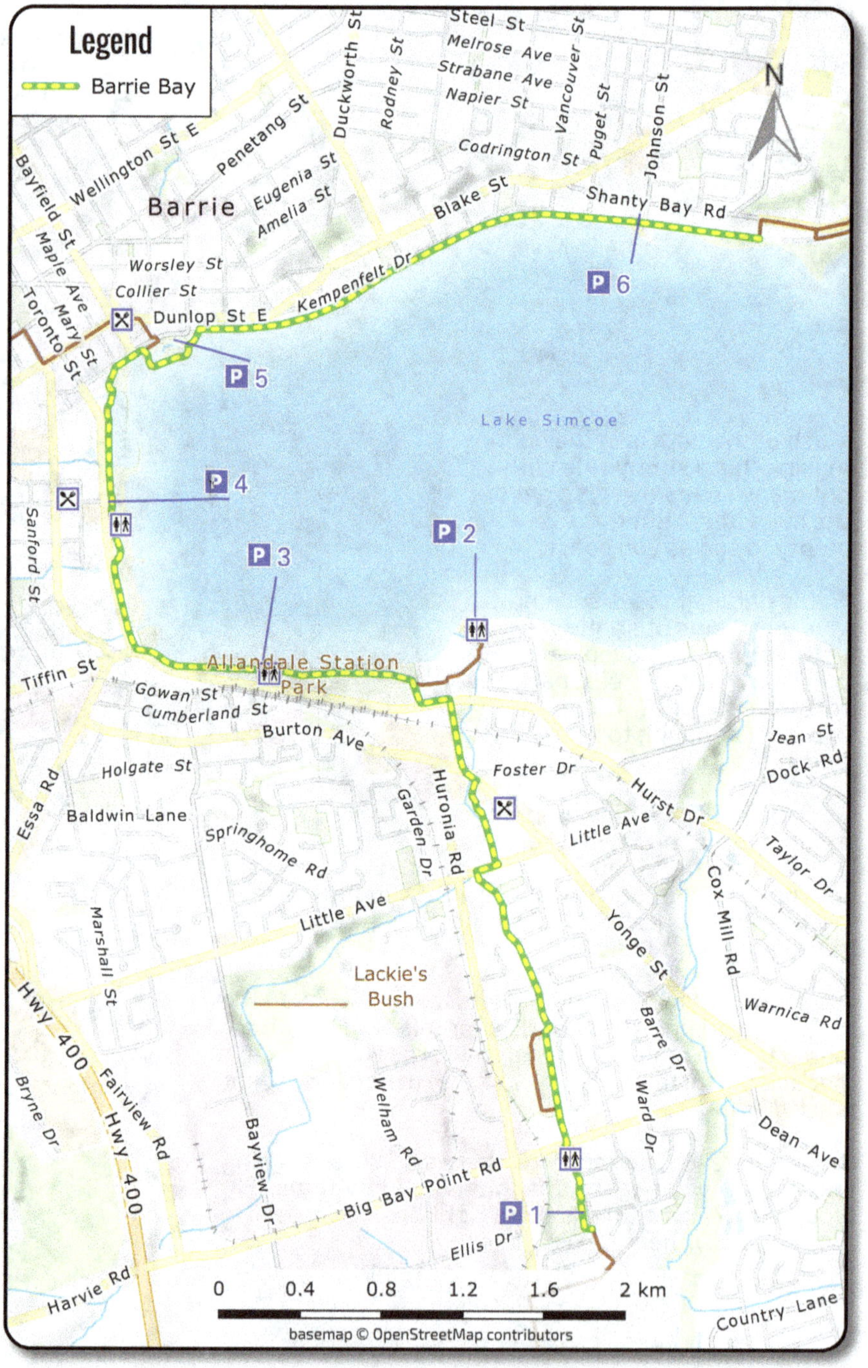

Legend
— Barrie Bay

basemap © OpenStreetMap contributors

Review:

The ever-growing city of **Barrie** has developed a **6.4 km** waterfront bike trail that's fun to cruise on a hot summer day. This is a short ride around **Kempenfelt Bay**, on the west side of **Lake Simcoe**. Unfortunately, Barrie has no other long off-road riding I can see, so I have added an optional extra **3 km** to it heading south to make it a longer route.

My **Barrie Bay** route passes by **parkland, beaches,** and a **marina** and continues onto a **rail trail**. Also, because it starts away from the beachfront, you may be able to find some free parking. The lots at the waterfront are very expensive ($10/hr).

My brother and I started from the south end at **Lennox Park.** The bike path going straight up to the bay was not well marked, a surprise considering this is part of the **Trans Canada Trail**. Nor was the terrain always easy to manage.

Willoughby Park was soggy going; you may wish to circumvent it by riding around the block instead. Granted, we rode it at the beginning of May, after a week of rain.

We had to **use a map** and you will, too, to get to the water as half of it was road riding. (There were some bike lanes.)

The paved waterfront path starts just west of **Minet's Point Rd** and **Lakeshore Dr**, taking you into a woodlot where we were fortunate to see a giant woodpecker.

You will notice at this point the **Allandale GO station** stop, perfectly located for those who might take the train up from **Toronto.**

Soon enough you are out of the woods on to basic manicured parkland (I'd wish for more trees and flower beds). Large **metal sculptures** along the way may grab your attention. They're not all art: the smaller ones are fitness workout stations that will give you more exercise than this short spin.

You'll also find benches, a playground, volleyball players, fast food options, sailors out on the water, and sun worshippers lounging about, taking in the rays.

An **outer path** designated for cyclists goes around the bay. On the south side, the path is shared with walkers. The **dividing line** is a welcome concept but makes the bike part a little too narrow for bikes to pass each other.

The rest of the way, walkers have the **best views** on the inner path closest to the shore. It's not always clearly marked where you can ride on "their" path. A brief detour to the edge for a peek is fine, but you may get dirty looks if you ride too far on the walkers' side, as pedestrians easily outnumber cyclists.

As you round the bay to the north bank, **downtown Barrie** is only one block up on **Dunlop St.** Go for a bite and walkabout if inclined.

Once **Heritage Park** ends, your trail changes to a fine crushed stone path. I like this more natural stretch to **Johnson's Beach,** in the shade of a tree-lined rail trail. Actually, the bay's waterfront had train tracks running around it once, but now, only the **train station remains.**

Easy going, as rail trails tend to be, this is the beginning of a much longer route if you detour on the road for about **2 km** to connect with the **28 km Oro - Medonte RT** that goes over into **Orillia.**

Here is where I'll mention again the better known, and much larger, **Simcoe RT loop.** Look it up—it's a great weekend two- to three-day ride.

Whether you're passing through or staying a while in **Barrie**, check the events calendar before your visit. There is always something going on by the water, so you can time your ride to a festival, race, concert, market, art show, fireworks, or whatever you fancy. (Then there will be no parking at any price.)

The **GO Train** can take you from Toronto to **Barrie's Allandale** waterfront, right where you need to be.

Bartley Greenway – Park Trail

GTA - Vaughan

Length - 15 km (one way)

80% park path
20% road crossings, detours

Elevation - Flat along the creek, with short climbs to street-level crossings.

Terrain - Half is paved or concrete slab; the rest is crushed stone with no large rocks; a few bridges. a little hillier than one expects following a creek.

Skill - Easy to Intermediate

Maps - New, well-posted map boards; trail markers

Traffic - Not busy, especially the north end; typical path users

Facilities - Parking lots, benches, picnic tables, rain shelter, toilets on the south end

Highlights - Keffer Marsh, 12+ small ponds, interpretive signs on the route, look for wildlife

Phone - 905 832 2281

Website - City of Vaughan

Similar Trails - Oak Ridge, Morrison Valley,   Oshawa Creek

Local Clubs - Toronto Bicycling Network - TBN

Access - You can find parking at:

⊕ **P4** Ross Lord Park - 4777 Dufferin St, four large lots
P3 Dufferin Clark Community Centre - 1441 Clark Ave W
P2 Langstaff EcoPark - Langstaff Rd & Planchet Rd
P1 Mackenzie Glen Park - 220 Cranston Park Ave
⊕ Teston Rd & Cranston Park Ave

GO station in Vaughan is nearby. On the south end, the Finch Hydro Corridor bike path can get you there.

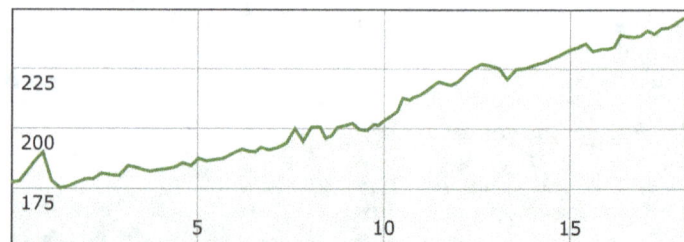

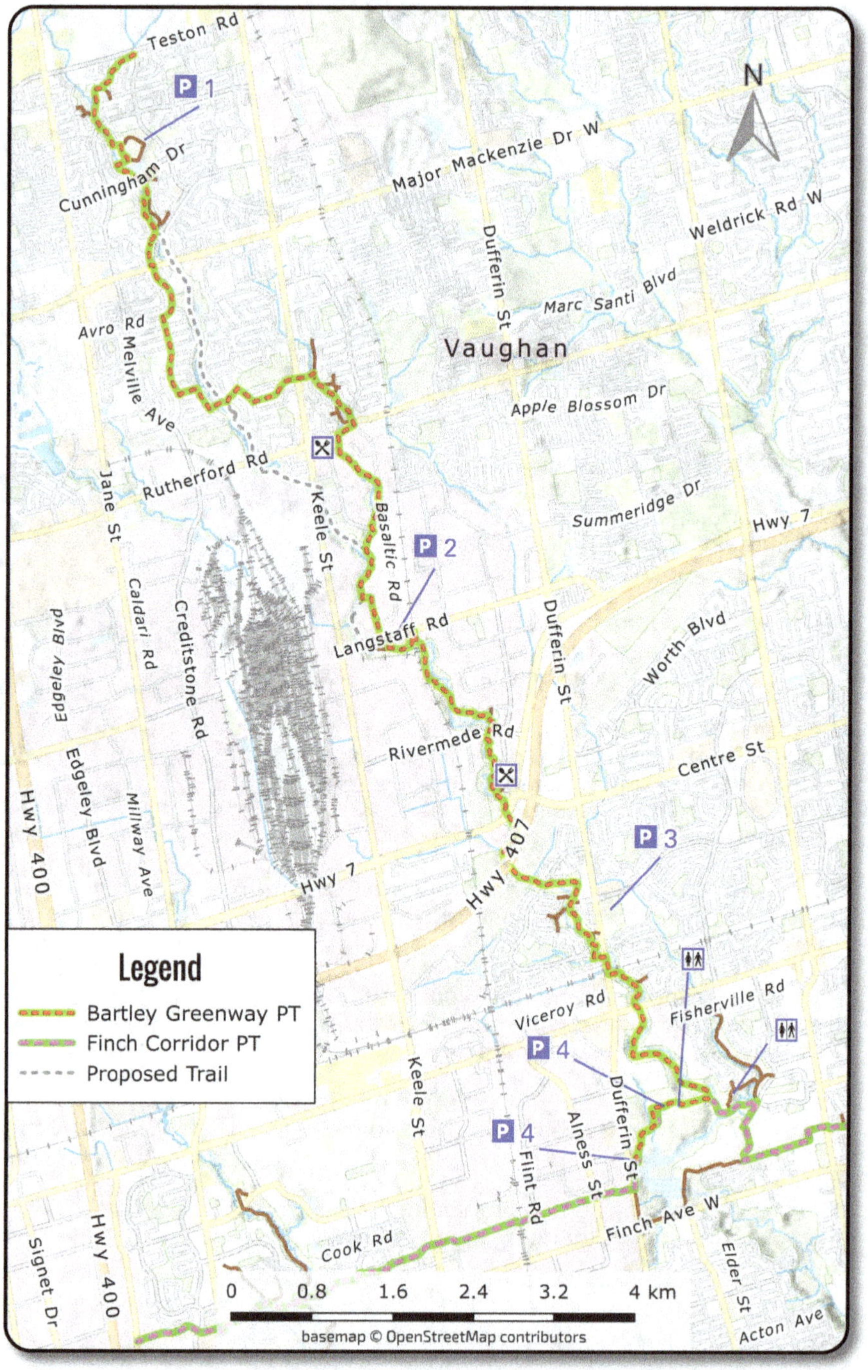

Legend

━━━ Bartley Greenway PT
━━━ Finch Corridor PT
╌╌╌ Proposed Trail

basemap © OpenStreetMap contributors

Review:

The **Bartley Smith Greenway** (BSG) is a **15 km** park path in **Vaughan**, a suburb **northwest of Toronto**. This trail heads north following the source of the **West Don River**.

I recently revisited the route and found little changed except for new signage. It offers an **enjoyable ride** with a variety of open parkland and natural wooded scenery and a few **more hills** than one would expect for a riverside trail.

We started our day by parking in **G. Ross Lord Park** above the reservoir. I included this **2 km** paved **Hidden Trail** section to get you to **Steeles Ave,** a busy road with few opportunities to park or breaks in traffic to cross. For safety, I recommend using the lights at the corner. The official start of the **Bartley Greenway** is on the other side of these six lanes.

Your other major crossing will be **Dufferin St**, where you can go under the train tracks and across another wide road at the lights. If you can spot it, there is a tunnel under **Glen Shields Ave** which continues north on a concrete trailway to the pond, a lovely, tranquil setting to stop at (one of five along the way).

Once you are crossing under **Hwy 407,** the path turns to **crushed limestone**. Some call it stone dust, or is it limestone screening? Is not a problem for most riders, just watch your turns, as there are pockets of loose grit.

The city has paved most of the sloping portions of the pathway with asphalt, a thoughtful addition, and **added new signs** that answer a lot of directional questions for cyclists.

When you cross over **Rivermede Rd**, down you go again for about **1.5 km** through a secluded ravine. Right away there is a deck with a bench overlooking a pond, an ideal snack stop. Further up at **Langstaff Rd**, Metrolinx has been working on track repairs for years (soon to be finished), and you may be asked to detour.

Another project in the works will be a **more direct 5 km path** following the west branch of the creek to **McNaughton Rd**. This will be a major addition and a welcome off-the-road ravine connection to the northern section when done. Exciting stuff!

While we wait for that, there are still a few road detours. This one is through an industrial area, which is quiet on weekends. Jog west, then north, on **Planchet Rd** to the end and look west for the ravine valley entrance. This path seems less used heading north and perhaps would not be as appealing on your own, in the dark, on a full moon, when the wolves are howling.

For whatever reason, the path goes up a wooden ramp to **Basaltic Ave** ever so briefly, then takes you down into the ravine again. Odd, but fun.

At **Rutherford Rd**, cross to connect with the last **1 km** through residential parkland to see your **fifth pond.** Or head west to discover assorted fast-food options at a mall.

The **Bartley trail 2.5 km northern section** requires a long **3 km detour** ('til they build that west branch path I mentioned) to see seven more small ponds! If you choose to do it, it is well marked on side streets with the familiar **BSG green and brown signage** that you would have seen on the trail, all the way to **Teston Rd.**

The **Bartley Smith Greenway** will eventually connect to the proposed Vaughan Super Trail loop which will offer more than **100 km** of riding. But for now, this is **Vaughan's longest park path**, a worthy jaunt on a summer's day all on its own, for those living **north of Toronto.**

Birkdale – Park Trail

Toronto - Scarborough

Length - 5 + 2 + 10 km (one way)

75% park path
10% hiking trail
15% road crossings, detours

Elevation - Mainly a flat, meandering park path with a few short hills

Terrain - Paved on the main routes, some dirt and gravel sections, many bridges

Skill - Easy rolling for most of the route

Maps - A few signs; needs more/better signage to avoid having to stop and check your map

Traffic - Not busy; typical city path users.

Facilities - Parking lots, toilets, benches, picnic tables, rain shelter, playgrounds, shopping mall on the east end

Highlights - Pioneer homes, pleasant parkland route, no outstanding features, just an average city park path.

Phone - 311

Website - City of Toronto

Similar Trails - Upper Humber River,   Taylor Creek, Upper Humber

Local Clubs - Toronto Bicycle Network - TBN

Access - Parking lot start points:

⊕**P1** Birkdale Community Centre - 1299 Ellesmere Rd
P2 Birkdale Park - 1101 Brimley Rd
P3 Thomson Memorial Park - 1011 Brimley Rd
⊕**P4** Cedarbrook Community Centre - 91 Eastpark Blvd
⊕**P5** Knob Hill - 625 Brimley Rd

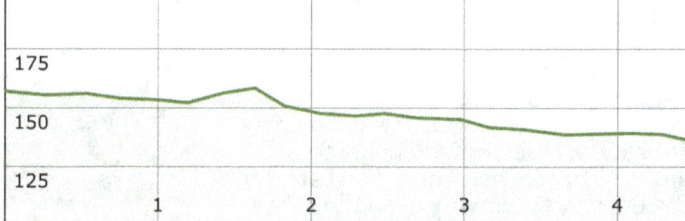

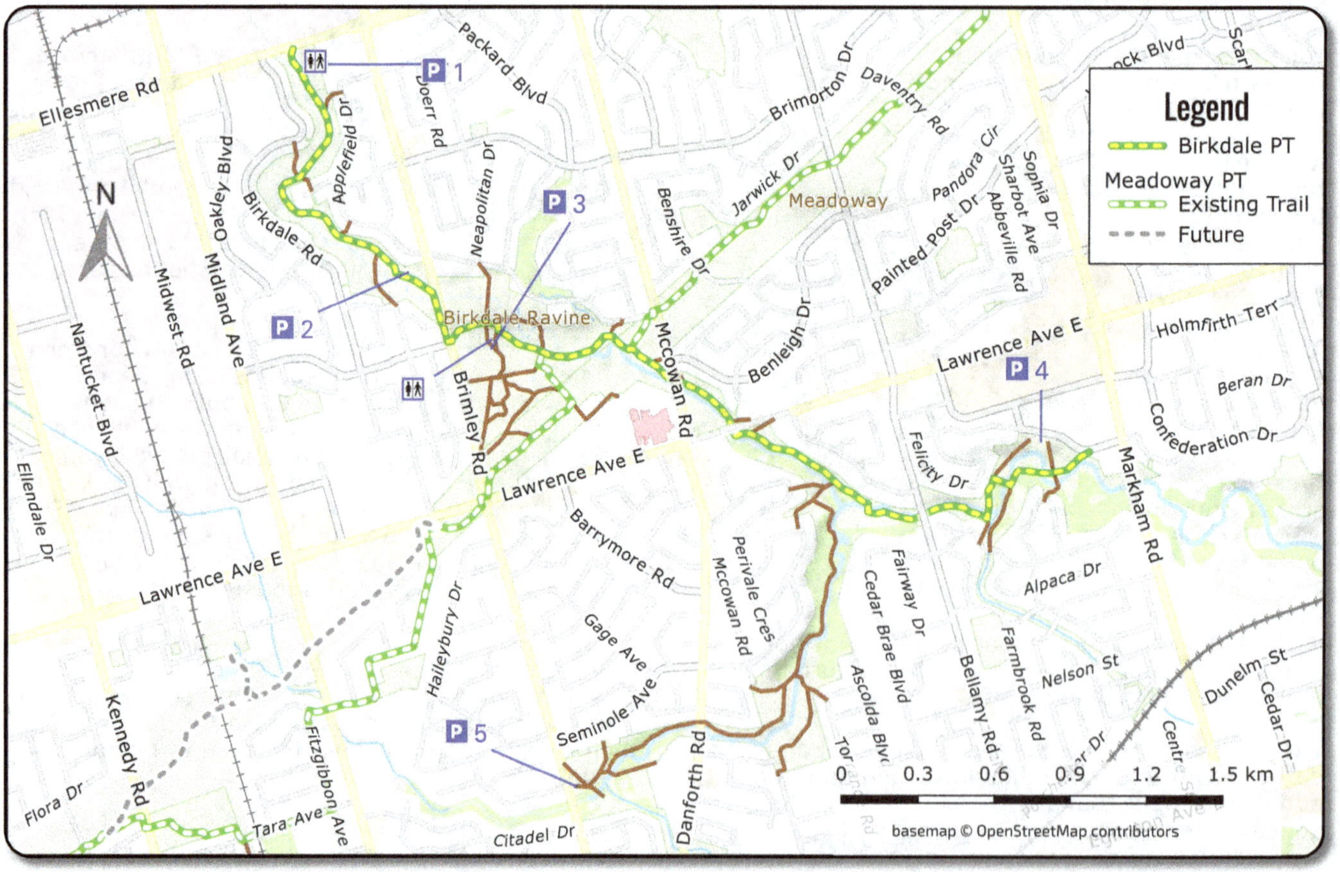

basemap © OpenStreetMap contributors

Legend
- Birkdale PT
- Meadoway PT
- Existing Trail
- Future

Review:

Right in the heart of **Scarborough**, on the east side of **Toronto**, the **Birkdale Trail** follows the **West Highland Creek** for **5 km**. Though a short cycle, it has two other routes that intersect to add **12 more kilometres** to your journey if you are so inclined.

Explore a collection of **parklands** and **natural ravines** typical of this area, somewhat connected together by a path that is certainly better paved than it was a few years ago.

The route starts from the north end at **Ellesmere Ave.** Down into a small ravine valley we meandered on a wide, paved trail. It offered a **quick escape** from the concrete of the big city as we traversed bridges and cruised along the banks of the treed creek.

In the spring there are cherry blossom trees in bloom near **Pomeroy St.**

Brimley Rd is the only road crossing, go south to cross at the lights. Then enter the large **Thomson Memorial Park** grounds.

Here you could consider looping around to explore the park, or having a look at a few pioneer buildings at the **Scarborough Heritage Museum.**

You could also branch off onto the new **11 km** (16 km in the future) **Meadoway** (Gatineau Hydro Corridor). Not the prettiest trek, but it gets you places.

In a few years to connect with the **Don Valley paths** and on the east end the **Rouge Valley** and **Highland Creek** trails.

Staying on the main path takes you south under **McCowan Rd** and **Lawrence Ave E** through a wooded ravine following the creek again.

There is on the way a **2 km side trail** for the more adventurous. No signs make it obvious, so use a map. It's a dirt trail in **Hague Park** that follows the creek tributary. At first, it seems a little rough but it does improve.

We had to ride over boulders lining the edge of the creek bank. **Mountain bikers can do it**, but many may walk this section. It's a quiet, more natural, and narrow side trail that will open up towards the end as a paved path to the **Knob Hill Park** car lot.

So back on the main trail it eventually takes you east to **Markham Rd, Cedarbrae Collegiate,** and a **large mall** to the north, where you are assured of finding refreshments (and ice cream).

This trail system is a little short on directional signs; we had to refer to our GPS phone map more than once at a few three- and four-way junctures. Defaulting to **take the trail that stays low** by the water usually works for me.

The **Birkdale Trail** is not outstanding, but it is a pleasant, easy outing. There are a few **play-grounds for your restless kids** to stop at. It's good enough for most cyclists looking for new byways to ramble on when the weather is inviting.

Chinguacousy – Park Trail

GTA - Brampton

Length - 9 + 6 km (one way)

90% park path
10% road crossings, detours

Elevation - Flat with quick dips; climbs for road and water crossings

Terrain - Wide, paved path with gravel patches, bridges, and benched tunnels

Skill - Easy

Maps - Limited amount of map boards, trail markers, bring your phone map app

Traffic - Underused path with occasional cyclists, or walkers with dogs

Facilities - Parking lot, toilets, snack bar, benches, picnic tables, rain shelter

Highlights - Bridges, ponds, main park area, zoo

Phone - 905 874 2000

Website - City of Brampton

Similar Trails - Upper Etobicoke Creek, Upper Humber River, Nokiidaa

Local Clubs - Brampton Cycling Club

Access - Large parking lots at these Brampton lots beside the path; many side streets have access paths:

⊕1365 Countryside Dr
P1 Brampton Soccer Centre - Sandalwood Pkwy E & Dixie Rd
P2 Ellen Mitchell Rec Centre - 926 N Park Dr
P3 Chinguacousy Park - Hanover Rd & Central Park Dr
⊕ **P4** Victoria Park Arena - 20 Victoria Crescent
P5 Earnscliffe Rec Centre - 44 Eastbourne Dr

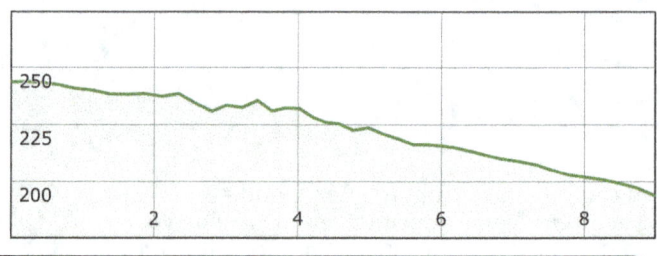

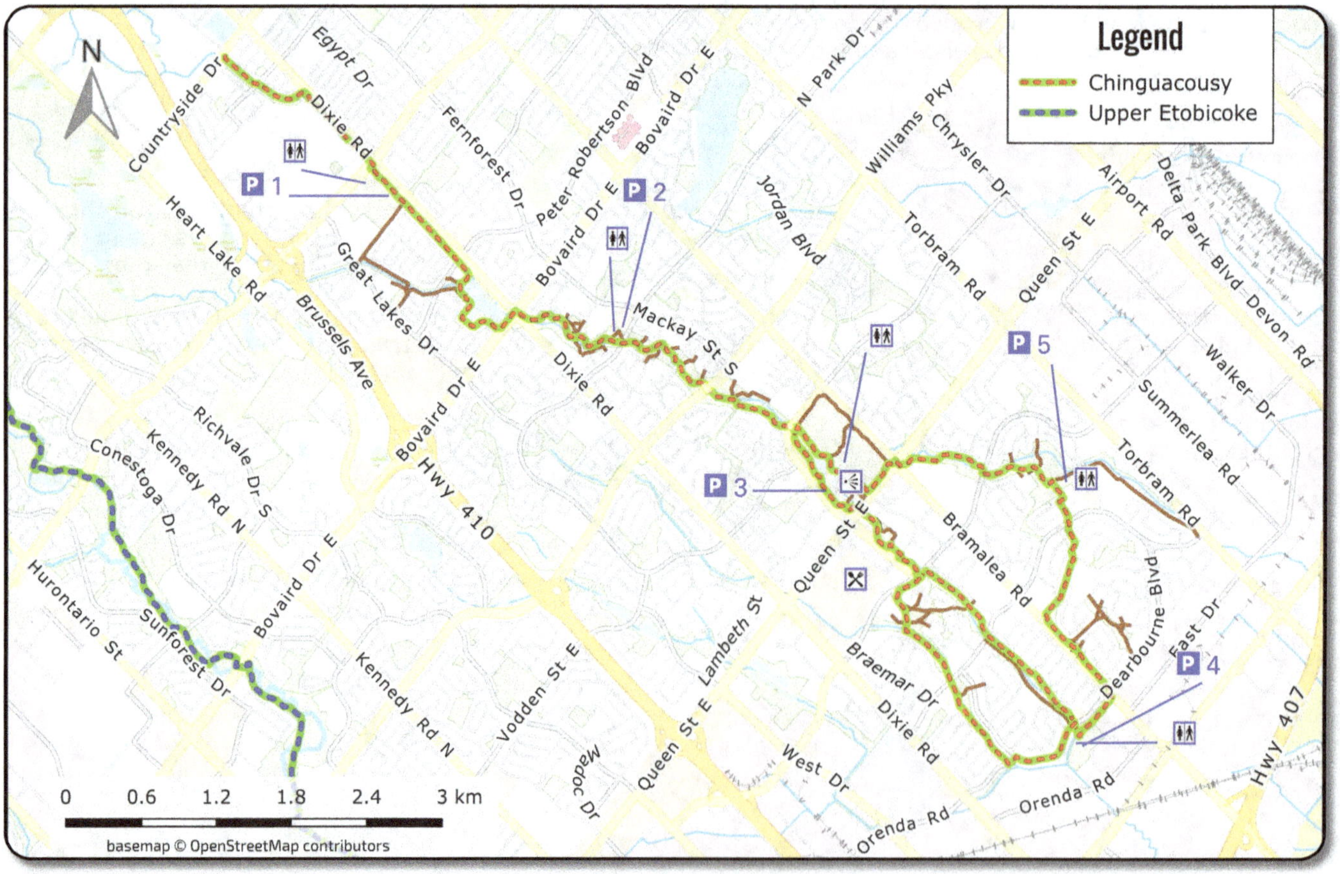

Review:

In the centre of **Brampton** lies the **9 km long Chinguacousy Park** path, a trail worth cycling on any sunny day to wash away your worries.

In the middle of the summer on a beautiful Sunday afternoon, we were cruising the length of this fine trail. **All was good,** car-free, quiet, and easy going, **except for one thing**—where are the cyclists, I kept wondering?!

This was an odd occurrence considering the path is accessible to many neighbourhoods, easy to ride, scenic and long enough to make it a good outing. Yet there were few bikes to be seen.

Exactly why is a mystery, as I have travelled enough routes to **recommend this one.**

The **Chinguacousy** path runs north/south following a creek with a paved trail linking numerous parks.

Halfway along it connects with the well placed large main **Chinguacousy Park** area that has ponds, gardens, a petting zoo, refreshments and washrooms.

There are alternate paths to cycle back, benches to rest, and neighbourhood backyards to eye as you cycle along.

I would speculate a few **things are not up to par** on the trail which may have earned it a poor reputation and kept some cyclists away, but it has been getting better over time**.**

On my 2019 ride, I encountered broken bridges and overgrown paths. Those have been fixed and new curb cuts have been added.

Yet there's still no painted trail line down the middle or enough **signage/maps** to deal with the confusion of first-time riders.

This route has a lot of connector paths; some are three-way junctions that keep you guessing too often.

We had to stop and refer to our phone GPS map more than once.

Perhaps the lack of cyclists and even walkers is due in part to a rather **sterile parkland landscaping.** Parts of the path follow the water in a dull, straight line, whereas these days park trails meander.

Even parts of the creek bed have been turned into an ugly de-naturalized cement channel. **Creek crossings** and **tunnels** use parts of this cement barrier.

We could manage to keep our balance riding the **concrete benches along the water's edge,** and it was even a cool feature. Perhaps some novice riders may get nervous doing them. And after a heavy rain, the water runoff will likely make these tunnel benches **impassable.**

So there you have it: a **decent Park ride** in the middle of **Brampton** (a bike friendly town), with no one on it. A friend who lives here admits Bramptonians **love their cars** and driveways are full of them. Discover a better way to beat the traffic: cycling on these paths this summer.

I have added **two bonus side loops** to this ride for variety that you can try when you get to the south end.

So do you go **east for 3.5 km** or **west for 2.5 km**? Yes! What's the rush? None of this is hilly and it is all paved and enjoyable on a sunny afternoon. Do 'em both.

Clearview – Rail Trail

Collingwood

Length - 12 + 4.5 km (one way)

90% rail trail path
10% road crossings, detours

Elevation - Flat with a 40 m slope towards the bay

Terrain - Fine crushed stone, gravel, some asphalt

Skill - Easy

Maps - Map boards, signposts

Traffic - Bicycles, hikers,

Facilities - Parking on the street, outhouse, benches

Highlights - Shaded path, Collingwood Station Museum, waterfront, downtown vibe

Phone - 705 445 1030

Website - Town of Collingwood

Similar Trails - Georgian RT, North Simcoe +Tiny RT, Thornton-Beeton RT

Local Clubs - Collingwood Cycling Club

Access - Only a few public lots to pick from or street parking.

⊕ Warrington Rd & Centre Line Rd
P1 Station Park - 208 Huron St, Stayner
P2 Collingwood Arena - 96 Hurontario St, Collingwood
P3 Sunset Point Beach - 79 St Lawrence St
⊕ 38 Huron St, Collingwood

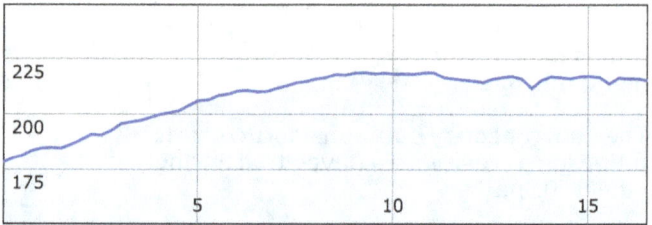

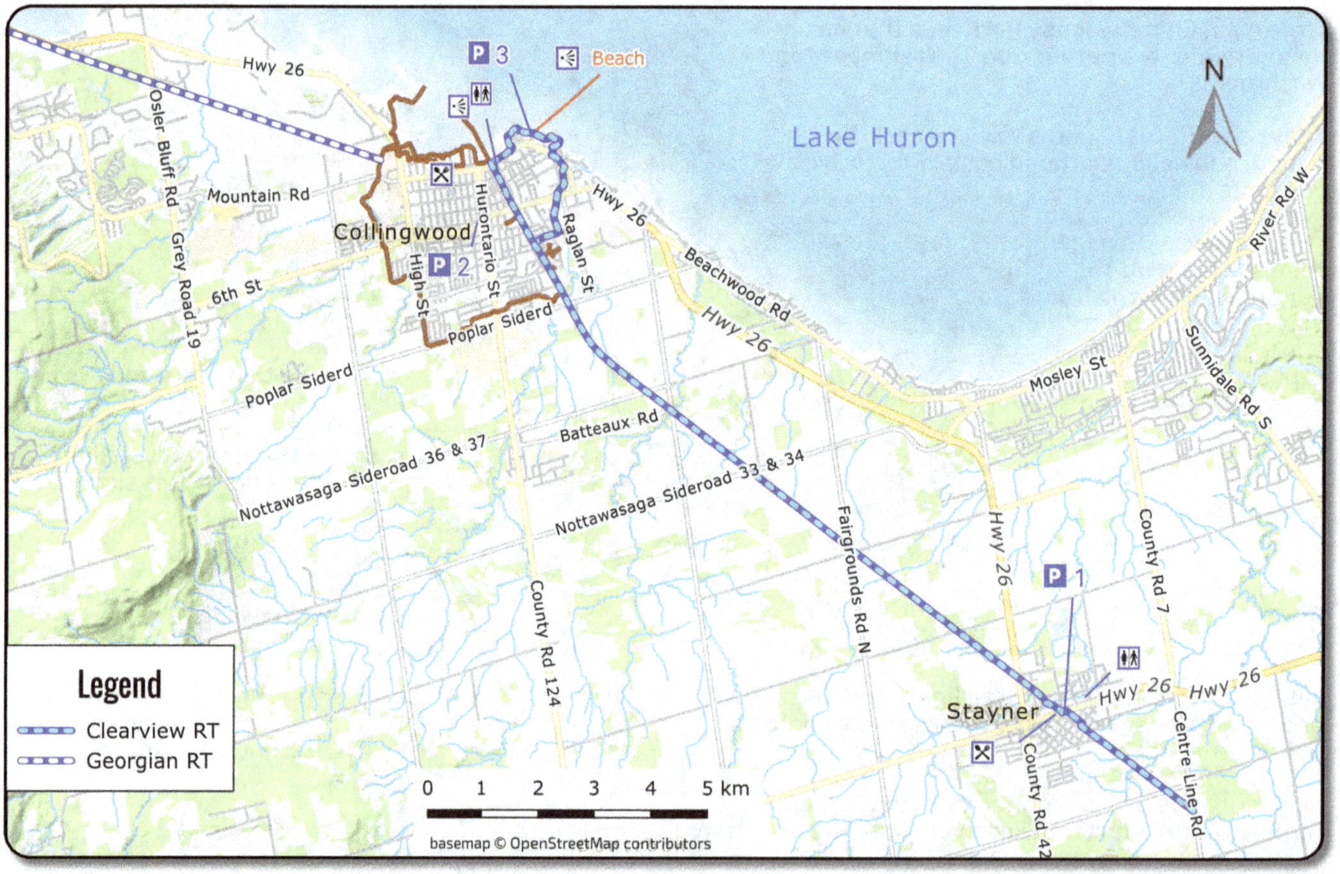

Review:

Here is a short 12 km rail trail that would make a great day trip for the family or with your spouse right into **Collingwood,** one of **Ontario's top tourist destinations.**

The **Clearview Collingwood Train Trail** runs southeast to the town of **Stayner** and is officially a little farther if you want to do the entire length. Actually, in the future it may even go beyond—potentially **to Angus one day??** As always, it will take time and money.

For anyone coming up from the big city, **Station Park in Stayner** is a good launch point for your group to head into **Collingwood** on bicycles. It's a short, easy ride into town with views of farms, equestrian activity on harness racing ovals, and the smell of lilac stands in the spring.

It's a **straight-as-an-arrow route** with only one bend in it, because this is the cheapest and fastest means to get a train from A to B. Last time I checked the **rusty rails are still there** and RT runs beside the abandoned tracks till **Poplar Sideroad.** Odd, since most of the time rails are removed in haste; perhaps a future consideration?

As you enter town, this fine gravel path becomes **shady with trees lining the route.** This tree canopy will continue until you reach the end at the **station museum near the harbour.**

To make it a little bit more interesting, I've added a **4.5 km side loop** to take you along the **Georgian Bay shoreline first.** When the old track curves to the right, take the path on the right that goes to the **Pretty River.** Follow this briefly to **Hwy 26** and then go up to the intersection at **Ontario St.** Turn right here onto **Raglan St**; a few more blocks you'll be at the **waters of Georgian Bay.**

Here you can have lunch in this large park, let the kids run wild, dip your toes in the water, or take a nap…. When you've had enough downtime, get back on your pony, ride to the other end of the park shoreline, and back on the road at **Huron St** (sorry about that).

A minute later, you'll see the **Collingwood Museum—a rebuilt train station** inspired by the old one—ahead of you. The RT starts behind it and heads south to **take you back to Stayner…**

Now, wait just a minute! You're in holiday mode, in **Vacationville,** where there's **no shortage of activities, waterfront strolls, patio pubs, great places to dine, and places to stay.** Wander down **Hurontario St** among the century old storefronts, stay a while, and wish you could retire sooner.

For those who want to **clock in a little more riding,** there are a number of trails circling the town that you can try. They're a little bit of a patchwork between street and park spaces.

And I should also mention the RT big brother to the **Clearview** and continuation to this rail line: the **Georgian RT,** a popular long route along the coast to **Thorold and Meaford.**

History - The **Ontario, Simcoe and Huron Union Railroad** first reached **Collingwood in 1855,** an extension of **Upper Canada's first steam line** that had originated in **Toronto** two years earlier. Not long afterwards, it was renamed the **Northern Railway of Canada.** It became part of the **Grand Trunk Railway in 1888** and eventually the **CNR.**

In its early days, the line primarily moved agricultural products, serving the port towns on **Georgian Bay.** Competition, the Great Depression, and widening of the **Welland Canal** decreased the use of the ports, and traffic declined.

Once **Collingwood Shipbuilding** closed in **1986,** the end was near for this section, but **the original line from Toronto lives on with GO train service to Barrie.**

Erin Sawmill – Park Trail

GTA - Mississauga

Length - 8 km

85% park path
10% hiking trail
5% road crossings, detours

Elevation - Half of the route gradually climbs 60 m; on the other half you coast back down

Terrain - Mainly a paved path, soil/wood chip base, bridges

Skill - Intermediate

Maps - Map boards, posted directions to many routes

Traffic - Cyclist, walkers, dogs, strollers

Facilities - Parking lots, toilets, benches, picnic tables, playgrounds

Highlights - Natural ravine valley, quiet suburbia

Phone - 905 615 4311

Website - City of Mississauga

Similar Trails - Morrison Valley, Upper Etobicoke,

Local Clubs - Credit Valley Cycling Club, Mississauga Bicycle Racing Club

Access - It's a loop trail, so start from any Mississauga side street where you can park, or try these lots:

P1 U of T campus - The Collegeway east of Mississauga Rd, fee
P2 Pheasant Run Park - 4140 Pheasant Run
P3 South Common Centre - 2233 South Millway
P4 Erindale Park - 1699 Dundas St W

Graph starts at P1 on the map

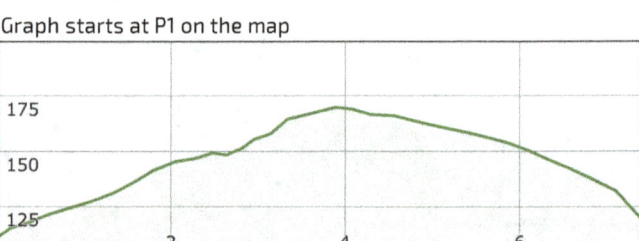

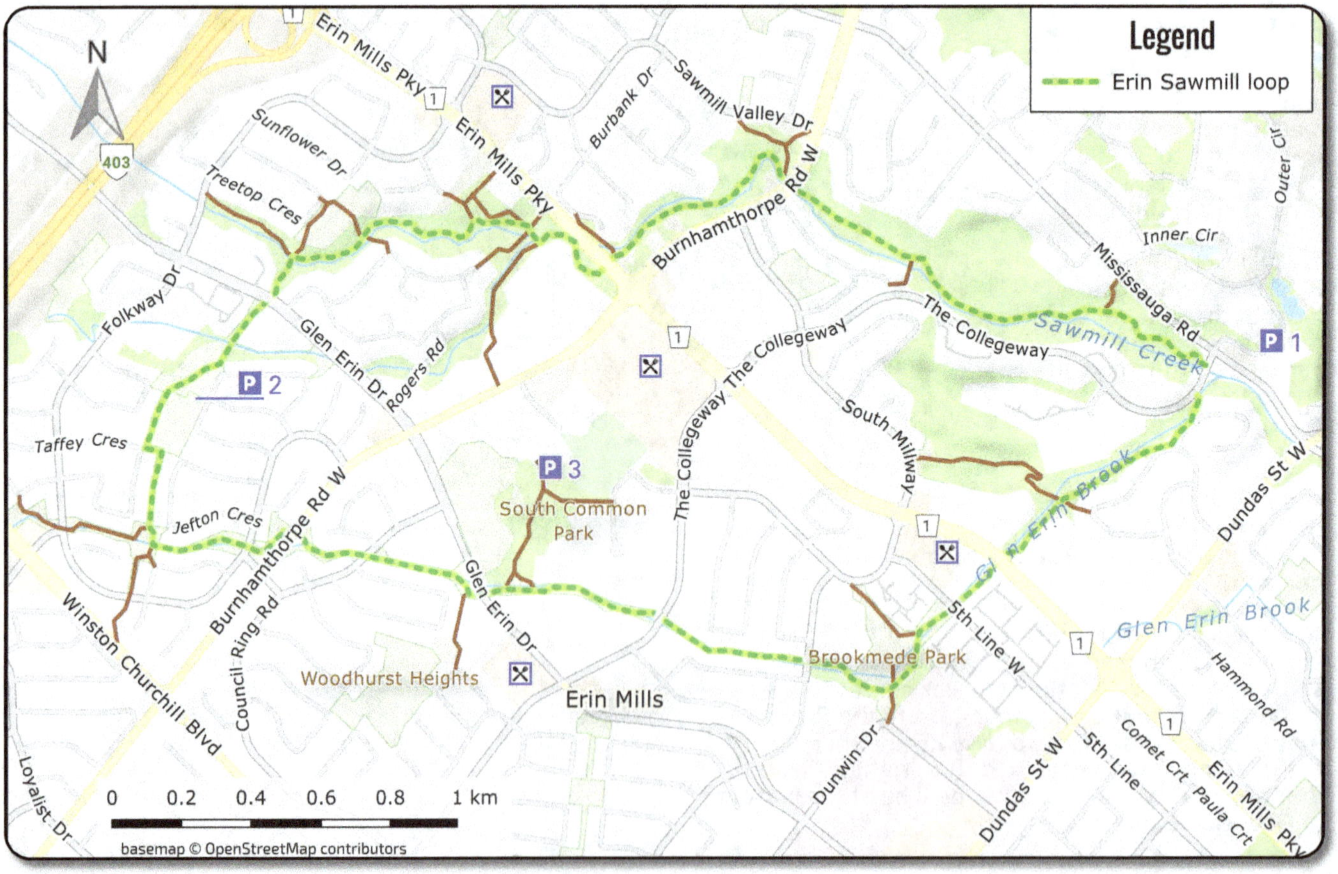

Review:

In **Mississauga**, explore an interesting, ever-changing **8 km bicycle loop**, which I designed because everyone loves loops.

This route encompasses a few different trail sections, so the name changes, and so does the terrain. I am calling it the **Erin Sawmill** Park Trail.

It **flows well** between one neighbourhood and the next with very few street crossings, as most roads have an **underpass** for cyclists. Hurray, we like seeing this!

That said, riding it for the first time **will require a map** to stay on course, as there are lots of side trails to keep you guessing.

Signs are posted, sometimes, but this is not a loop the city has mapped out. I put it together and gave it a name.

Starting from **Mississauga Rd** and **The Collegeway,** we took the **Sawmill Valley Creek** trail into the wooded ravine.

It is shady as it follows the water on a dirt/wood chip path you need to contend with. This is the more **natural, secluded** part of the loop.

As it curves around westward, it **rises gradually 60 m** to street level into more of an open parkland setting by the time you get to **Pheasant Run Park.** (Another good start point.) Here the kids can hit the playsets for a break.

For the rest of the route, which is all paved, you will be cruising the **Glen Erin/5th Line** pathways between townhouse backyards and school playing fields.

And cruise you will, as you **glide down the second half** of this loop as it now descends back to your start point.

This route at times has a **residential feel** to your ride (as it is in the city). It is quiet and laid back. Cars are in the distance to be ignored and you will encounter no commercial malls or industrial areas.

That said, a quick detour can get you to a variety store or pub patio for a pit stop at any time on this loop.

Though short, this **path is never boring** and it's one of the few off-road **Park loops** I know. I've rated more of an **Intermediate** Park ride as you have to sort out your route, manage the elevation, and there are unpaved spots.

This good city Park ride is convenient for those on the **west side of Toronto** when you've got to get moving.

*[By the way, we parked at **P1** the UofT lot, which offers access to the **13 km Culham Trail**, but we soon bailed. On the south end, it started as a promising paved path along the river, but it turned into a rough, loose gravel trail that slowed us right down (riding this requires a gravel bike or MTB).*

There were signs that this might be resurfaced with fine crushed stone to make it more manageable on a city bike but a recent chat with a local cyclist tells me not so. It's certainly a lovely riverside nature trail that would be beautiful in the fall, so it might be worth seeing how far you can get.]

Escarpment – Rail Trail

Hamilton - Caledonia

Length - 34 km (one way)

90% rail trail path10% road crossings, detours

Elevation - Gradual slope up escarpment for 30 minutes, then it levels out

Terrain - Sections of asphalt, crushed stone

Skill - Hill climb is Intermediate, the rest is easy going

Maps - New map boards and signs posted

Traffic - Bicycles, joggers, hikers, dogs, Nordic skiers in winter

Facilities - Parking on street, outhouse, benches

Highlights - Lookouts from the cliff climb, Albion Falls, Grand River

Phone - 905 546 2489

Website - City of Hamilton

Similar Trails - Hamilton Brantford RT, Oro- Medonte RT,   Caledon RT

Local Clubs - Hamilton Cycling Club, HBMBA

Access -

⊕**P1** Corktown Park - Ferguson Ave S and Forest Ave, Hamilton
P2 Mohawk Ice Centre - 710 Mountain Brow Blvd, Hamilton
P3 Albion Falls - on Arbour Rd, Hamilton
P4 Chippewa trailhead - 55 Dartnall Rd, Hamilton
P5 199 Haldimand hwy 66, Caledonia
P6 Gypsum Mine Tract trailhead - 62 McClung Rd, Caledonia
⊕ Haldmand Rd 9

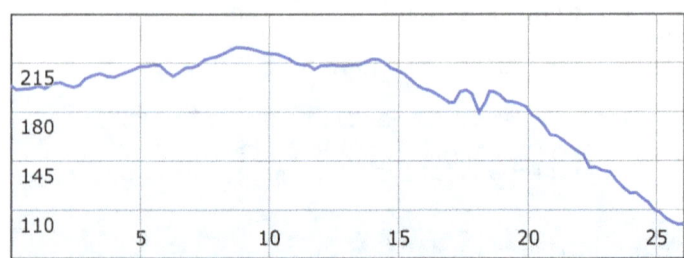

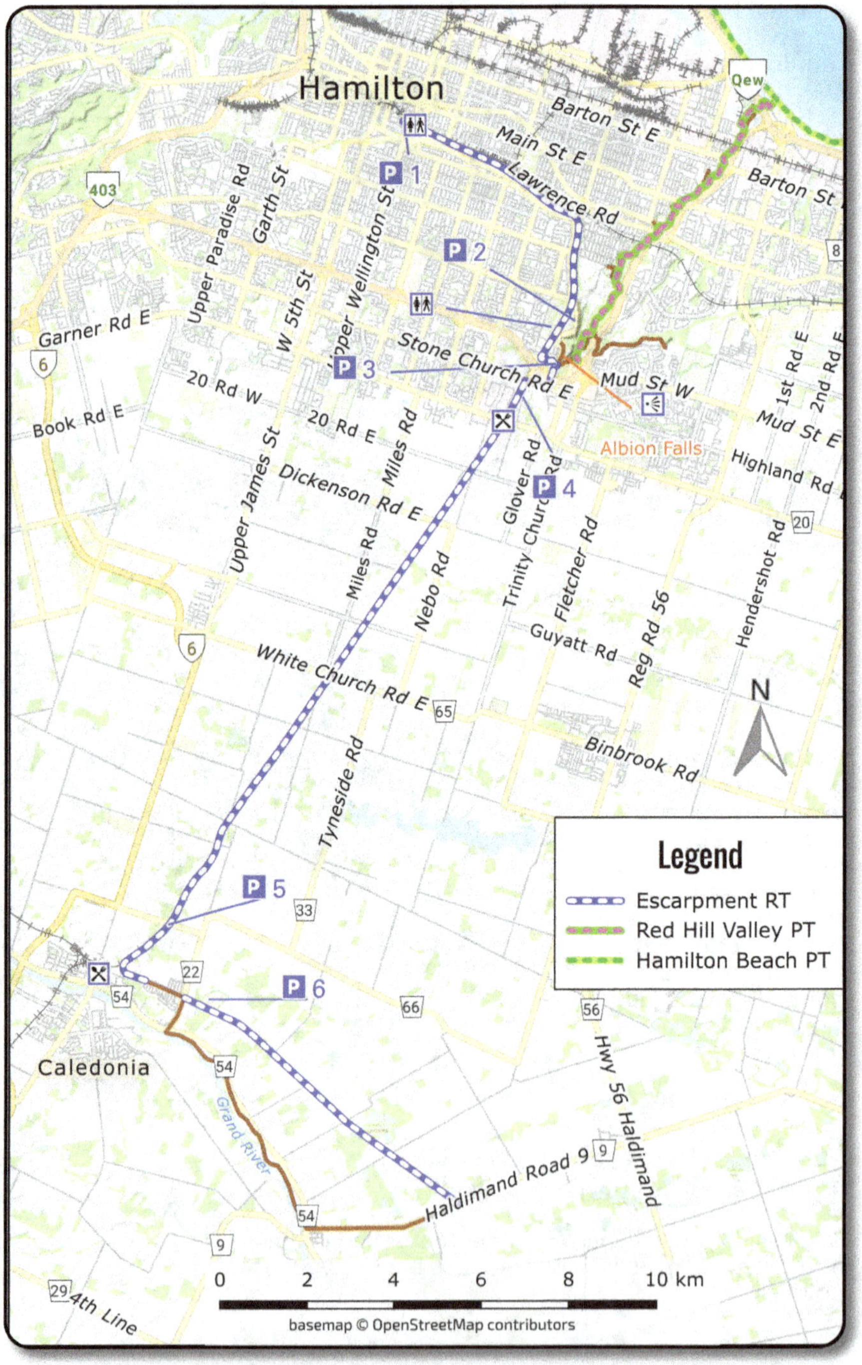

Review:

The **34 km Escarpment Rail Trail** starts from the base of the bluff ("mountain") in **Hamilton**. It's a long climb up a **gradual slope** that gets you to the top in about **40 minutes,** including a few stops to check out the views. It was probably more of a challenge for trains years ago than it will be for you to climb the **95 metres** on your bicycle.

This rail trail to **Caledonia**, on the **Grand River**, has three sections/names. The **Escarpment Rail Trail (Iron Horse)** segment takes you from the inner city across the escarpment to the top, where it flattens out considerably for the rest of the route.

Starting at **Corktown Park,** the path is paved and level, running alongside a set of tracks. Maybe the kids will see a freight train chug by. As the path heads up across the stony bluff for **8 km**, it leaves the other tracks behind at the bottom.

This is a **well-treed path** with only a few lookouts: many of the original grand views of **Hamilton** are now overgrown. On the other hand, the trees provide welcome shade to cyclists. The rest of the route is more open once you get to the top.

It's a popular trail for joggers, who test their stamina on various access staircases along the way.

This moderate climb turns south and takes you through a **limestone rock cut** as it levels out close to **Albion Falls**—a must-see destination, and one of **many waterfalls** in the area. This is an ideal time to have a snack at a park picnic bench.

You now have three choices. U-turn and coast down the hill for the big payoff. Smoke those brakes!

Or take the adventurous, steeper **Red Hill Valley Trail** past the falls and down to **Lawrence Rd** to head west back on the bike lane (at Gage Park, take Cumberland Ave, then rejoin the RT at Wentworth St S).

The **105 m descent** drops quickly, then levels out; it can take you **10 km** to the lakes edge for more riding. (You might be walking down the steep gravel incline at the beginning if you do not have a MTB.)

A third option is to continue on for **16 km** south to **Caledonia** on the recently resurfaced **Chippewa Rail Trail**. First, there is a road detour you will need to do to get over the freeway. A pedestrian bridge makes that easy.

Once in **Caledonia,** a third **8 km** section called the **Gypsum Mine Tract Trail** has just been added and newly resurfaced for you to extend your trip toward the southeast. It will be yet another straight-as-she-goes, pleasant-yet-uneventful ride through Ontario farm country.

Here is a **more scenic alternate** return. Head west on **Haldimand Rd 9** when you get to the end or the road before, **Stoney Creek Rd**. Both have paved shoulders to take you down to the shore of the **Grand River.** Find the path/road back north to **Caledonia** on the banks of the river. No need to stay on **Hwy 54.**

The larger part of **Caledonia** is on the other side of the **Grand,** all interesting touring you can add to the ride.

The **Escarpment Rail Trail**, combined with the other two sections, makes for a **pleasant exit** from the concrete and noise of urban living in no time. And that **hill climb is nothing much**—not a grind, nor even laborious, as I recall—so **if you are fit, give it a try.** The escape will be worth it.

History - continues on page 118

Etobicoke Creek – Park Trail

GTA- Etobicoke

Length - 3 + 17 km (one way)

85% park path
15% road crossings, detours

Elevation - Flat along water's edge, a few short hills

Terrain - Almost all newly paved; a small amount of gravel base; wide path; not a lot of shade

Skill - All levels

Maps - New trail signs and map boards

Traffic - Typical city path users, busy on the south end on weekends

Facilities - Parking lots, toilets, benches, picnic tables, rain shelter, tuneup stations, local malls

Highlights - Centennial Park, low-flying planes, many underpasses

Phone - 905 615 4311

Website - Walk & Roll in Peel, TRCA, Mississauga Bikes

Similar Trails - Upper Don, Highland Creek, Upper Humber

Local Clubs - Toronto Bicycle Network - TBN

Access - For the short trail from the lake, park at P1, the rest of the parking suggestions are for the longer route after the gap.

⊕**P1** Marie Curtis Park - Lakeshore Rd E at Forty Second St
P2 Etobicoke Valley Park - 72 Westhead Rd
P3 Fleetwood Park - on Burnhamthorpe Rd E
P4 Centennial Park - Elmcrest & Rathburn Rd
P5 Airport lot - Britannia Rd E near Courtney Dr E
P6 Mount Charles Park - 1265 Cardiff Blvd
P7 CAA Sports Centre - 7575 Kennedy Rd S, Brampton
P8 Nelson Park - 56 Neilson Dr
⊕10 Austin Dr, Brampton

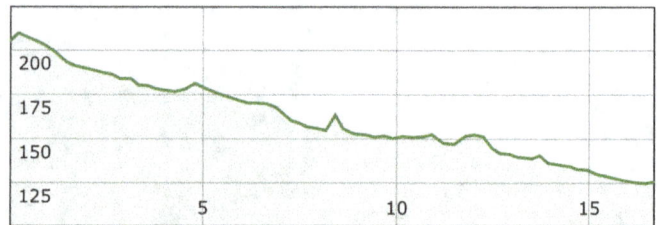

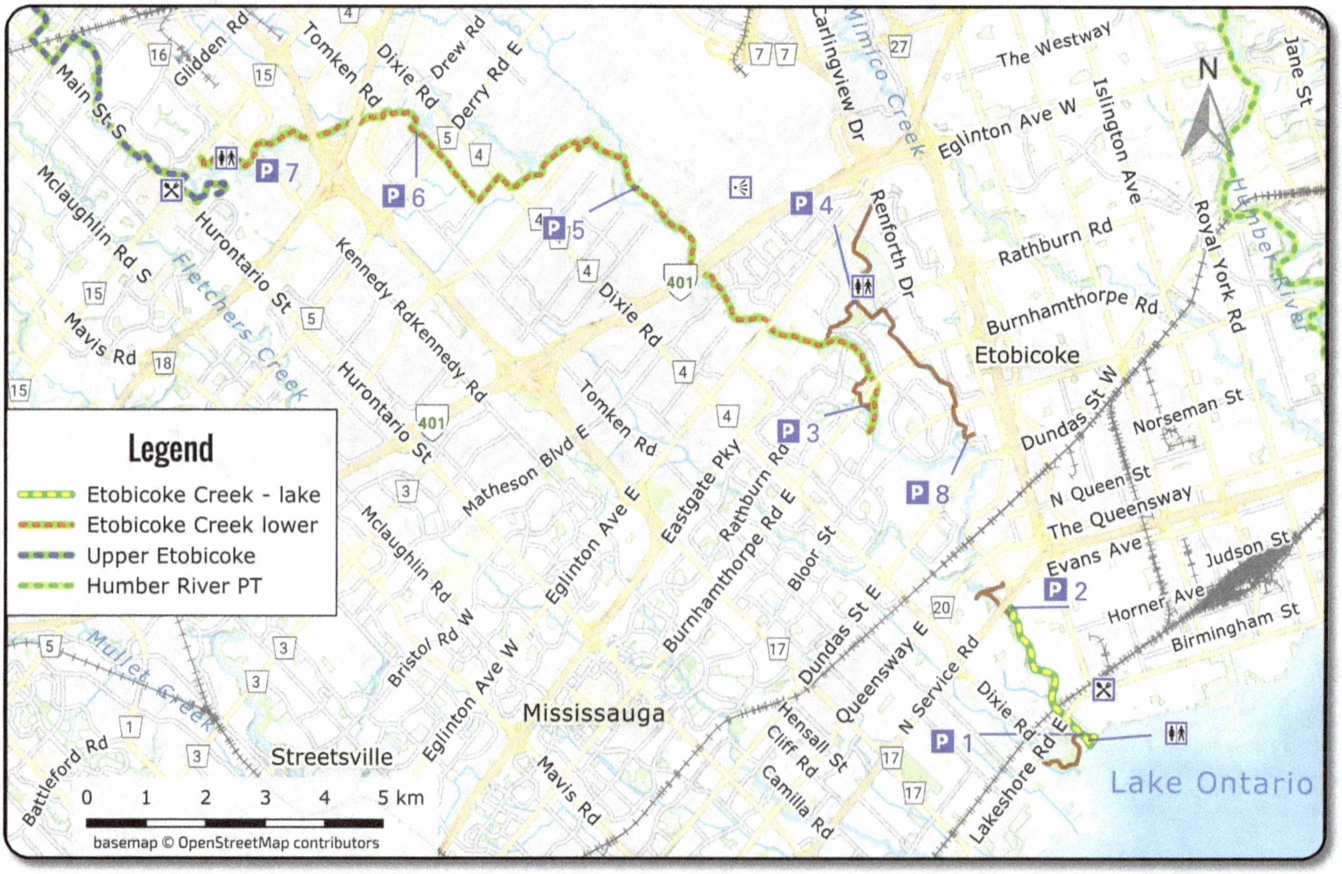

Review:

Ride the **17 km** of newly expanded bicycle paths along **Etobicoke Creek**, a route that has taken years to develop into an **excellent long cycling adventure**.

As you ride by the waters of this creek, there is little to remind you that there is a bustling city beyond the edges of the valley. **Assorted hills, curves, underpasses,** and **bridges** keep it all interesting. The scenery is a **naturalized ravine setting** typical of the Toronto area.

From **Lake Ontario**, this trail starts in **Marie Curtis Park**. It winds up the creek valley for an enjoyable **3 km** to the **QEW highway**. That's it for the south end. Beyond is a MTB adventure on a rough, unmarked track I have not done in years. The way is blocked by this untamed section and a golf course.

The master plan is to one day, someday, **connect the whole length**. Untill then, let me suggest a much longer section above this mere 3 km jaunt.

As of 2021, you can start from **Fleetwood Park** off **Burnhamthorpe Rd E** to catch this trail as it follows the west bank north. Most of it is **paved** and recently upgraded with **new signage, benches,** and **crossing lights.**

A highlight on the trip is **Centennial Park,** whose large parklands have many features like a conservatory, ski hill, **BMX race track**, and extra paths to explore.

Once the trail reaches the other side of Hwy 401, you may see **airliners coming in low over your head** to land at the airport. A thrill for any aviation junkie (like me!).

I am not sure why the path does not continue to follow the creek. At **Dixie Rd**, there is a road bypass where the trail veers off onto **Mid-Way Blvd.** Head north on

Columbus Rd, which becomes **Cardiff Blvd,** then back into a natural environment at **Mount Charles Park.**

Here, you are not actually riding on the road, but just beside it, on a raised curb. It's a **brief 2 km stretch** for a few blocks through a bland, ugly industrial area. At least it should be quiet on weekends.

Once on the trail again, this part of the new path takes you under **nine highway bridges!** An unusual, cavernous sight indeed. Then it travels beside a golf course into **Brampton**, ending at **Steeles Ave E.** But there is more…

A mere minute going west is the Upper Etobicoke trailhead, where you can access another **20 km of parkland riding**. Or you can just relax, grab a bite at the mall, and head back home.

It may take a few more years 'til they sort out a way around/through the middle obstructions. When I surveyed my maps, I could not see a simple, safe road bypass that could connect both sections.

I would also like to suggest the **Elmcrest Creek Trail**, a tiny stream on a skinny **3 km** pathway. It's definitely a pleasurable side trail. It starts in **Nelson Park** and takes you north to **Centennial Park**, where you can ride west to catch the main trail.

The **Etobicoke Creek** route has been a ride I have wanted to mention for years. It's still not complete, but what there is, is fine riding for city cyclists with the north end all spruced up.

Finch Corridor – Park Trail

Toronto

Length - 16 km (one way)

90% park path
10% road crossings, detours

Elevation - Not flat as you may think; drops into four valleys; east end has a 40 m uphill

Terrain - Paved, bridges, road crossings, loose grit from winter sanding, watch your turns

Skill - All levels

Maps - Map boards, sign posts (some missing)

Traffic - Typical path users, the middle section is the busiest

Facilities - Parking lot, toilets, benches, picnic tables, rain shelter

Highlights - Very long, gets you places, car free, skyline views of the city

Phone - 311

Website - City of Toronto

Similar Trails - Meadoway,   Oakridge,   1000 Islands

Local Clubs - Toronto Bicycle Network -TBN

Access - Many side trails and streets lead into or cross this path. You can ride in from other bike trails mentioned in my reviews. Take the subway there to Finch or Finch West subway station. Here are a few parking lot/starting point suggestions at various spots along the trail.

⊕ 75 Norfinch Dr
P1 Bayview Arena - 3230 Bayview Ave
P2 Finch Subway Station - Yonge & Bishop Ave or Hendon Ave
P3 Shiner Stadium - 5220 Bathurst Ave
P4 Ross Lord Park - 4801 Dufferin St
P5 Finch West Subway - 415 Tangiers Rd
⊕ 47 Pineway Blvd

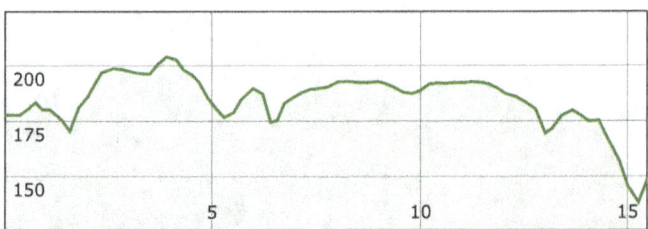

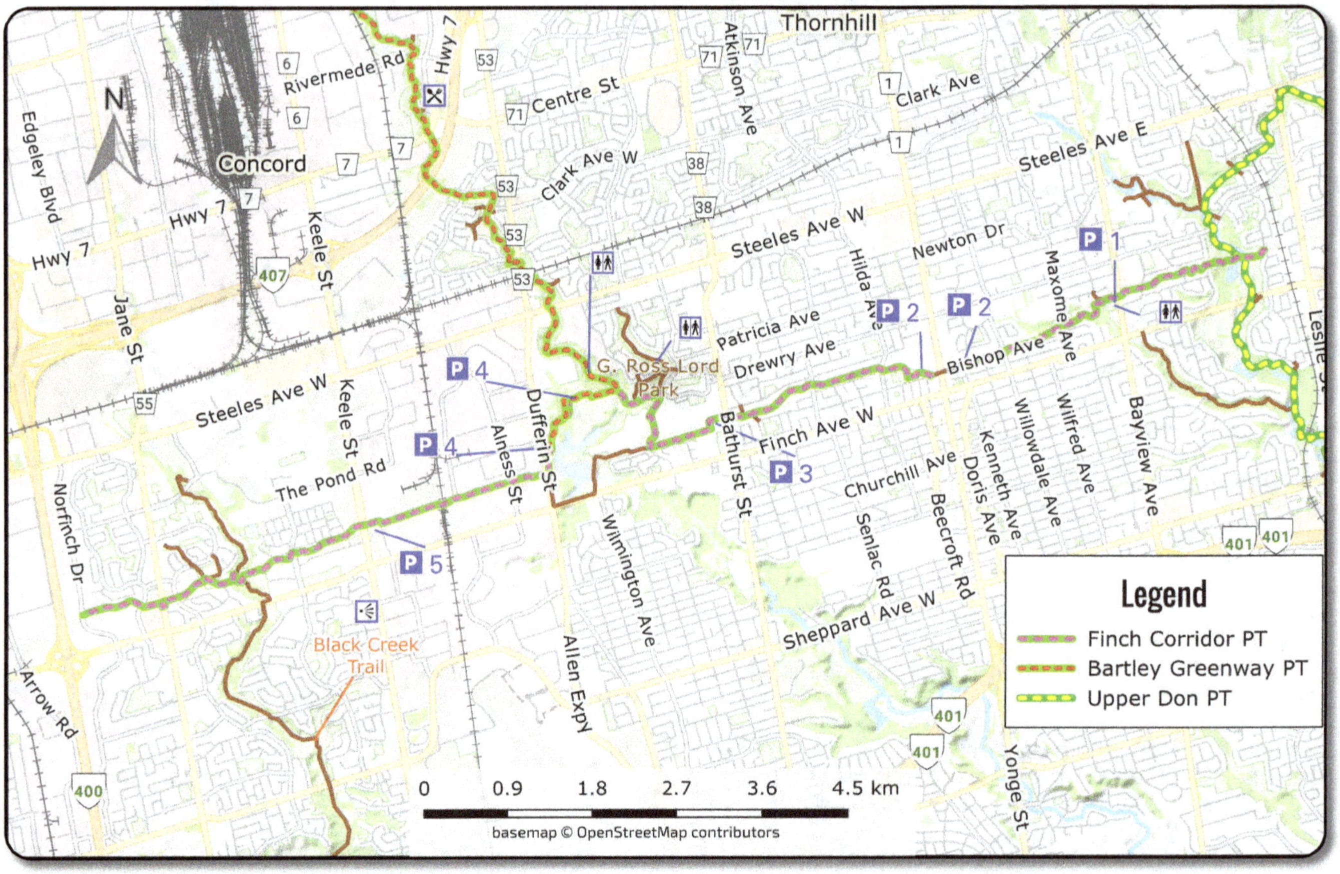

Legend
- Finch Corridor PT
- Bartley Greenway PT
- Upper Don PT

0   0.9   1.8   2.7   3.6   4.5 km

basemap © OpenStreetMap contributors

Review:

The **Finch Corridor Park Trail** runs parallel to/above **Finch Ave W** in **Toronto**. It is what I would consider **a bike path that gets you places.** It runs almost in a straight line across northwest Toronto for **16 km.** Cyclists who use it as a **bike highway** to go to work or visit friends can cover a fair bit of ground with no concern about the dangers of car traffic—and much of the time **you won't even see a car.**

This path enables cyclists to connect even further afield to other, more beautiful trail systems, like the **17 km Bartley Greenway** to **Vaughan**, the **6 km Black Creek Trail**, the **9 km Upper Don Trail** at the east end of the ride, and other smaller side trails.

This bicycle trail under the **hydro tower corridor** was built a few decades ago and suffers from an **old design** that lacks creative landscaping; I don't find it too inviting. I know that if it were being built these days, the parks department would put in more bends, humps, and dips to keep it an interesting ride.

I thought the ride might be boring and flat, but actually **it does have a few hills to it**, and those tend to be the interesting parts of the ride. Dipping down into **three deep valleys** gave us some quick descents and required some effort to get the top again. These small valleys had trees and shade. So does the large **G. Ross Lord Park** section that makes up the middle portion of this ride. I think the valleys and this park are the **most scenic parts** of the journey.

The parkland was very **sterile**, just a sea of **green grass** following the towers, with a strip of asphalt down the middle. This almost barren, treeless landscape does offer **distant views of city skylines** and is likely **dramatic at sunrise or sunset**. Some sections are lined with homes and playing fields, while further west it feels more **industrial** thanks to views of white fuel tanks and the sound of planes landing at the airport.

As you can tell, I prefer my rides to have **more going on visually** and a closed-in tree canopy. But for **road riders**, this wide-open feel may be what you seek—or at least not an issue during a ride.

I must say, for an old path, the **asphalt is in good repair**. Not a crack or pothole to mention. Plus they've recently added fancy bicycle crossing lights and curbed bike lanes to improve connections, so there is change underway.

We were less impressed with the signage. Though plentiful signs (some sunbleached) point riders to many side streets, they were **missing at key moments** when we needed directions to stay the course. Parts of the routes did have a painted line to follow; some were so faded we were not sure. I think the general rule here is: "When in doubt **follow the 60 m tall towers**; ya can't miss em."

Crossing over **Yonge Street**, the trail ends just before the subway station. It's a busy intersection, and you have to believe it continues on the other side of the lights at some point. This is not stated in any signs or with painted markings, so you have to **look for the opening.**

The **Ross reservoir** is another place where things get a bit unclear. You can go down and cross the **dam** to get a better look at the size of it, but to get back to the main route, you have to go onto the road, and it's not very seamless. The better route is up and around the **north side of the reservoir** through the park. It's not well marked, but you need to turn north when you get to **Torresdale Ave.**

The last thing to be aware of is the **40 m hill climb** from the **Upper W Don** trail to get onto the Finch path. Do I even need to mention that on a windy day you will feel it? And you'll get tons of sunshine, too.

Now, to be fair, **Hydro One has landscaping limitations** for maintenance and emergency service, so planting a forest is not going to happen. Look up Secondary Land Use: they need a 15 metre working radius under each tower and trees are to be no higher than 4 metres. You don't want arcing trees set ablaze on your ride, do you? But the **Meadoway** path in **Scarborough** has found **ways to beautify.**

All in all, it's **not the prettiest path in Toronto**, and it's certainly not one I would recommend to tourists. Why even put it in the book? Well, it has potential, and with a facelift, it would be more inviting. It is also too long to go unnoticed on a map. So now you know more about it and can make an educated choice. And that's the purpose of this book: **to send you off in the right direction.**

Granger Greenway – Park Trail

GTA - Klienburg

Length - 8 km (one way)

100% park path

Elevation - Hilly path with three to four large climbs

Terrain - Packed crushed gravel; coarse gravel where it has washed out; some slopes are paved; a few bridges to cross

Skill - Intermediate to Advanced

Maps - New map boards, numbered trail markers (signage is being replaced)

Traffic - Hikers, cyclists, joggers, Nordic skiers, snowshoers

Facilities - Parking lots, benches, picnic tables, rain shelter, no toilets!, amenities nearby

Highlights - Superb scenery, pastoral vistas, challenging Park style ride, McMichael gallery, Kleinburg, Boyd Conservation Area

Phone - 416 661 6600

Website - TRCA, Boyd Conservation Area

Similar Trails - Oak Ridge, Dundas Valley, Upper Don River

Local Clubs - Toronto Bicycle Club, Veneto Cycling Club

Access - Only a handful of car lots and entry points by bike. Parking lots fill up fast on sunny days. Check Boyd Conservation Area (closed to cars in the winter). Cyclists can pick up the trail from Rutherford Rd or Major Mackenzie Dr access ramps. Suggested parking:

✦**P1** Boyd Conservation Area - 8739 Islington Ave, Vaughan (south lot) expensive fee
P2 4700 Rutherford Road, new lot
P3 Foster Woods - 10110 Islington Ave dirt side trail
P4 McMichael Gallery - 10365 Islington Ave, Kleinburg - fee
✦**P5** Bindertwine Park - 299 Stegman's Mill Rd, Kleinburg

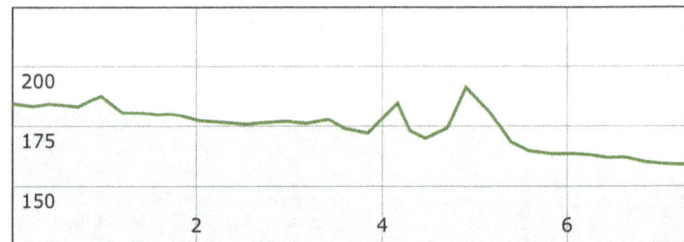

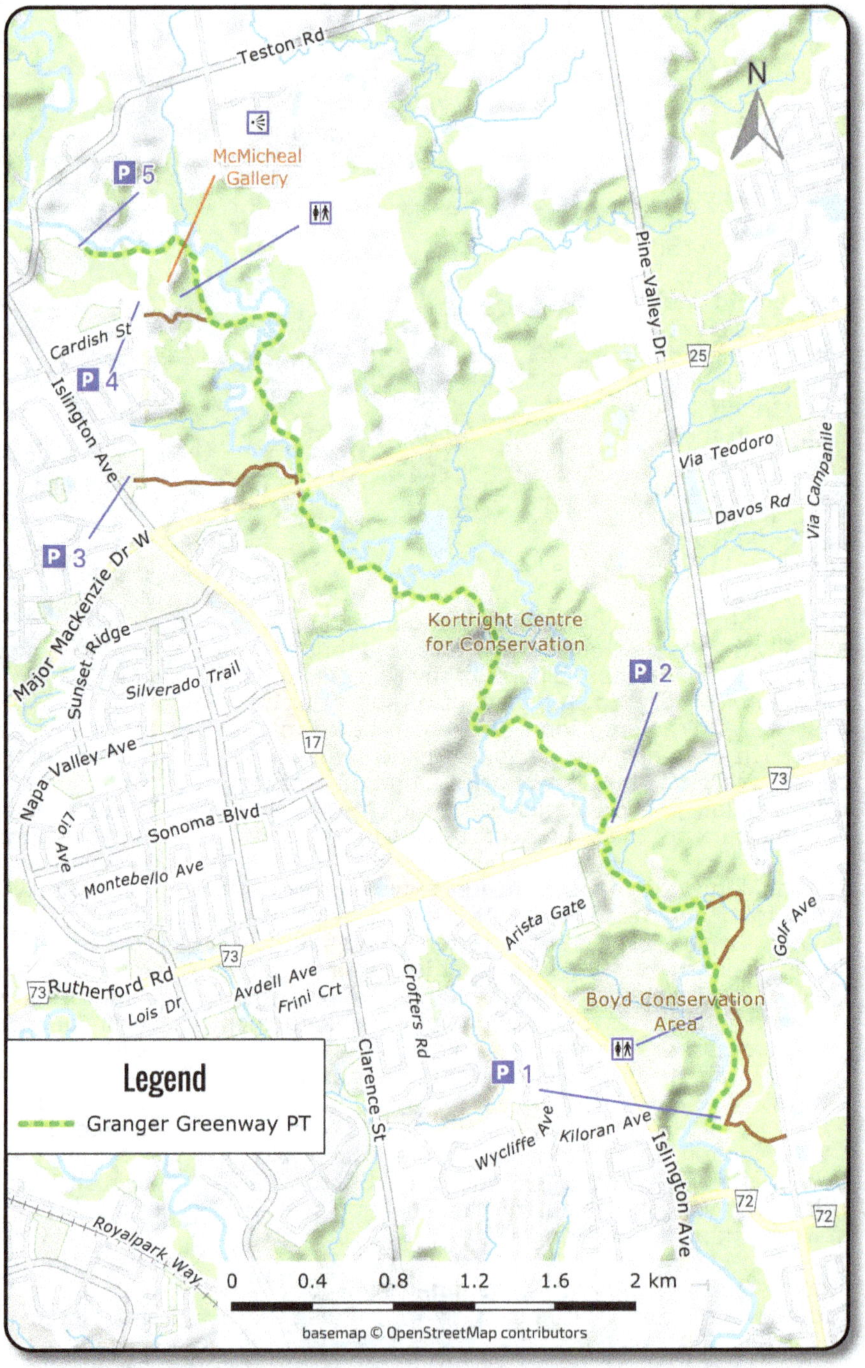

Review:

The **Granger Greenway** is the new name for an older **8 km** hiking trail in **Kleinburg. Nestled in valleys** where the upper reaches of the **Humber River** and **Cold Creek** meet, it's **one of the most beautiful Park rides I have seen in the province.**

A serene array of **woodlots, open fields, and hilltop vistas** greeted us on our sunny spring morning outing. An exceptionally beautiful bike ride was had. We were delighted at how lovely the surroundings were, so **peaceful and natural,** far removed from homes and congested roads, with trees all around.

The path winds along with **ever-changing scenery** over the river numerous times and under street bridges. **No traffic to worry about**: it's a 100% car-free trail riding venture. There aren't even many cars to be seen from a distanc

I know some of you seasoned, off-road Park riders may sometimes wish for a ride that provides **more exercise**. I'm pleased to share this one with you!

This **cruise through Shangri-la** is **more challenging than the usual mellow outings** offered in Ontario parks, requiring more skill and effort to enjoy. I rate this route for most as a **Intermediate - Advanced Park** ride because it has a **loose gravel base** and is

very hilly, compared to the more than 80 other Park trail rides I have reviewed.

The **Granger** is not paved except for a few of the hill climbs. The crushed gravel is a mixture of packed fine crushed stone and coarse aggregate (a product of numerous **washouts on slopes**). You just have to be cautious, knowing this gravel could be **unstable and chunky**. We managed without incident on our hybrids and MTB.

It is also unusually hillier than the norm, so **you need good legs** or you'll walk it. (Not an issue if you are a road rider or mountain biker, you'll see hills like this daily.) I counted **three large climbs** with a total **elevation gain of 74 m** from the south end.

We started in **Kleinburg** at the **McMichael Gallery parking lot**, which **added another large ascent** to our menu. Well worth it! I highly **recommend a gallery visit;** it will enrich your day with superb **Canadian artwork** in a relaxing atmosphere.

The **historic village of Kleinburg** next to the gallery is a tourist attraction in itself; I would suggest you walk about and enjoy it!

For family outings, **Boyd Conservation Area** is a popular summer spot with **picnic facilities**. It's a great place to start your ride from. Entrance fee is currently $20 per car.

I had known about these hiking trails behind the gallery for quite some time and I'm so glad that I tried them out for cycling. They have been slow to develop into an accessible, bike-friendly path. Does the **new name** signal better riding conditions in the future? The gravel path badly needs grading and a few more hills could use some asphalt traction.

I have read proposals to extend the length of this trail further north and south in the future—all very promising. As we know, it takes time, money, and political will to execute. It's a terrific idea that could connect this to the main Humber River trail network, **right to Lake Ontario!**

This is a **very idyllic Park setting**, indeed, perhaps the best I've ever ridden. I'll be back to see the splendour of the **valley's fall colours**. It's a destination you are sure to savour, any time of the year.

Lower East Don – Park Trail

Toronto

Length - 9 + 3.5 side trails = 12.5 km (one way)

100% park path

Elevation - Relatively level along river's edge, large hill to get out of the Don Valley

Terrain - Paved path, fine crushed gravel, 20+ bridge crossings, 3 tunnels

Skill - Easy, except the valley hill

Maps - New map boards, trail markers… more eventually

Traffic - Typical city path users

Facilities - Parking lots, other future amenities unknown

Highlights - Profusion of bridges, tunnels, quiet ravine wilderness, interpretive placards and artwork

Phone - 416 661 6600

Website - Toronto Conservation Authority - TRCA, City of Toronto

Similar Trails - Upper Don River, Upper Humber River, Highland Creek

Local Clubs - Toronto Bicycling Network - TBN

Access - Cycle in from Wigmore Park, Wynford Heights Cres, or the Meadoway trail. Street parking on side streets suggested. Here are car lots that currently exist:

P1 Sauriol Park - east off Don Mills Rd, down by river, N of DVP on ramps
P2 Moccasin Park - 55 Green Belt Dr
P3 Sauriol Park - Lawrence Ave E, southeast side from DVP bridge

More parking lots may be established in the future.

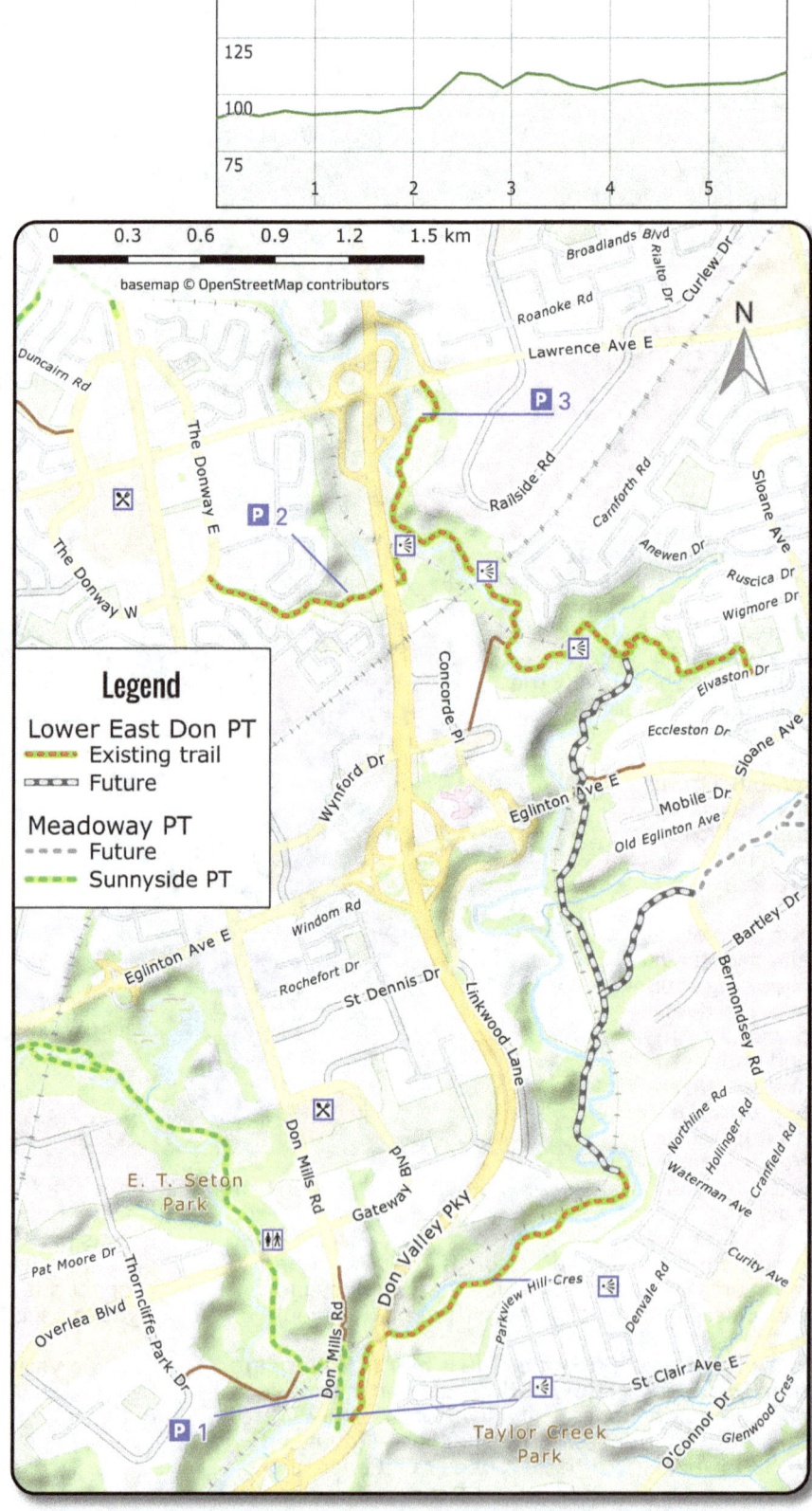

Review:

The new **9 km Lower East Don** River Trail is a **significant addition to Toronto's** cycling trail network. Once complete, it will become a **nature oasis** in the big city and an **important bike path** to connect much of **Toronto.** Portions of the trail are ready to ride, while others are almost done. I can't wait!

For years, I was curious about this strip of wild ravine, in the **centre of town,** with no marked paths. While looking at Toronto maps, I could see it below the **Eglinton Ave bridge.** I went in decades ago with friends on mountain bikes to explore. We didn't get far; **much of it was impassable.**

What we encountered impeding the way,—and city planners still have to contend with—**is a CN rail line, a winding river,** and a **golf course,** all squeezed into one **narrow ravine** with **steep, eroding banks.**

By 2011 the top end (the easy part to build) was finished. It goes south briefly from **Lawrence Ave & the DVP** (where the **Rainbow Tunnel** is visible from the highway).

At that time a city master plan for cycle paths prioritized continuing the trail south to meet the **Lower Don** trails. The benefits were many, the challenges were great and the cost was going to be high ($20M+).

When it is finished, I counted 21 medium sized bridges, 5 underpasses and 4 tunnels to make the connections. **A major undertaking** that is more than a **decade in the making.**

The goal was not only to create access through this remote ravine for the surrounding communities, but also to **link it to important connector paths,** thus adding a way to cycle off road from downtown to **Pickering** and beyond via the new **Scarborough Meadoway** path.

As of 2023, bike riders can **pedal the paved top third 3 km of the way,** from **Lawrence Ave** down to where it comes out at the apartments at **Wynford Heights Cr.** You can go farther by taking the **1 km Wigmore Park side trail**. You can also take the **Rainbow Tunnel to go 1.5 km** under the highway to **Moccasin Trail Park. All routes have a major climb** to get out of the valley if you do not drive there.

Did you know the **Rainbow Tunnel** was once a creative bit of graffiti? For years, the **city kept painting it over** and street **artists would paint it back.** This went on forever, 'til the city gave up, and now it has become an **iconic landmark.**

At the beginning of the ride, you may not see the highway, but you will hear its drone through the trees. Once you go under the massive **iron trestle rail bridge,** nature is upon you, the highway is forgotten, and **all is peaceful and serene.**

At the second rail underpass, you may notice **rocks on bars.** They're more than artwork: **each rock has a year carved into it.** These mark the **water lines for major floods,** and some are quite high.

The switchback to go up to **Wigmore Park** is where the middle section (still being built) will come out.

Phase 3, as they call it, (the middle section) is currently under construction and the **most challenging to build,** with the completion date already pushed to 2025. Bridges are in place and tunnels under the tracks will be added in 2023.

The bottom third, where the **other tributaries of the Don River meet with Taylor Creek,** is half ready. Started years ago, it needs tunnels and bridges to keep going. I checked it out in the spring of '23 and it is still a dead end. Eventually it will reach **Bermondsey Rd** and the **Meadoway** by the end of '24, sooner than right through to the other end.

It's open to the public but **not paved**; you can ride around the puddles and cycle for 15 minutes if you're curious to see what progress has been made. Even better, check the TRCA website for trail updates.

I would think the city will keep this part of the valley wild when the trail is completed. I have not seen any plans to put in flower beds and playgrounds. **Better for us to get back to nature in the big city, whenever we can.**

I am so excited this will be complete in two to three years, in my neck of the woods! Can't wait! And I wanted to prime your engines about something this good that's near completion.

Meadoway – Park Trail

Toronto - Scarborough

Length - 16 km eventually (one way)

85% park path
15% road crossings, detours

Elevation - Not as flat as you may think; a few hills help give you some exercise

Terrain - Wide, newly paved path; some loose grit; bridges (including one tall metal one)

Skill - Easy going

Maps - This trail project (part of the Pan Am Path) has yet to be completed on either end, but map boards and trail markers are starting to appear; most of the route is easy to follow

Traffic - A typical mix of path users; not busy

Facilities - Parking lot, toilets, benches, picnic tables, rain shelters

Highlights - LRT metal bridge, large Thomson Memorial Park, future connection to a much larger cycling network

Phone - 416 661 6600

Website - The Meadoway

Similar Trails - Finch Corridor, Chinguacousy, Centennial Bikeway

Local Clubs - Toronto Bicycle Network - TBN, Morning Glory Cycling Club

Access - You can find parking lots here, more are planned. Take the subway with your bike to Kennedy station (during non rush-hour periods).

⊕182 Bermondsey Rd
P1 Wexford Park - 898 Pharmacy Ave
P2 Goodlad Park - 940 Kennedy Rd
P3 Kennedy Subway - 24732 Eglinton Ave E
P4 Thomson Park - 1005 Brimley Rd
P5 Botany Hill Park - 236 Orton Park Rd
⊕**P6** Toronto Zoo - Meadowvale Rd & Zoo Rd

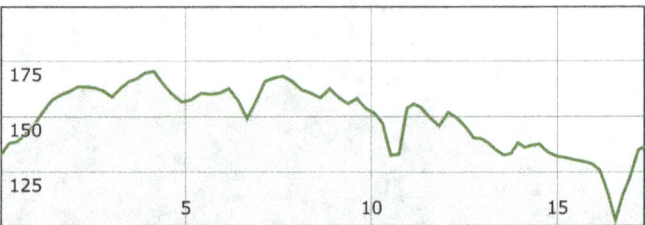

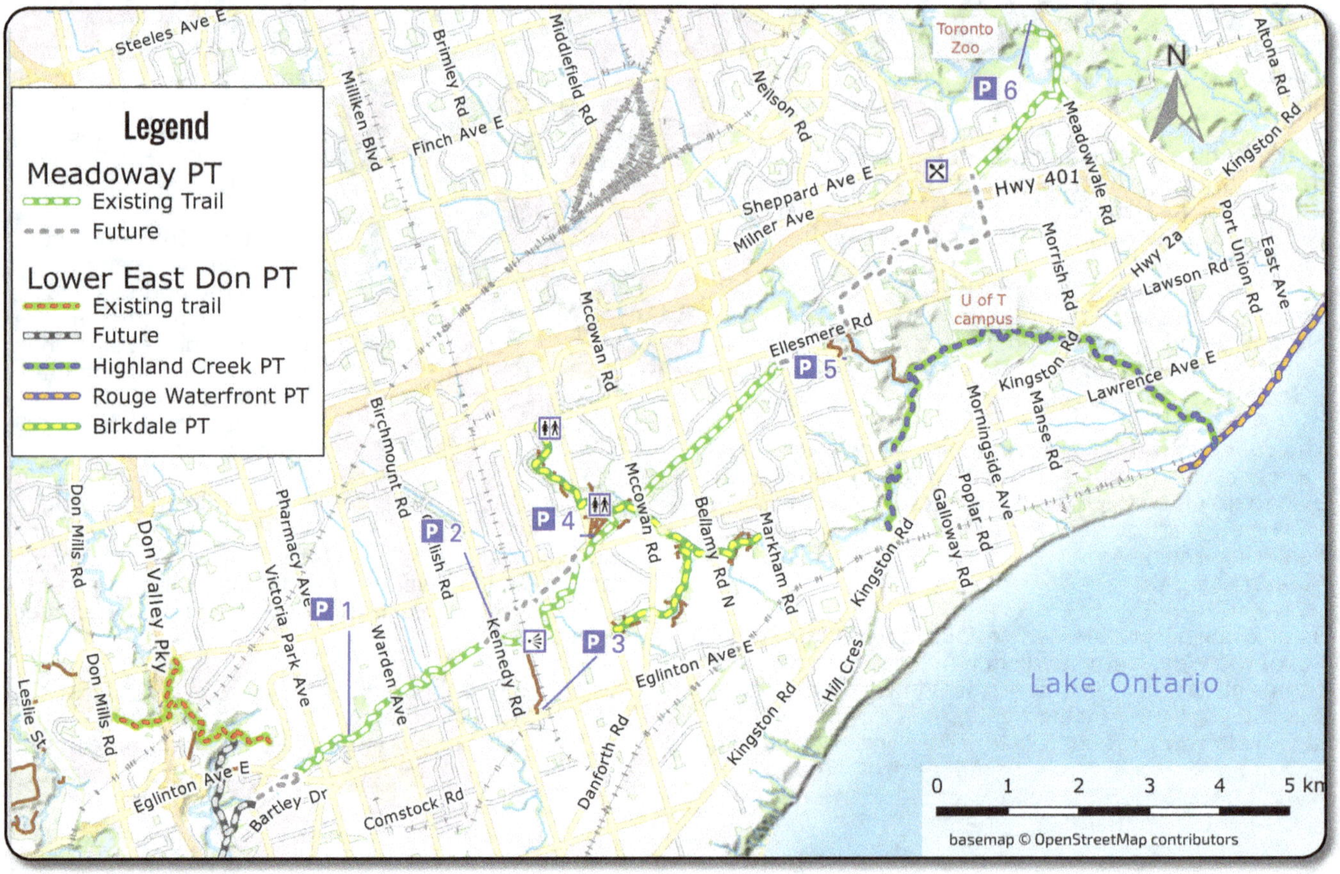

Review:

The **Meadoway** (formerly the Gatineau Hydro Corridor) trail cuts diagonally across **Scarborough** for about **10 km** (currently). This newly paved trailway is a **linear route that helps connect cyclists** to other parts of **Toronto.**

There are some **grand plans in the works** to revitalise this dead space under the **hydro corridor power lines** that deliver electricity from the nuclear plants east of **Toronto.**

The grand vision is to eventually go to the **Rouge National Park ravine** on the east end. On the west side cyclists will be able to connect with the East Don Trail also under construction (to get downtown). When the route gets finished in 2024-25 (hopefully), it will be **16 km in length!**

Recently a connection was made to **Morningside Park** that leads rides to the **Highland Creek trail.** From here you can ride bike paths down to the lake and far **out to Oshawa,** if you have the legs. Wow! That's another **50 km off-road.**

photo - TRCA

This rather uneventful, utilitarian path follows the power lines for much of its full distance. Thankfully, **the route is not too straight,** as it does wind around these tall towers, and it has (surprisingly) **a few good hills**. It's very much in the open, so you may experience wind gusts and get **plenty of sun**, so be prepared.

Not the most picturesque views among the electrical grid towers... but it is **a car-free ride** that **gets you places**. Well, sort of... it still has road crossings and a section in the middle that connects via side streets.

A fairly tall, elaborate **metal bridge** crosses the **Scarborough LRT tracks** and could be considered the

highlight of the ride, lol. Yup, not much to see on this route compared to other trails in this book.

At the bridge, there is a side path that goes south for a **kilometre to the Kennedy subway station,** which would be ideal for cross-town bikers to get here to start the ride.

In the future, the road detour at the bridge will be gone and the path will continue. The LRT service will be **closed by 2024** and replaced with a subway extension. So after the construction is done, a new bridge or tunnel will exist, maybe a closer station will be built?

But for now, if going east, take **Tara Ave**, then go north on **Fitzgibbons Ave**, then east on **Marcos Blvd**. and follow that to the end.

Almost in the middle of this ride is large **Thomson Park**, which offers another route you could consider, the **Birkdale** path.

The hydro fields have been ploughed under and **reseeded to promote native plant meadows**. Give it time to grow in so that the **scenery is enhanced.** It will take a few years to pave the full length, build bridges, and install signage, benches, and other little extras.

Because there's such a large population surrounding this path, efforts have been made to improve this sterile strip, and the fact that it will be an important connector route in the future, this trail merits inclusion for all to know. **It does hold promise!**

Oak Ridge – Park Trail

GTA - Richmond Hill

Length - 8 + 3 km (one way)

95% park path 5% road crossings, detours

Elevation - Rolling hills, with steep hills at Bond Lake and in Jefferson Woods

Terrain - Crushed fine gravel (still new and loose), and some asphalt on hill sections

Skill - Intermediate Park rider

Maps - Map boards, numbered trail markers

Traffic - Bikes, hikers, busy on nice weekends.

Facilities - No toilets! Parking lots, rest areas, food close via Yonge St, swim at Lake Wilcox beach

Highlights - Quiet, scenic, varied terrain (sunrise and sunset should be nice)

Phone - 416 661 6600

Website - Toronto Region Conservation Authority, Richmond Hill

Similar Trails - Jefferson, Nokiidaa, Upper Humber R

Local Clubs - Toronto Bicycle Network, Toronto Bicycle Club

Access - Parking lots in Richmond Hill at:

⊕ 49 Gamble hwy 29
P1 Bathurst Glen Golf Course -12481 Bathurst St
P2 Grovewood Park - 25 Grovewood St
P3 Bond Lake Trailhead - 12611 Yonge St
P4 365 Old Colony Rd
P5 Oak Ridge Com. Centre - 12895 Bayview Ave
⊕ **P6** 1245 Bethesda Side Rd

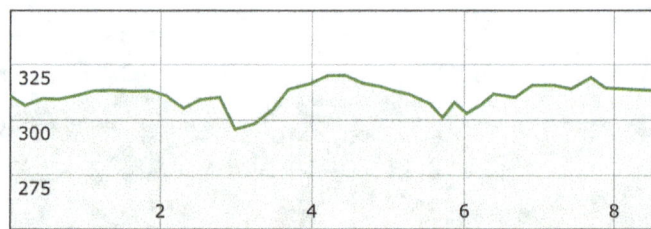

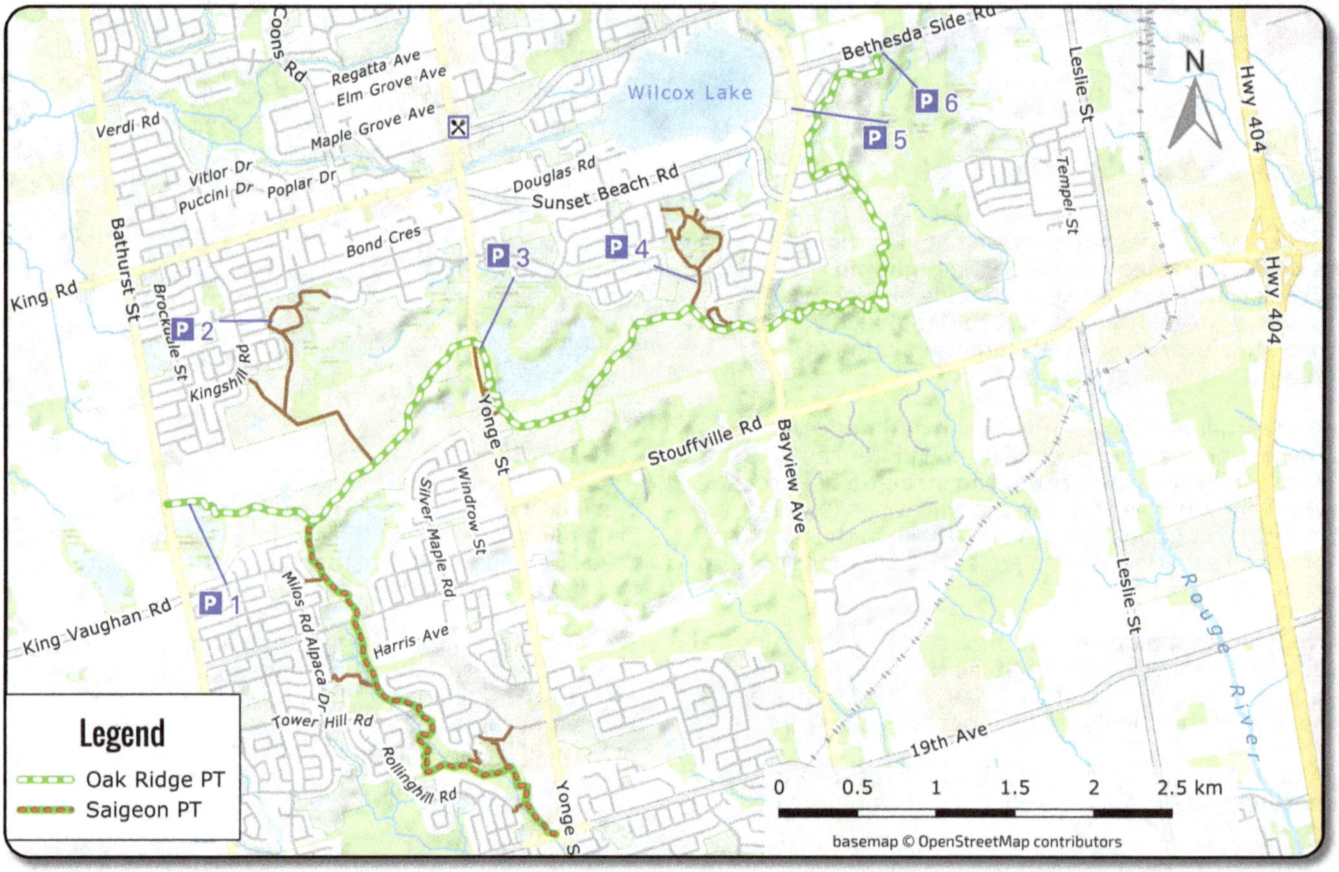

Review:

I am excited to note a new and wonderful reason to get out on your bike. Since my last book was published, a new **8 km Oak Ridges Corridor** trail has been completed and is ready for riders! Just north of **Toronto**, in **Richmond Hill**, this old favourite hiking path has now been upgraded to carry bicycle traffic, too.

Not only is this a **close, central location** for many **Toronto (GTA)** folks, but it also runs east-west through quiet, scenic woodlots and fields interspersed with small lakes.

Though most Park cycle paths follow a relatively flat river trail, not so on this route. Expect **a different type of Park ride** with more hills and open spaces to it, with no water to follow.

Some hills are quick and steep, others can be circumvented or

walked if you are feeling lazy. These extra challenges and the **fine gravel base** make this an **Intermediate Park** rated ride.

We started our outing on the top east end, at the **Bethesda Side Rd** parking lot. The gravel path is so new that it was **loose in sections** and will need a few winters to pack down. New map boards and path signage point the way, luckily, as other branching trails can take you off course.

The route skirts the west edge of Jefferson Forest, passing new townhouse developments (that look actually well designed). Riding south and then west is where you'll find **most of this trail's hills.**

Much has changed here in the 20 years I have been mountain biking the area. This path meets many dirt trails that may tempt you. Unless you have a **MTB** and **good legs**, stick to the main route.

At one point, the gravel path dips down and right back up a narrow valley. Odd sight? I think a wished-for bridge is not in the budget yet. **A lovely treed** and winding section takes you down and out of the woods.

When you leave the tree canopy and cross under the **large Bayview bridge,** you are met with a **major climb** up an asphalt switchback. Some may walk this part.

At the top, there is an optional small **loop around a pond,** and then the terrain flattens out through open fields, bush, and many newly planted trees. As you wind your way along, you reach **Bond Lake**, one of the many kettle lakes produced by the Ice Age.

Then another **steep hill!** Take it on, or bypass the quick down and up section by riding north on **Yonge St** to the lights and the only road crossing on the ride.

The sudden road noise tells you how **tranquil** the ride among the distant subdivisions has been. As you cycle another few kilometres, three side trails break out. The first leads you north to **Grovewood Park.**

The path then splits at one of the many new resting spots, ringed with boulders to sit on. Going right, down the field, and along the boardwalk takes you to the end of the **Oak Ridges** path at the **Bathurst public golf course** parking lot.

Going south offers **3 km** more to ride on the **Saigeon Trail** to **Gamble Rd.,** a more shady path. Some of this has a woodchip base and again is rated an Intermediate Park adventure.

So there you have it: a new stretch of trail. You could make a day of this sort-of out-of-town trip, just north of **Richmond Hill**. I saw families riding, joggers pushing strollers and hikers out there enjoying it. Why don't you join them?

Red Hill Valley – Park Trail

Hamilton

Length - 9.5 km (one way)

85% park path
10% hiking trail
5% road crossings, detours

Elevation - Level at the water's edge; gradual climb; steep at the top end—you might walk it

Terrain - Paved, gravel paths and sand, bridges

Skill - Easy to Intermediate climbs for 90% of it

Maps - Map boards, trail markers, easy to follow

Traffic - Cyclists, hikers, dogs and kids, not busy

Facilities - Parking lots, toilets, snack bar, benches, picnic tables, rain shelter

Highlights - Albion Falls, beach waterfront, long bridge, fast descent

Trail Fee - Free

Phone - 905 525 2181

Website - Hamilton Conservation Authority

Similar Trails - Lower Don River, Niagara River

Local Clubs - Hamilton Cycling Club

Access - Many side trails and streets lead to this route. Here are a few suggested parking lots to start from:

⊕**P1** Red Hill Trail - 169 Mud St
P2 Rosedale Park - Whitehouse Rd
P3 1060 Lawrence Rd
P4 Hwy 8 bridge, west side
P5 East end of Brampton St
⊕**P6** Confederation Beach - Van Wagner's Beach Rd

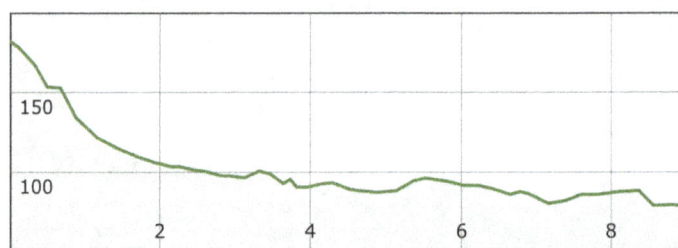

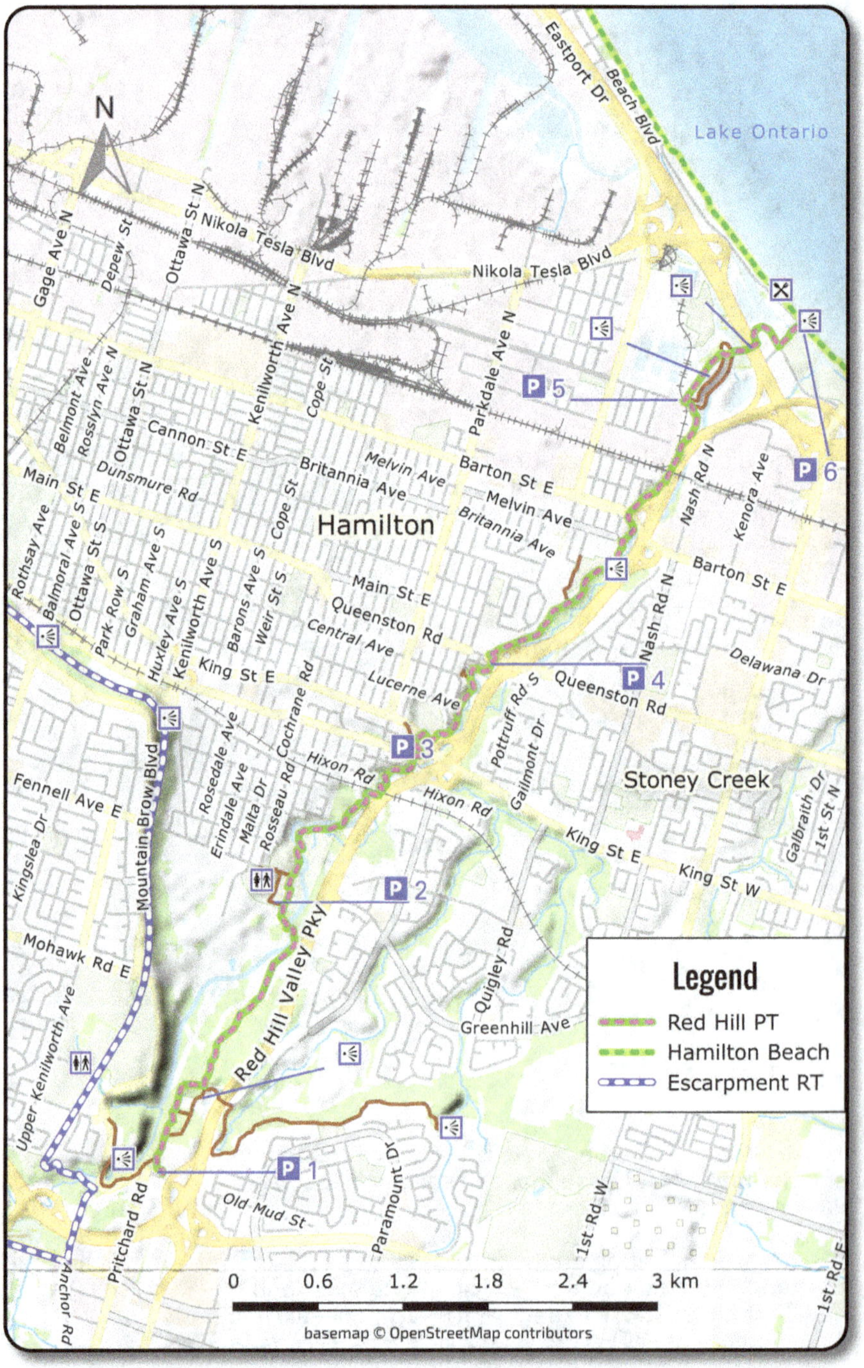

Legend

●●●	Red Hill PT
●●●	Hamilton Beach
□□□	Escarpment RT

basemap © OpenStreetMap contributors

Review:

The **Red Hill Valley** trail in **Hamilton** is a **9.5 km** ride that takes you, as the name implies, along the **Red Valley** and up a **big hill**, the **Niagara Escarpment**. I don't mean to scare you off with the **105 m climb**. It is a **gradual** one for most of the way until **the last kilometre**, which you can skip.

But why would you skip it? If you carry on to the top, **the big reveal is Albion Falls**, a spectacular **cascading waterfall** you can best view from the parking lot around the bend in the road. Psst: it's worth it.

Let's start from the shores of **Lake Ontario**, either from the car lots at the beach or coming off the **Hamilton Beach bike trail**. The signs will guide you sufficiently to weave your way up the **Red Hill Creek**.

Take **Van Wagner's Beach Rd** to the trail entrance just up the street on the right. It will curve around to get you up and across the **twelve lanes of the QEW!** This substantial pedestrian bridge crossing offers a few good lookouts.

Once across, you can't help but notice the **Red Hill Valley Parkway** that shares the valley with the trail. There was plenty of controversy when they built the highway; it's an eyesore and a marvel at the same time.

Highways are a reality in cities and certainly cyclists have learned to accept the one running up the **Don Valley in Toronto**. These roads have no impact on your safety when you're on the path, and that bridge was expensive, so let's use it, lol. The hum from it will dissipate the further along you ride. And the free views from it go on for miles.

The rest of the bike trail is a **lovely, slow, treed ascent,** alternating through woodlots and sports playing fields. The **Red Hill** Creek is on the east side (to your left as you ride), crossed by a few bridges. On the banks, you will see the **red clay soil striations** which must have given the trail its name.

The route design manages to do a decent job of getting riders across intersections and there is a cool (in more than one way) **tunnel under King St E.** Signs are getting a little old and battered, but they still give you the info you need. There are three road crossing**s, but the ride itself is free of car traffic.**

At some point, the incline may get steeper than you wish, and **walking up or heading back** are your options. Or take a street like **Lawrence Rd**, which has bike lanes to get you into town.

If you were to start from the top, it would be somewhat easier, because **gravity is your friend.**

After the parking lot at the top, the trail runs flat for a few minutes, then there is a **quick 20 m drop**, a hard climb up, and a loose gravel descent coming down. Some may walk it either way. I was just happy to be on a MTB when I came down.

Of the three trails on this section, the **west one seems to be the most tame.** Just don't do the dirt MTB trails with jumps.

The **Red Hill trail** has many parking lots to start from and even more exits from which you can head off in all directions, like east to **Felker's Falls**. You can combine it with the **Escarpment RT** (an easier way to get up) or carry on along the **Hamilton Beach park trail to Burlington.**

I saw the **Bear** and **Turtle meeting places**—the **Nest** and **Eel** meeting places are yet to come as of this writing. See if you can spot them. These Indigenous-inspired spaces are a collaboration between the **City of Hamilton** and the **Haudenosaunee Confederacy Chiefs Council.**

In the fall, the **colours are showy** and the leaves can be slippery and could hide ruts. The creek has been known to **flood**, so be aware of that.

The long beach strip on **Lake Ontario** has fast food and **Hwy 8** has some, too, and at the top, you can find picnic tables. Enjoy this connector route on your wayward journey.

Rouge Valley – Park Trail

GTA - Markham

Length - 12+ km (one way)

97% park path
3% road crossings, detours

Elevation - Flat along creek; short, gradual hills; a few quick, steep climbs over bridges

Terrain - Patchy surface; partly paved; some sections are gravel or wood chips. Path varies in width. Bridges, boardwalks, and short road crossings with traffic lights

Skill - Easy rolling for everyone

Maps - Some signs say Villages & Valleys; none yet say Rouge Valley. (Expect new signage soon.) You may need to refer to a map app on your phone.

Traffic - Typical path users, tourists; busy on weekends

Facilities - Parking lot, toilets, benches, picnic tables, shelters, bike repair stations, swimming at Milne Dam

Highlights - Boardwalks, large ponds/lakes, many bridges (some grand), old homes, ever-changing scenery, tourist stops, art gallery

Phone - 905 477 5530 ⊕

Website - City of Markham

Similar Trails - Oshawa Creek, Nokiidaa, Speed River

Local Clubs - Toronto Bicycle Network - TBN

Access - On the north end there are two entry points for this trail south of 16th Ave (we parked on a side street as there are no lots). Parking access is easier on the south end. Suggested car lots:
⊕16th Ave east of Village Pkwy
P1 Toogood Pond - 280 Main St
P2 Carlton Rd. & Main St, Unionville
P3 Milne Dam Cons. Area - 8251 McCowan Rd
P4 Rouge River Comm. Centre - 146 Rouge Bank Dr
⊕ **P5** Roxbury Park - 80 Roxbury St
P6 Tomlinson Park - 96 Boxwood Cres

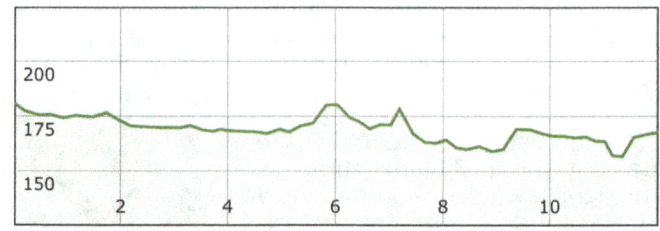

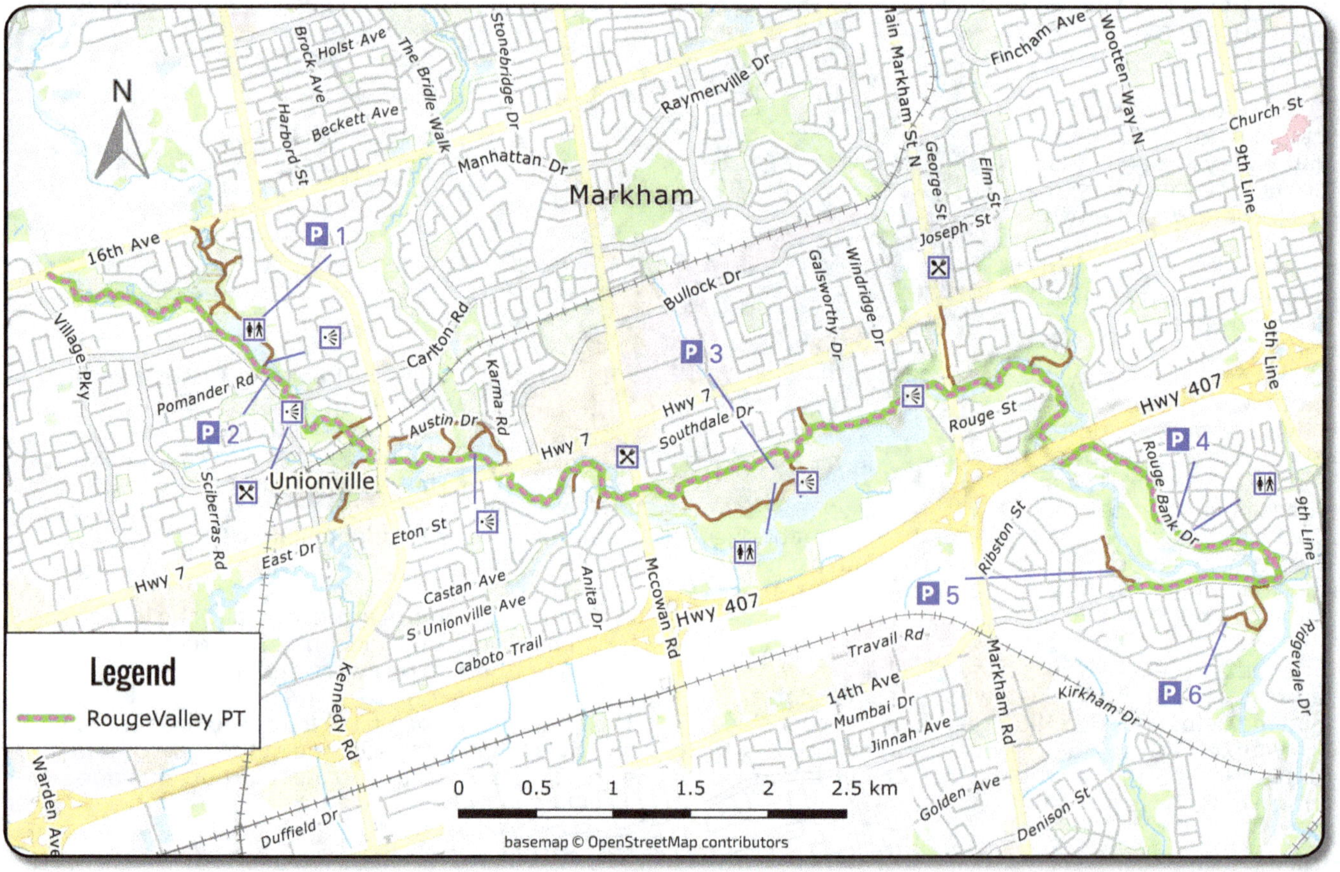

Review:

In **Markham**, a suburb on the northside of **Toronto**, we found a surprisingly pleasant **12 km** bike cruise called the **Rouge Valley Trail**. Following the **Bruce Creek** into the upper **Rouge River** tributaries, we encountered a **patchwork** of trails—not to mention **ponds, a lake, boardwalks, large bridges, and a dam—that we loved.**

We set out on a spring day and found the trek full of winding, **ever-changing landscape** that **kept us interested in going further.** Much of it was still natural, open parkland, not overly cultivated.

At the top, the path starts at **16th Ave** and heads southeast, following the creek on a twisty and easily navigable narrow path. Onward through ravines, and over many boardwalks and bridges, it takes you to **Toogood Pond.** Much of this I remember being a rough, cracked asphalt hazard. It's now **been repaved and widened,** but not by much.

This area by the pond and the **old Main St of Unionville attracts a lot of tourists**/walkers on the path.

A few road crossings are required, but **none seem overly hazardous**; the larger crossings have lights, except for one spot right where **Main St & Carlton Rd** cross and there is a gap.

I was hoping this **short gap** would have been resolved by now. **Puzzling.** There is nothing to tell you the trail continues in the same direction beyond the parking lot.

The path changes often from paved to crushed stone and back. A few loose **washed-out sections** on the hills will be easier on **wide tires,** but the entire route is manageable on a **gravel or a hybrid city bike.**

Onward we pedalled, past another pond, through park land bordered by trees that made any neighbouring homes invisible. Once we got to **Milne Dam Conservation Park,** a popular **picnic area** in the summer, we did a small climb to reach **lookouts over the lake.**

Recently **two massive, modern** (expensive $$!) pedestrian **metal bridges** were built to connect the route to more riding to the south, creating the longest bike trail in **Markham.** I am glad they installed them, since **this pretty wooded path** is the **best part of the ride,** and it's not crowded.

The trail goes under **Hwy 407** and wraps around the **golf course** to end at **Roxbury Park.** There are **a few long hills,** but they're **worth doing.** When you get to the golf clubhouse parking lot, **stick to the path along the road** and don't inadvertently ride towards the first tee, like I did, lol.

I wish I didn't have to tell you this, but here comes the **biggest problem** with this **terrific ride.** The **signs are a mess!** I was hoping this would be fixed, but it's **gotten worse since I was there** three years ago, when the path looked almost finished.

So many issues. The first one is the **trail name.** Signs posted along the route call it the **Villages and Valley Trail** and the **Forest Therapy Trail;** signs referring to the **MPL Trail Project.** Who is this? I looked it up later. It's the public library doing something.

Yet its official name, **Rouge Valley Trail,** has **little presence** on the trail. It gives riders mixed messages and **creates visual clutter** on the path. And the worst part is, **some junctions have no signs!** We figured out eventually to follow **everyone's** signs, as they all went the same direction.

There are **other missteps** and blunders on this route I will bitch about at the back of the book on **my experiences with trail signage.**

Just one last volley about this name. When I hear **Rouge Valley Trail,** I think of the larger, better-known **Rouge National Urban Park** trails east of here, in a **much more significant valley.**

When I rode this route in **Markham, I never felt I was in a valley,** so the name doesn't describe the ride, either. Anyway, that aside, **it is a scenic ride with other great qualities.**

Stop at **Toogood Pond,** find a bench, and watch the geese swim about. Or visit the **Varley Art Gallery** or meander by the old storefronts in **historic Unionville** further **south on Main St.**

Plan a lunch there or at the **Milne Reservoir,** which has picnic tables for your group. Or cycle just beyond this park 10 minutes up **Markham Rd** to walk about the **old Markham village area.**

A quick drive up the DVP will take you to the north end of the trail on **16th Ave** or use the **407** to get to the other end in no time. This ride is a great find within the GTA, and a highly recommended jaunt for local Torontonians.

Sunnybrook – Park Trail

Toronto

Length - 15 km (one way)

90% park path
10% road shared cars in park

Elevation - Flat along the water's edge, a large hill to get in or out of the valley

Terrain - Predominantly wide, paved two-way paths; some gravel and sand; bridges

Skill - Easy

Maps - Map boards, numbered routes

Traffic - Cyclists, walkers, rollerbladers, dogs, kids, a few cars

Facilities - Parking lots, many washrooms, snack bar, benches, picnic tables, rain shelters

Highlights - Deep, wooded ravines; tall bridges; horse stables; botanical gardens

Phone - 311

Website - City of Toronto

Similar Trails - Humber River, Etobicoke Creek,   Highland Creek

Local Clubs - Toronto Bicycle Network - TBN

Access - Many entry points; of the eleven car lots you could use on this route, I suggest these ones to unload your bikes:

⚓ **P1** C Sauriol Park lot - east off Don Mills Rd, down by river, north of DVP on ramps
P2 Seton Park - 73 Thorncliffe Park Dr, bottom of hill, turn north, two lots
P3 Wilket Creek - 1132 Leslie St, first lot on right
P4 Sunnybrook Park - 1132 Leslie St (same entrance as P3, drive north to barn)
P5 Edwards Gardens - 755 Lawrence Ave E
⚓ York Mills & Scarsdale Ave

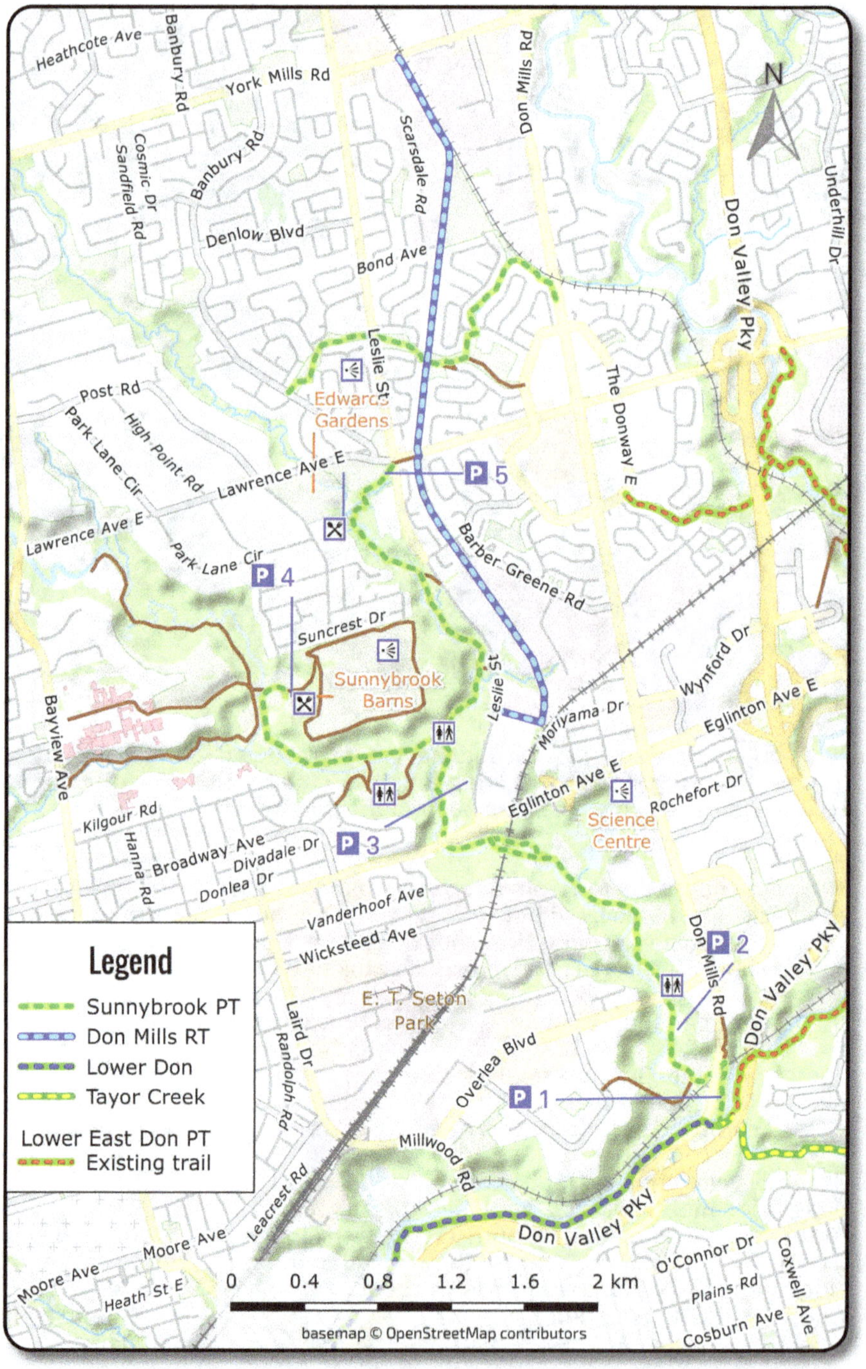

Legend

- - - Sunnybrook PT
••• Don Mills RT
••• Lower Don
- - - Tayor Creek

Lower East Don PT
- - - Existing trail

basemap © OpenStreetMap contributors

Review:

The **West Don** tributary has some of the most popular scenic bicycle paths in **Toronto**. None of them are very long, so I grouped a **cluster of five** together to offer you about **15 km** to enjoy. I call them the **Sunnybrook** Park Trails.

At its southern hub by the **DVP**, the trail is an important thoroughfare connecting with the **Lower Don River** and **Taylor Creek** bike paths (and soon the E Don).

From there, heading north over the river and rail tracks, this trail starts with a **steep hill**, bridge and ramp to overcome. Sounds impassable, yet everyone does it.

Once over, you are in **E T Seton Park** on a wide paved roadway (**bike route 45**). Cars also share the route, briefly, to find parking.

From this deep valley you will see the tall **Overlea Bridge**; as you ride under it, the vista opens up and you enter the parkland behind the **Ontario Science Centre**. Here you can picnic, play disc golf, or **find some easy MTB dirt trails** in the woods to scoot around on.

Riding further, the path splits briefly (you can take either route) over the water and under another sizable iron railway bridge. You have now reached **Eglinton Ave E** The path underneath takes you to **Serena Gundy Park**. I find this twisty, paved path gets a little narrow in places, an issue on busy weekends.

Soon you will see where **Wilket Creek** meets the **Don River**. At the washrooms, take **bike route 26**, a **2 km** side trail to **Edwards Gardens.** This secluded ravine ride, a favourite of mine, takes you to the botanical gardens, a great spot for a lunch break, a walkabout and some **flower photos**. It's a must-do. And for the curious, streets west of here have Toronto's **largest mansions.**

At this point, a tiny **new stretch of rail trail** east of **Leslie Ave** past **Lawrence Ave E** leads you north. The **4 km Don Mills RT** is straight, as former train tracks tend to be, with a nice shady lane going north,

connecting to **3 km** of more scenic paths in **Talwood Park,** so it's worth considering the out and back.

Cycling the other way from the washrooms at **Wilket Creek,** the path continues as a flat valley ride by the west arm of the **Don River** onto **Sunnybrook Park**. Here you can watch horse riders train at the stables and **buy ice cream** (good for kids of all ages).

For the curious, the road that climbs up the hill past the stables leads to a large playing field. You could ride the dirt path around the perimeter, but there is little other reason to do that climb than for cardio.

Onward, by crossing the river again you can reach the end at **Bayview Avenue** by riding west up a grunt hill three different ways. There's the service road up through the **Sunnybrook hospital** complex, or you can ride further up the river on a gravel path through **York University Glendon Campus**.

The third option is the more natural **1.5 km gravel path** past the dog park; this is a prettier, but rougher, way to the road. It may still not go through. But many continue on a dirt trail anyway. The last climb is steep—some cyclists will walk it.

I thought I would suggest this well-established **central Toronto location** because many of you can get there by bike and drive to it without burning too much (expensive) gas.

It's a wonderful **relaxing urban scenic ride,** bustling on weekends with **picnics, sports activities,** and **tourists** out for a walk.

There are many offshoots beyond what I already mentioned. A quick scan of a map shows that you can easily get by bicycle to the **Aga Khan Museum** or go north beyond that short RT with a minor detour to the **West Don** trails.

On the south end of the **Sunnybrook** segment, bike trails branch out onto another arm of the river to clock in for more fun-times city cruising. The main **Lower Don** trail takes you to the lake and waterfront, where it, too, splits into numerous choices.

Taylor Creek continues to **Warden Woods** for **10 kms** and there is a third new trail almost done on the **East Don** tributary. Oh, the possibilities! Lube that chain and get going!

Tay Shores – Rail Trail

Midland - Waubaushene

Length - 17 + 7 = 24 km (one way)

90% rail trail path
10% road crossings, detours

Elevation - Flat as a pancake, with one notable small hill

Terrain - All asphalt; smooth, wide path; well maintained; many road crossings; seldom busy

Skill - Easy cruising

Maps - Map boards and plenty of signs

Traffic - Busy on nice days, with cyclists, hikers, dogs, rollerbladers, Nordic skiers. Watch for turtles!

Facilities - Parking on street, toilets, benches, picnic tables, places to buy snacks and refill water bottles, outhouses, bike repair stations, eateries, lodging nearby

Highlights - One of the best RT rides! Scenic views of the bay and wetlands, historic Fort Ste. Marie, Midland waterfront, a beach every 20 minutes

Phone - 705 534 7248

Website - Tay Township, Tourism Simcoe

Similar Trails - Georgian RT, Greenwa RT, Speed River

Local Clubs - Barrie Cycling Club, Collingwood Cycling Club

Access - Car parking lots in:

⊕**P1** Bridgeview Park - Fallowfield Ln, Waubaushene
P2 101 Coldwater Rd, Waubaushene
P3 Albert St & Veterans Ln, Victoria Harbour
P4 15495 Hwy 12
P5 Sainte Marie among the Hurons - 16164 Hwy 12, Midland
P6 287 Bayshore Dr, Midland
P7 550 Bayshore Dr
⊕**P8** Peterson Park - 162 Marina Park Ave

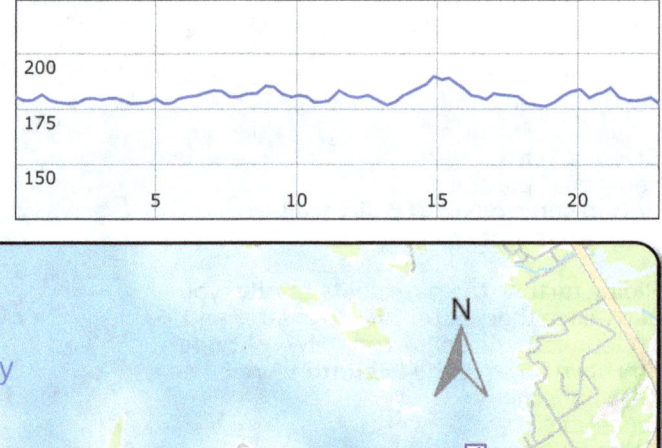

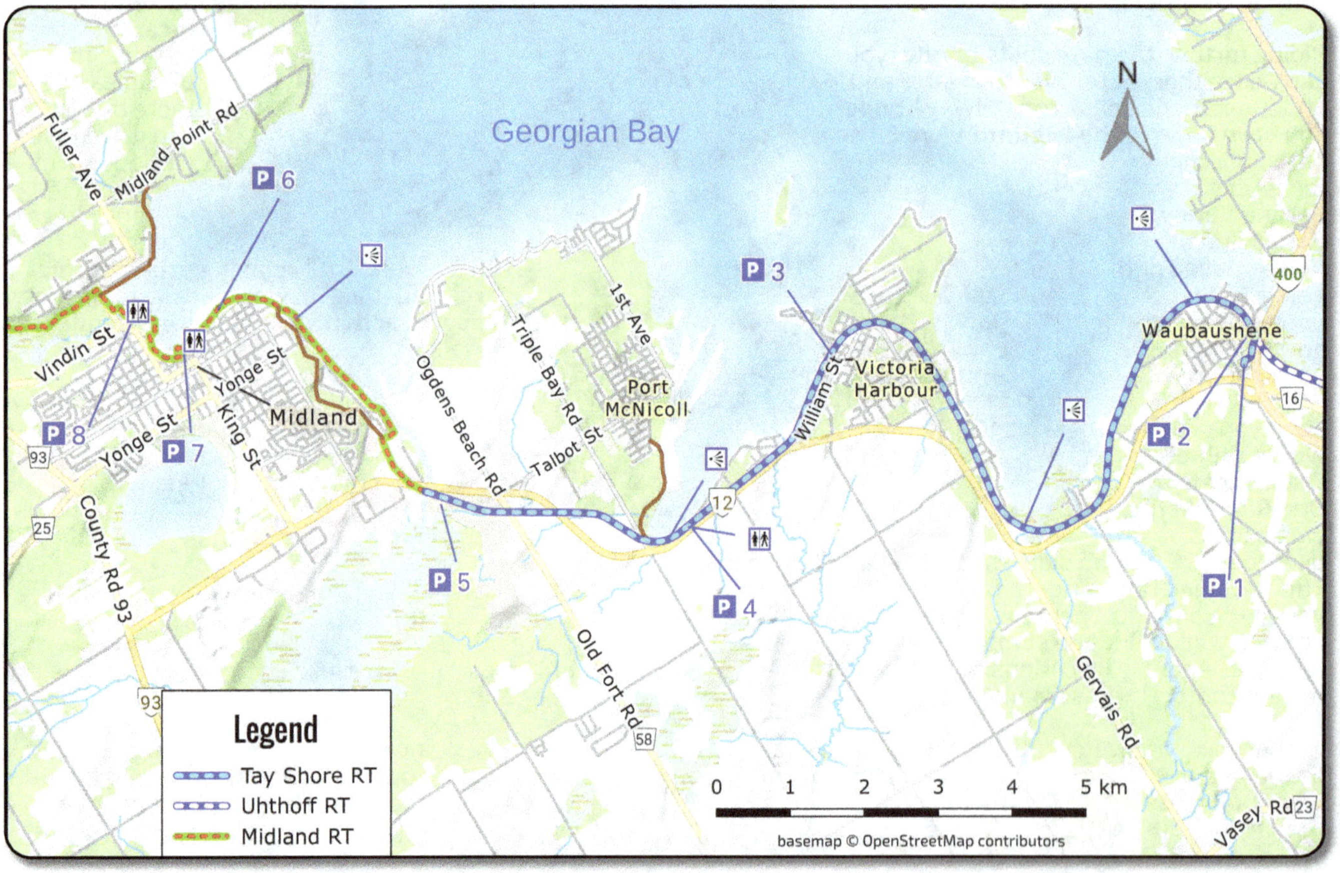

Review:

Experience the **best in Rail Trails** as you cycle the **17 km** of the **Tay Shore Trail** on the **Georgian Bay** coast. I have yet to encounter a better developed and scenic Rail Trail to enjoy on a sunny Sunday afternoon. (And enjoy it is exactly what we did!)

As part of a **much larger trail system**, this section is well-signed, flat, easy riding, with plenty to see, and it's all paved! Yes, a paved Rail Trail which truly has turned into a **Park trail** and is **good for any type of road bike.**

Evenly placed along the route are **benches to rest, picnic tables, outhouses, and interpretive signs** to take in the **local nature and history.** For train buffs, someone has placed small white signs with a detailed history of what was once a busy rail line.

As the route curves, it runs close to the shore from **Waubaushene** on to **Victoria Harbour** and into **Midland**. You will see many cottages and retirement communities, and pass through **two large wetlands** with grand views of the bay.

Well-shaded by trees, you might think you are riding in the country, but a quick look at a map shows homes and amenities close at hand. Plenty of small road crossings offer the chance to veer off and **discover small marinas** and **beaches** and alternate roads for your return.

A short **2 km** spur trail on the right takes you up to the town of **Port McNicoll** as an alternate route.

Actually, this area has many other routes to try. The trail officially ends when you cross the large bridge and see the **rebuilt historic fort—Sainte-Marie among the Hurons** (worth visiting).

After the fort, if you have the time, keep going. The **Midland Rotary Waterfront Trail** takes you **7 km** along the shore into town, where the waterfront is developed and varied. It's an enjoyable Park trail pedal to the **small harbour for a walkabout** and a chance to get a bite to eat.

From there, a short ride on the road and on the **Mid-Pen Link** trail connects you with the Tiny + N. Simcoe Rail Trail in **Penetanguishene**. On the other end of the **Tay Shores RT**, this trail continues south to **Orillia** as

the **Uhthoff RT.** Add the Oro-Medonte RT leg and you have a weekend of riding known as the **Simcoe County Loop**.

The **Tay Shore** section of this large loop is the smoothest part. As mentioned, it is all paved, rather than the usual fine crushed stone. Seems an **unnecessary expense.** Expect some other parts of this **2 to 3 day loop** to be rougher; wide, gravel bike tires will be needed.

Consider camping overnight up at **Awenda Provincial Park**; there is a 19 km loop to ride in there.

I noticed the trail barriers are a **tight squeeze to pass** at each road crossing. I can't see how wider bikes for the disabled can cope if I find these gates so narrow. And another odd observation was that, when I rode the trail, most of the signage was facing west. Maybe they have since fixed this.

The trailhead in **Waubaushene** is conveniently right by a **Hwy 400 exit**. So pack your things, load the bikes, and motor up the highway one day with friends to cruise this beautiful bikeway, where the **cool Georgian Bay breeze** blows your worries away.

History - In **1869,** the **Midland Railway of Canada** (MRC) was established, one of many small railways in this area that changed hands more than once over the years. It would eventually be part of the **Grand Trunk Railway** and then **Canadian National Railways** (CNR).

The MRC absorbed part of an older line that had begun northeast of **Toronto in 1846** in **Port Hope** on **Lake Ontario** and made its way first west, then towards the north en route to **Orillia** and beyond. At the **Sturgeon Bay** flag station, the signalman would wave a flag (or a lantern at night) to have the train stop for passengers.

The line served local lumber mills and connected with the **busy shipping Georgian Bay ports** of **Port McNicoll, Midland**, and **Penetanguishene** to move prairie grain and freight inland to the southeast markets.

In **1912**, during a blinding **snowstorm**, one train rear-ended another, causing much damage and several crew deaths.

The last CNR steam locomotive ran in October **1958** and then was sold for scrap. Much later, in **2007**, this route was opened as a paved recreational path, part of the **Trans Canada Trail**. The **Uhthoff RT** that connects to the Tay was actually a **separate CPR route** that was competing for the same business.

Thornton - Beeton – Rail Trail

Thornton - Beeton

Length - 28 km (one way)

95% rail trail path
5% road crossings, detours

Elevation - Flat—actually it slopes up north 80 m

Terrain - Crushed stone, bridges, road crossing

Skill - Easy

Maps - Map boards, trail posts, signage

Traffic - Cyclists, hikers, horseback riders, snowmobilers, Nordic skiers

Facilities - Parking lots, outhouse, benches on trail, amenities in Cookstown and Thornton

Highlights - Many bridges, scenic views, towns of Thornton and Cookstown

Phone - 705 435 3900

Website - New Tecumseth, Simcoe County

Similar Trails - Caledon RT, Sutton - Zephyr RT, North Simcoe RT

Local Clubs - Toronto Bicycling Network - TBN

Access - Parking can be found at:

⬧**P1** 7883 5th Line Sideroad
P2 Hwys 27 & 21, Thornton
P3 4497 5th Side Rd, Cookstown
P4 Behind the Antique Market on Hwy 27, north of Cookstown
P5 4585 15th Line, Cookstown
P6 11th Line & 10th Side Rd, north of Beeton
⬧42 Lilly St W, Beeton

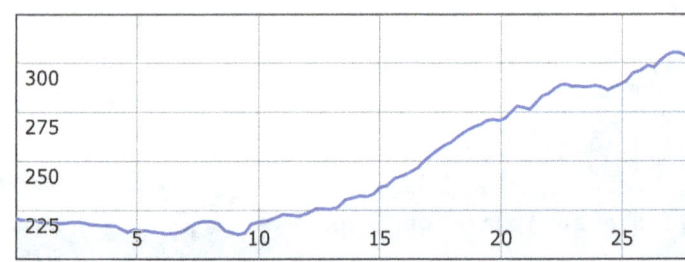

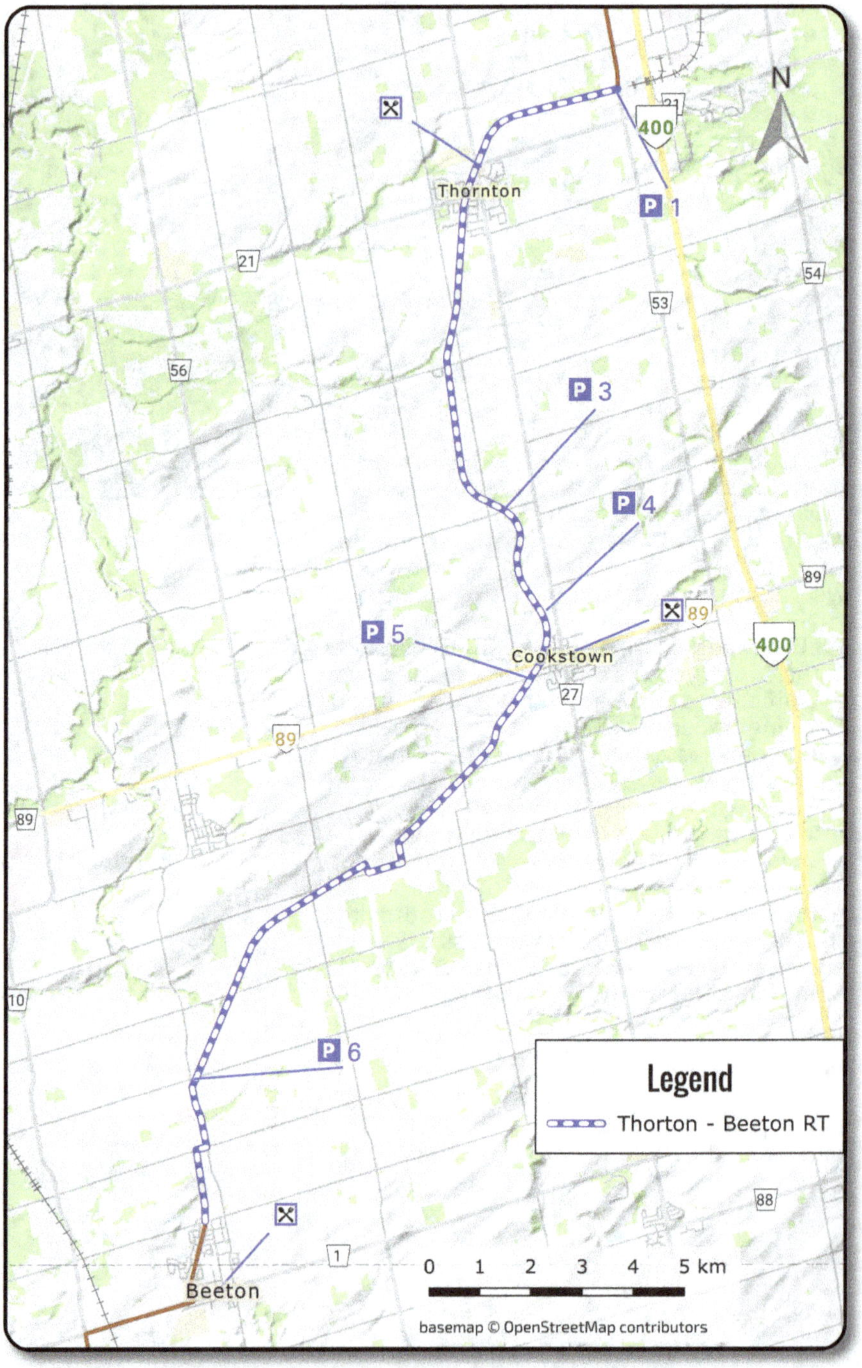

Legend

⬤⬤⬤⬤ Thorton - Beeton RT

0 1 2 3 4 5 km

basemap © OpenStreetMap contributors

Review:

Winding its way up towards **Barrie**, the **Thornton - Beeton** Rail Trail is another section of rail line repurposed for some fine leisure cycling.

This **28 km** segment of the line was once part of a much longer route from **Hamilton** to **Collingwood** and beyond.

My friend Bernie and I started the ride at a parking lot on the edge of **Cookstown,** the midway point. I was uncertain how far south the path could go, so we **rode north to Thornton first**. This was my first time on the trail, but it seemed already well known and **used by many** hikers, joggers, and cyclists.

I could see why: it was **well maintained, scenic,** and easy to follow. The trail base is your typical **fine crushed stone** all the

way. A gravel or hybrid road bike can manage this terrain nicely, but watch out for the occasional bit of loose grit.

There are a few road crossings. Some are quiet, but at others you'll need to pay attention to oncoming traffic. We crossed **Cookstown Creek** many times; I think I counted **eight trestle bridges,** all in good shape, and all nice spots to stop and perhaps take a picture.

The **landscape changes frequently** from treed sections to open fields. Most of the **route is not shaded**, giving expansive views of crop fields, pastureland, and marshy areas.

Those who like to stop along the way for a coffee and muffin will appreciate that both Thornton and Cookstown offer **opportunities to indulge**.

As we **headed back south** past our start point at **15th Line,** we continued for **4 more kilometres** before the fine gravel suddenly ended at a green gate. Had they run out of money? LOL.

Actually, in the last year, the next municipality has developed their part of the trail to now extend the RT down to **Beeton**. The **extra 8.5 km** has two small detours I hope get sorted out. It is essentially more of the same pastoral scenery.

Between **Beeton** and **Tottenham,** track still exists; tourists and rail buffs can take a vintage steam train ride at the **South Simcoe Railway.** Further along, this old rail line turns back into another cycling route, the very popular and longer **Caledon Rail Trail.**

On the north end, the rail trail goes **3 km** beyond **Thornton,** curving east to end at the highway where the casino is. From looking at aerial photos, I wonder if it could one day go right into **Barrie,** maybe to the waterfront. That would be great! I am unsure if and when, as the tracks are still used by trains.

This bike ride is about **50 km north of Toronto** and can be reached quickly being just west of **Hwy 400**. After your ride, there are plenty of places to find lunch on a patio and play the tourist travelling around to the local towns like New Tecumseth (Alliston), Tottenham, Bradford...

History - Originally the **Beeton Sub Branch Line** was built in the **1870s** by the **Hamilton and North-Western Railway** to bring produce and lumber to markets further south. Over the years this line was acquired first by the **Grand Trunk Railway** (GTR) and then the **CNR** in **1923**.

The last passenger train to run was in **1960**, and by **1986** the last freight train's journey ended a hundred-odd years of rail use. (This excludes the **South Simcoe Heritage Railway**, which purchased the track between **Tottenham and Beeton** and began running a vintage steam train in **1992**. This attraction is still running more than 30 years later.) The **CNR** sold most of the rest of the track to other local townships in **1996**.

Toronto Lake Shore – Park Trail

Toronto

Length - 18 = 9 + 9 km side trails (one way)

95% park path
5% road crossings, detours

Elevation - Flat along the water's edge, a few short hills, bridges

Terrain - Wide paved paths of asphalt and concrete

Skill - Easy

Maps - Map boards, blueish painted divider line

Traffic - Cyclists, walkers, joggers, kids, dogs, and rollerbladers; can get very busy

Facilities - Parking lots, toilets, snack bars, benches, picnic tables, rain shelters, beaches, swimming, bike share rental stands, kayak rentals, BMX park

Highlights - Beaches, boardwalks, lake views, many historical points of interest, Humber Bay Arch Bridge, Ontario Place

Phone - 311

Website - City of Toronto

Similar Trails - Harbourfront, Beaches Boardwalk, Hamilton Beach

Local Clubs - Toronto Bicycle Network - TBN, Toronto Bicycling Club

Access - Try to cycle there, as there is little free parking. Paid parking is found at:

⊕ end of Norris Crescent
P1 Humber Bay Park - 2225 Lake Shore Blvd W, Etobicoke
P2 Sunnyside Park - 1998 Lake Shore Blvd W
⊕ **P3** Ontario Place - 955 Lake Shore Blvd W

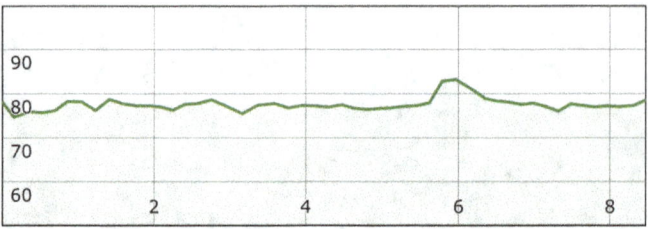

Review:

Cycling the **9 km Lake Shore** section of the **Martin Goodman Trail** may seem short, but veering off on **side trails** can double that distance. This enjoyable and **very popular route** around **Humber Bay,** on the **Toronto waterfront**, draws riders for many reasons.

As some of you may know, it is a **major cycling connector** for the city. But are you aware that this route has lots of **historic stops** and tempting **trip diversions?**

What brings riders down to the lake is not only the **cool breeze** and **beach sand** but a sense of **getting away** from the urban chaos.

Well, not completely, mind you: a glance to the north can reveal lanes of backed-up traffic. (You will be glad you are on a bike when you see it.) Still, half of the time there is enough parkland to separate cyclists from the sight of cars.

I start this ride on the west side, at **Mimico Waterfront Park.** Sadly, going further west from here is a patchwork of detours and on-road **bike lanes**, not the focus of this book. I stick to **off-road, car-free cycling,** where as much as possible riders cannot see or hear cars, much less encounter them.

Heading east, the first side trails (at about **4 km**) will loop you around both the **east and west peninsulas** at **Humber Bay Park:** perfect for **cityscape photos** across the bay (especially at twilight).

Then continue over the iconic white **Humber Bay Arch Bridge.** From here, you can ride up the **Humber River Trail & Upper Humber** right to the top ~**24 km,** one of the most **popular cycling routes in Toronto.**

Once across the bridge, you've reached the **Sunnyside Beach** area, which has a long history of attracting Torontonians. The old **Bathing Pavilion** is a favourite

for photo shoots, and the nearby **pool**—built in **1925**—was once one of the largest outdoor pools in the world.

A century ago, big bands played at dance halls, the **Palais Royale,** is now the last concert hall still standing. Kids could ride the streetcars for free to get here, and they even **set old ships ablaze** in the harbour and set off **fireworks** to attract people to come!

The **wooden boardwalk** (which you are not to ride) once had couples walking it on Sundays in their finest. Parkettes along the way have **placards posted** informing you about everything from **battles in 1812** to the first swimmer who **crossed the lake**. Yours to discover.

On the north side of **Lake Shore Blvd,** you'll find the **Sunnyside BMX park,** and further along is **High Park,** one of the largest city parks, where you can ride about **5 km of loops.**

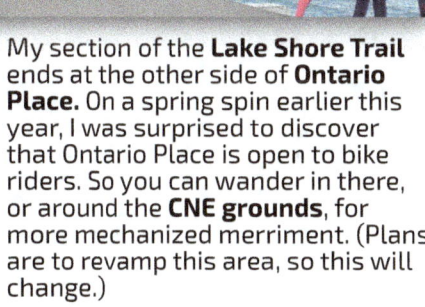

My section of the **Lake Shore Trail** ends at the other side of **Ontario Place.** On a spring spin earlier this year, I was surprised to discover that Ontario Place is open to bike riders. So you can wander in there, or around the **CNE grounds,** for more mechanized merriment. (Plans are to revamp this area, so this will change.)

Beyond this point, you are now joining up with the **9 km Harbourfront** segment and then another **9 km** along the **Beaches Boardwalk** section of the **Goodman Trail**. This very lively urban city tour of Toronto is **a must for bike tourists.**

The trail is well maintained and signed. It's also a **virtual bike highway** at times, which means riders need to **pay attention** to other cyclists, rollerbladers, joggers and those absent-minded, phone-staring zombies.

Personally, I wish the city would **define two paths,** one for pedestrians and joggers and the other for **bikes and bladers only.**

Pack a picnic or find a patio; this is **the heart of the city's relaxation zone.** Slow down, chill, and stay a while. There is lots to see and do any time of year..

Uhthoff – Rail Trail

Orillia - Waubaushene

Length - 42 = 32 + 5 + 5 km (one way)

90% rail trail path
10% road crossings, detours

Elevation - Flat, with a very gradual slope down to Georgian Bay

Terrain - Paved in town, out of town a mix of crushed stone, gravel, sandy soil, tall grasses, and doubletrack sections

Skill - Intermediate ('til they finish resurfacing the path)

Maps - Map boards and signposts keep you on track

Traffic - Cyclists, hikers, naturalists, equestrians, Nordic skiers, and snowmobilers

Facilities - Parking lots, washrooms in Orillia, benches, rain shelters, food

Highlights - Lively waterfront, shaded woodlots, quiet country cruising, communities of Coldwater and Waubaushene

Phone - 705 326 4585

Website - City of Orillia

Similar Trails - Simcoe + Tiny RT, Thornton-Beeton RT Clearview RT

Local Clubs - Mountainview Cycling Club

Access - My list of suggested parking lots:

⊕ **P1** Bridgeview Park - Fallowfield Ln, Waubaushene
P2 101 Coldwater Rd, Waubaushene
P3 Coldwater Area - 11 Michael Anne Dr, Coldwater
P4 2728 Burnside Line
P5 Division Ed E & Carlyon Line
P6 Couchiching Beach Park - 140 Canice St
P7 Orillia Waterfront - 50 Centennial Dr
P8 Tudhope Park - 450 Atherley Rd
⊕ The Narrows bridge north of 672 Hwy 12, Orillia

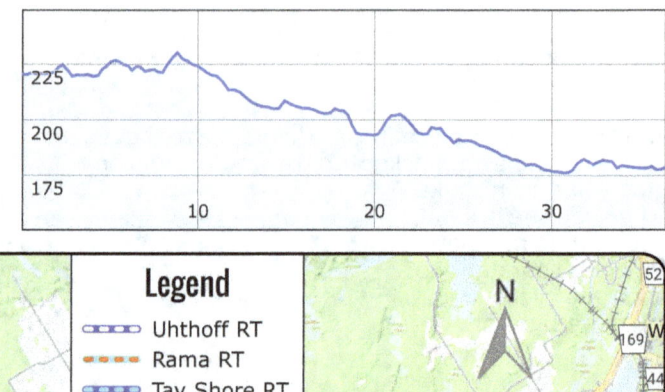

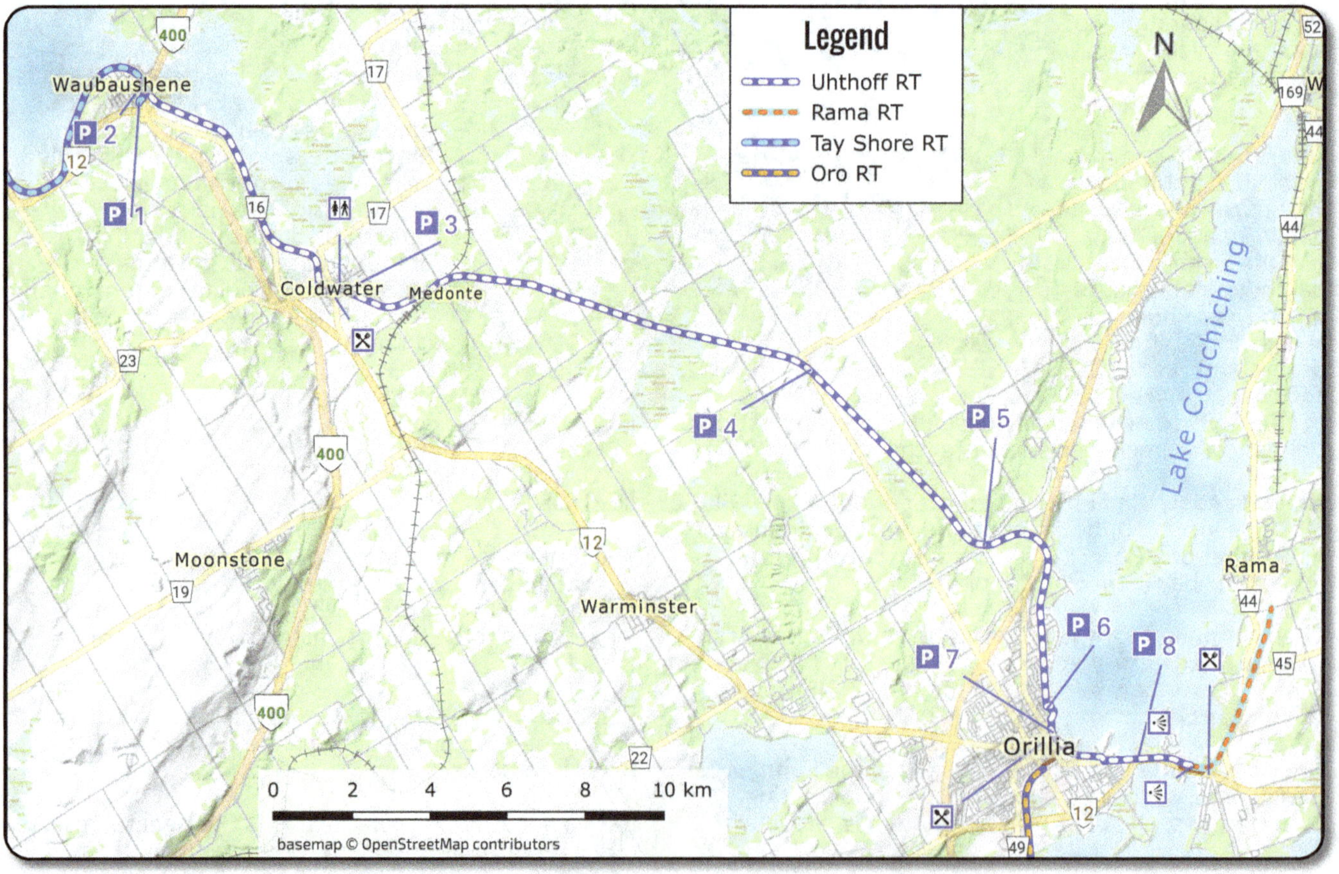

Review:

The **32 km Uhthoff Rail** Trail is a section of a much longer old rail line (as all rail trails tend to be). So I am including the **5 km** portion along the **Orillia waterfront** in this review, as they merge well and it's the best part, and another **5 km RT** past the waterfront.

Most riders will be driving up from southern homes, so I will start my description of the trek at the south end. You can park and start your ride on the waterfront anywhere along the **Orillia Millennium Trail.**

You can start east up to the narrows or on the other side, which requires you to cross on the road bridge (until they replace the unsafe swing bridge within a few years).

Wherever you pick up the trail, it is a very **pleasant paved tourist cruise**, with the **original train station** and other signs showing it was once a rail line. Other parts on this strip are manicured parklands, busy marinas, kids' playgrounds—it's all here, with a beach, of course.

Frankly, you could make this area the sum of all you are going to ride. Enjoyable park trails lead to the end of the **Tudhope Park peninsula**, one of four points you could explore at the bottom of this lake.

Venturing east across the narrows will connect you to a short extension: the tiny **Ramara RT** that just ends after **5 km**. You could carry on along gravel roads if that's your thing: perhaps to Washago, then back down, looping around **Lake Couchiching**.

However, if your intent is to go on the **Uhthoff RT** (which, after all, is what I'm suggesting), then ride the other direction: north to **Couchiching Beach Park**. Here the bike path veers off the shoreline onto **Jarvis St** into the woods.

There may be a bit of confusion, as you will notice two paths start here. These used to be two **parallel train**

tracks heading into Orillia. You can ride either one for a kilometre, but after that the left trail veers off and ends. So get on the **right-hand (east) trail**—there should be a sign—to continue up and out of town on the RT to **Waubaushene.**

The first part of the ride snakes into the forest for 30 minutes, a cool, shady spin. The sky opens up as you pass a very **large quarry**, which may not be so evident until you glance at your phone map.

You would think that with such an abundance of local material, the trail would be completely resurfaced with crushed-stone screening. Alas, it's better than I remember from years ago, but it is not completely redone.

Consider this a cue that maybe a **hybrid/gravel bike** or **mountain bike** will help you enjoy your tripping. There are **pockets of singletrack and overgrown, sandy, muddy, or rooty bits** to keep an eye out for. Not impossible terrain—I just know some riders like a fair warning. And in time this will all get resurfaced.

After this, the trail opens up, offering views of farmland, barns, and wetlands. Half of it is still shady woodlots. At **Dunns Line** the trail crosses over train tracks and another grown-in, abandoned CPR line intersecting. See if you can spot it, just past where you crossed the tracks. **It is the same line** as the one that ran parallel into **Orillia.**

By the time you get to the **quaint little town of Coldwater** there's a little detour in town to get over the creek and you're almost there. Grab a snack (ice cream) or drink and relax a while in town, as the end of this RT is only **7.5 km** away.

This rail trail has been gradually descending to **Georgian Bay**. When you get to **Waubaushene**, the name changes to **Tay Shores RT.** This is an all-paved and very scenic RT you could continue on, so why turn back now?

On the other hand, if you head back to **Orillia**, you could tackle the **Oro - Medonte R**T that leads to **Barrie**. Either way, there is plenty to pick from to suit your fancy around **Orillia**, and afterwards, **Mississaga St E** makes for a **nice downtown walk**, with patios, cafes, a craft brewery, and an opera house to visit .

History - continues on page 118

Upper Don – Park Trail

Toronto

Length - 9 +2 +13 km

85% park path 10% hiking trail 5% road crossings, detours

Elevation - Gradual slope north along the water's edge; a few short climbs to road crossings; big hills on Finch Corridor path

Terrain - Paved asphalt, natural base, wooden bridges

Skill - Easy to Intermediate

Maps - Limited map boards & trail markers; you may need to use a map

Traffic - Popular route - cyclists, hikers, children, dogs

Facilities - Parking (one lot), toilets at Sheppard Ave, benches; no playgrounds or picnic areas on this trail

Highlights - Many bridges; close to creeks; natural, treed ravine setting

Phone - 311

Website - City of Toronto

Similar Trails - Highland Creek, Taylor Creek, Lower East Don

Local Clubs - Toronto Bicycle Network - TBN

Access - This great ride surprisingly lacks free parking lots. There is only one I can suggest on the route. You will have to refer to a map to find street parking nearby.

I myself have street parked on Valleybrook Dr (free on weekends) when starting from the south end.

⊕ 3700 Don Mills Rd
P1 East Don Parklands -
 1240 Sheppard Ave E
⊕ 275 Duncan Mills Rd

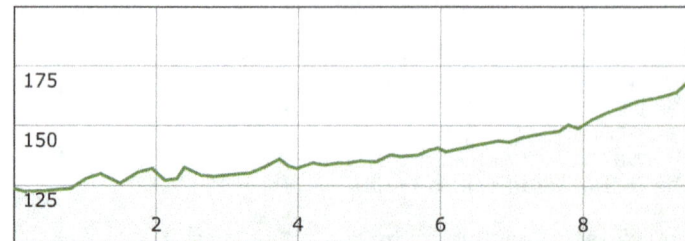

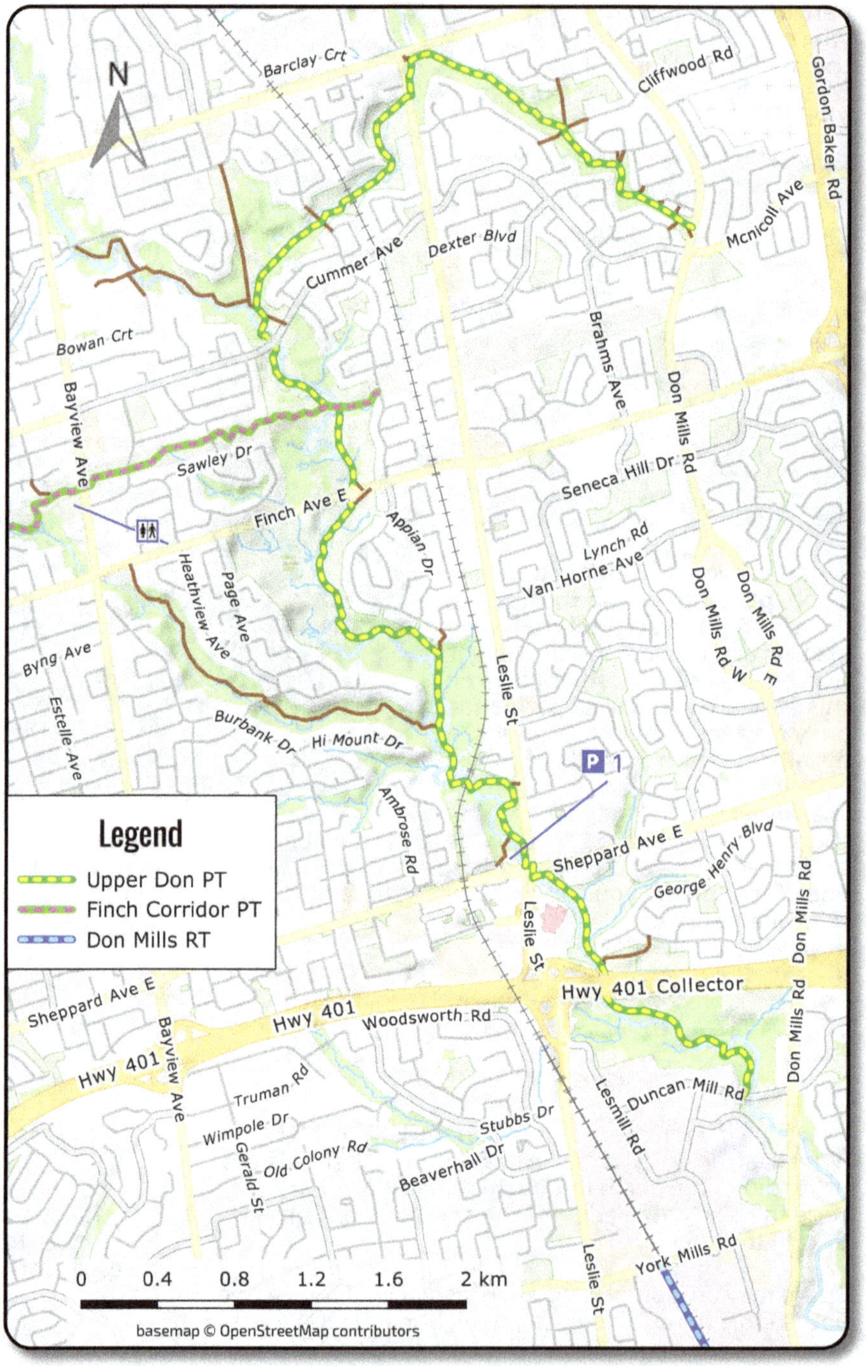

Review:

On the north end of **Toronto** resides a shady bicycle path through ravines along the **Upper East Don River**. This **9 km** Park trail makes for a nice relaxing outing for many who live close by in need of a getaway.

This meandering path follows the east arm of the **Don River** (one of four) from just below **Hwy 401** onto **Steeles Ave** and then curves back down to **Don Mills Rd.**

We started our trek on the south end, entering from **Duncan Mills Rd** to ride the short **Betty Sutherland Trail**.

It's more than a bit surreal to ride this route that travels under **sixteen lanes** of highway!

At **Sheppard Ave,** we came across an odd bridge. Actually, this trail has a **multitude of bridges** to cross, both over water and under roads and train tracks.

You have to use the lights to cross the large intersection at **Sheppard Ave**. On the opposite corner, the

trail—now officially called the **Upper Don** trail—continues down into the woods again.

What makes this path so pleasant is the sense of **being out of the city, in nature.** It has **very little manicured parkland** and none of the usual open playgrounds and picnic areas. You will find this to be **a nice change from a familiar city park tour.**

I found the **pavement is in good shape** though the signage is a little disjointed. You may have to refer to a map. I know the city is replacing its cycling signs and I hope they paint a line down the centre, too.

It also offers numerous **side trails** you can check out to make it a longer ride. The first fork is the **2 km Newtonbrook path** to the northwest. It's been kept as a natural surface and will be a bit of a rougher ride.

Another is a long path following the hydro field towers. The **Finch Corridor** trail goes winding up a large hill due west for **16 km** and can take you far across town to connect with other routes. (Frankly, being out in the open on a rather straight path with acres of sterile grassland is a totally opposite vibe to the **Upper Don** trail.)

Eventually, at the top end, the path meets **Leslie St**. You will need to cross at the lights to take the **Duncan Creek** ravine trail southeast **2 km** to **Don Mills Rd.**

You may take the option to loop back down to your start point by road riding south on **Don Mills Rd.** for **5 km** or head back the way you came.

I did not see any deer on my most recent ride here—just many walkers and cyclists using the trail on a fine summer day.

Make your way over to this neck of the woods to enjoy one of the many Toronto park rides, this one in a more **natural ravine setting.**

And there will soon be a lower **Lower East Don trail** to ride. Construction is almost complete! Can't wait...and they may even connect one day if they can sort out a way past the golf course.

Victoria – Rail Trail

Lindsay - Haliburton

Length - 85 km (one way)

90% rail trail path
10% road crossings, detours

Elevation - Flat as she goes, with a few noticeable inclines

Terrain - Crushed stone, gravel, asphalt, very sandy and rocky north of Kinmount

Skill - Most is easy; north part is difficult

Maps - A few map boards, well marked

Traffic - Cyclists, hikers, horseback riders, ATV enthusiasts, dirt bikers, snowmobilers, Nordic skiers

Facilities - Limited parking; towns of Lindsay, Fenelon Falls, Kinmount, and Haliburton have food, lodging, & toilets; bike share station by locks in Fenelon Falls

Highlights - Wilderness; waterfront cottages; Fenelon Falls & locks; Highlands Cinemas & station in Kinmount; old train stations and old locomotive in Haliburton

Phone - 705 324 9411

Website - Kawartha Lakes

Similar Trails - Victoria South RT , Uxbridge Lindsay RT, N. Simcoe RT

Local Clubs - Peterborough Cycling Club

Access - These parking lots are good:
⊕150 Victoria Ave N, Lindsay
P1 At the end of William St N and Champlain Blvd
P2 By the entrance of the Ken Reid Conservation Area - 277 Kenrei Rd
P3 Old Station Gallery - 103 Lindsay St, Fenelon Falls
P4 Garnet Beach Park - 98 Francis St W, Fenelon Falls
P5 Fell Station - Hwy 121 Superior Rd
⊕**P6** Austin Sawmill Heritage Park - 5 Station Rd, Kinmount

P7 Gelert Rd, Haliburton
P8 134 Highland St, downtown Haliburton
+66 Maple Ave, Haliburton

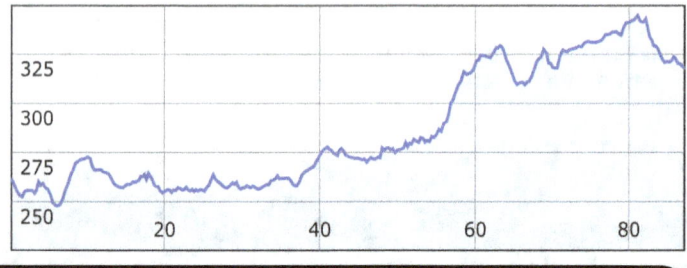

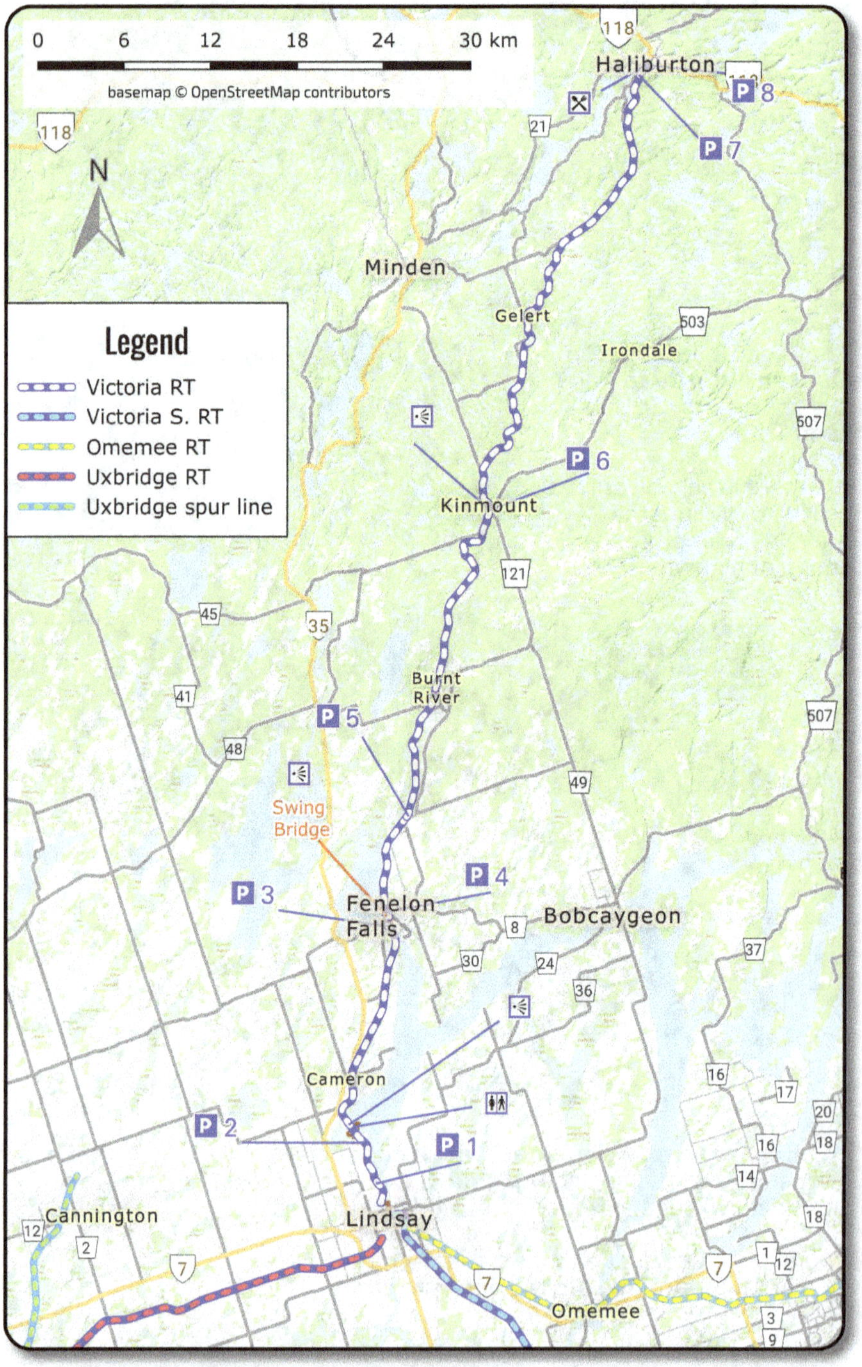

Legend

- ▱▱▱ Victoria RT
- ▱▱▱ Victoria S. RT
- ▱▱▱ Omemee RT
- ▱▱▱ Uxbridge RT
- ▱▱▱ Uxbridge spur line

Review:

The **Victoria Rail** trail is a **popular 85 km route** running north through Ontario farm fields into the forests of cottage country. It's a **long and winding path** that keeps cyclists engaged with the ever-changing geography between **Lindsay** and **Haliburton**.

Over the years I have ridden separate sections and it being so long and different, I think it best to **divide the Victoria RT into three parts.**

From the south end in **Lindsay**, it starts as a paved path but soon enough, as you leave town, it becomes that familiar, crushed, fine gravel railbed that riders are used to. There is the odd larger stone to avoid, but little else to be concerned about.

Soon you pass through a **rock cut** to cross the open wetlands of **Sturgeon Lake**. Stop for a moment on the bridge to take in how large this marsh is (and take a picture).

After that, there is a little bit of a climb to some nice **scenic vistas** over farms and fields. This part is an open trail, with **no shady woodlots** to pass through. The going is pleasant right to the old train station in **Fenelon Falls, 20 km** away.

To get to the next section of the trail a short road ride is required, as the **train swing bridge** is only in use in the winter for snowmobiles. No matter. Take **Lindsay St** (in Fenelon Falls—confused?) to cross the only bridge in town; this leads you to the **locks** and **waterfalls**, a worthwhile sightseeing stop.

If you start your ride in this **summer tourist town,** head north of the locks along the waterfront. Take note of the pizza, craft beer, and ice cream storefronts by the locks, a perfect triad you'll want to return to after your ride. Yum!

This trail takes you further north, along the waterfront of **Cameron Lake** with its fancy cottages and docks, then up the **Burnt River** through forests and fields to **Kinmount** for **30 km**.

Along the way, there are opportunities to stop and take in a snack break when you spot a set of **rapids** or **waterfalls**.

This Rail Trail is **well used by everyone,** so expect to encounter more travellers, cycling and hiking on the path closer to any of the towns.

In the village of **Kinmount**, there is a park with a dam, an old train station, and a sawmill museum. This can be another start point to go south or further north to **Haliburton**.

The route to **Kinmount** should be fine for mid-sized bike tires, but beyond, it gets really rough with stones and sand. It becomes frustrating as you try to head toward **Haliburton**.

I (and others) have tried to push farther north, but the sand is so loose, I would only suggest it on a mountain bike... or even better, on a **Fatbike**. If you can make it up **4 km** to the large bridge, the riverside route is worth seeing.

We were surprised at how **well maintained** and level the terrain was, considering the number of **ATVs** that passed us. And this trail has **lots of them!** Just take note of their presence, give them space to pass, and hope the dust is at a minimum.

This route is well suited for an overnight stay on your trek, be it in **Lindsay, Fenelon Falls,** or **Haliburton,** and the trail runs through the Log Chateau Park campground as well.

Another Rail Trail I reviewed in my first book goes by the same name and continues SE from **Lindsay**. I called it the **Victoria South** section for **29 km** more, if you want to do it all. Use a MTB.

History - At one time, **Lindsay, Ontario** was an **important train hub,** with lines from other railways running in all directions. The **Victoria Railway,** with its terminus in **Lindsay,** started running trains to **Haliburton** in **1878**. Interestingly, as the railway made its way north from **Kawartha Lakes**, a contingent of recently arrived settlers from Iceland served as its workforce in the years **1874-75**.

Most eventually moved on to **Manitoba** due to the various hardships they endured in that time, including sickness and lack of work when the railway unexpec-tedly ran short of funds. By the time the railway made it to **Haliburton,** though, it was more profitable and it carried on as a means of extracting **lumber and minerals** from the north.

The line was acquired by the **Midland Railway in 1882,** and eventually by the **CNR** in **1923**. Regular passenger service ceased in **1960** and freight service lasted until **1978**. Today, sadly, there are **no tracks left in Lindsay**—but you can start a great Rail Trail ride from here.

Whitby Waterfront – Park Trail

Whitby

Length - 19 km (one way)

90% park path
10% road crossings, connections

Elevation - Small, gradual elevation changes with one larger hill near Oshawa

Terrain - Wide, paved path; bridges; boardwalks

Skill - Beginner

Maps - Map boards; follow the painted line

Traffic - Typical path users, can be busy on sunny weekends

Facilities - Parking lots, toilets, snack bar, benches, picnic tables, rain shelters

Highlights - Quiet; scenic lake views; wetlands; beaches

Phone - 905 430 4300

Website - Town of Whitby, Great Lakes Waterfront Trail

Similar Trails - Ajax Waterfront, Rouge Waterfront, Hamilton Beach

Local Clubs - Durham Cycling Club, Oshawa Cycling Club

Access - Lots of parking options on this route. Here are a few:

⊕**P1** Lynde Shores Cons. Area - south end of Halls Rd S, Whitby
P2 Lynde Shores Cons. Area - north end of Halls Rd S
P3 Port Whitby Boat Launch - 301 Gordon St, Whitby
P4 Whitby Promenade - 250 Water St**P5** 1202 Phillip Murray Ave, Oshawa
⊕**P6** Lakeview Park - 55 Lakeview Park Ave

GO Transit - Whitby Train Station - 1350 Brock St S

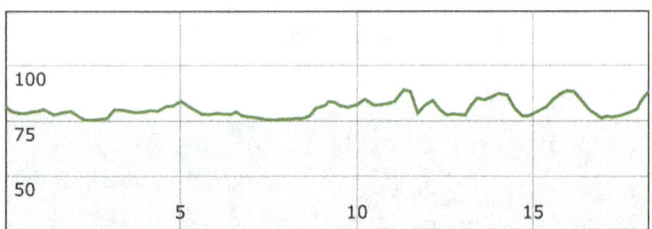

Review:

Relax and forget your worries as you cruise along the **19 km Whitby Waterfront** trail on the shores of **Lake Ontario**. It's the perfect new destination for a summer cycle with family and friends.

This meandering park bike path winds through open fields and parklands, up and around bays, and bridges over wetlands.

A wide, paved park path in **decent shape** follows the edge of the lake. **The water is not always within sight,** but certainly the stillness and cool breeze that come from the lake are apparent.

Stop at some point to **walk to the edge**. There are small clay bluffs along the way with opportunities to look out over the water or climb down to the beach.

Map boards posted show you the way, but simply following the **painted divider line** on the path keeps you on track. This parkland is a **popular area,** so expect traffic on nice sunny days. I saw plenty of benches, rain shelters, and a few washroom stops along this ride.

Twice you need to ride through **quiet neighbourhood streets** to reconnect back to the park path; it's all **very enjoyable** on this well-established bicycle route.

We did not start this ride at the very beginning, which is on the other side of the **Lynde Shores Conservation Area** (a good place for **birdwatching,** my brother tells me).

This time the three of us opted to take the **GO train** to **Whitby**. Friends came in from the Mimico GO station and joined us.

Taking bikes on the **GO train** is a simple enough endeavour; once we arrived at the **Whitby station,** we used the elevator to get over the tracks, then a short ride across the parking lot connected us up to a bike path on **Henry St** that would take us down to the waterfront.

From there our bicycle trek went eastward from **Whitby Harbour** to **Lakeview Park Beach** in **Oshawa.**

Our fall ride was a little chilly, and on the return trip, we did hit some **wind gusts.** With all the **open spaces and few trees**, you are exposed to the weather and **sun.** Be sure you go on a good weather day.

Think of **packing a jacket,** as it's always a little cooler by the water, and some **snacks** if you've got kids along. There is not much to be found on this route to eat, perhaps a food truck or snack bar. (The day we went, it just so happened there was a Ribfest going on. Anyone for lunch?)

This path is part of the larger **Great Lakes Waterfront trail system** and connects west onto the **Ajax Waterfront** section, which offers a similar experience.

Going further east is not as good, but it does attempt to keep going. Or you can extend your ride by cycling north via the **Oshawa Creek** trail and find a patio in town where you can dine.

Bruce + Saugeen – Rail Trail

Southampton - Clifford

Length - 90 = 82 + 8 km (one way)

95% rail trail path
5% road crossings, detours

Elevation - Flat, gradual slopes

Terrain - Crushed stone, gravel, asphalt (one section not resurfaced)

Skill - Easy

Maps - Map boards, posted signs, more to come

Traffic - Bicycles, eBikes, hikers, horses, ATVs, dirt bikes, snowmobiles, Nordic skiers

Facilities - Parking, outhouse, benches, shelter, repair stations on the Saugeen RT; the Bruce RT is still being developed

Highlights - Beaches, bridges, quiet farmlands, rural towns, Port Elgin, Southampton, Paisley

Phone - None

Website - Saugeen Shores, Bruce County

Similar Trails - G2G RT, Grey + Bluff RT,   N. Simcoe + Tiny RT

Local Clubs - None

Access - The Bruce RT is so new, it has yet to establish enough designated user parking lots (I asked). Look on their site in the next few years for locations.

May I suggest finding lots in parks or nearby arenas; any quiet country road crossing where you can safely park on the shoulder should work. And:

⊕ 248 Laird Lane, Southampton
P1 Beach lot - 289 Front St S, Southampton
P2 The Plex Community Centre - 600 Tomlinson Dr, Port Elgin
P3 Concession Rd 4 in Port Elgin
P4 Concession Rd 6
⊕ 45900 Huron Bruce Rd, Clifford

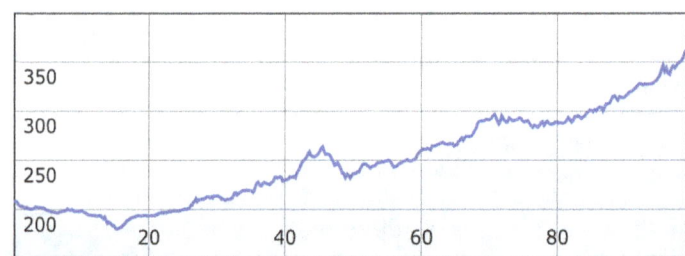

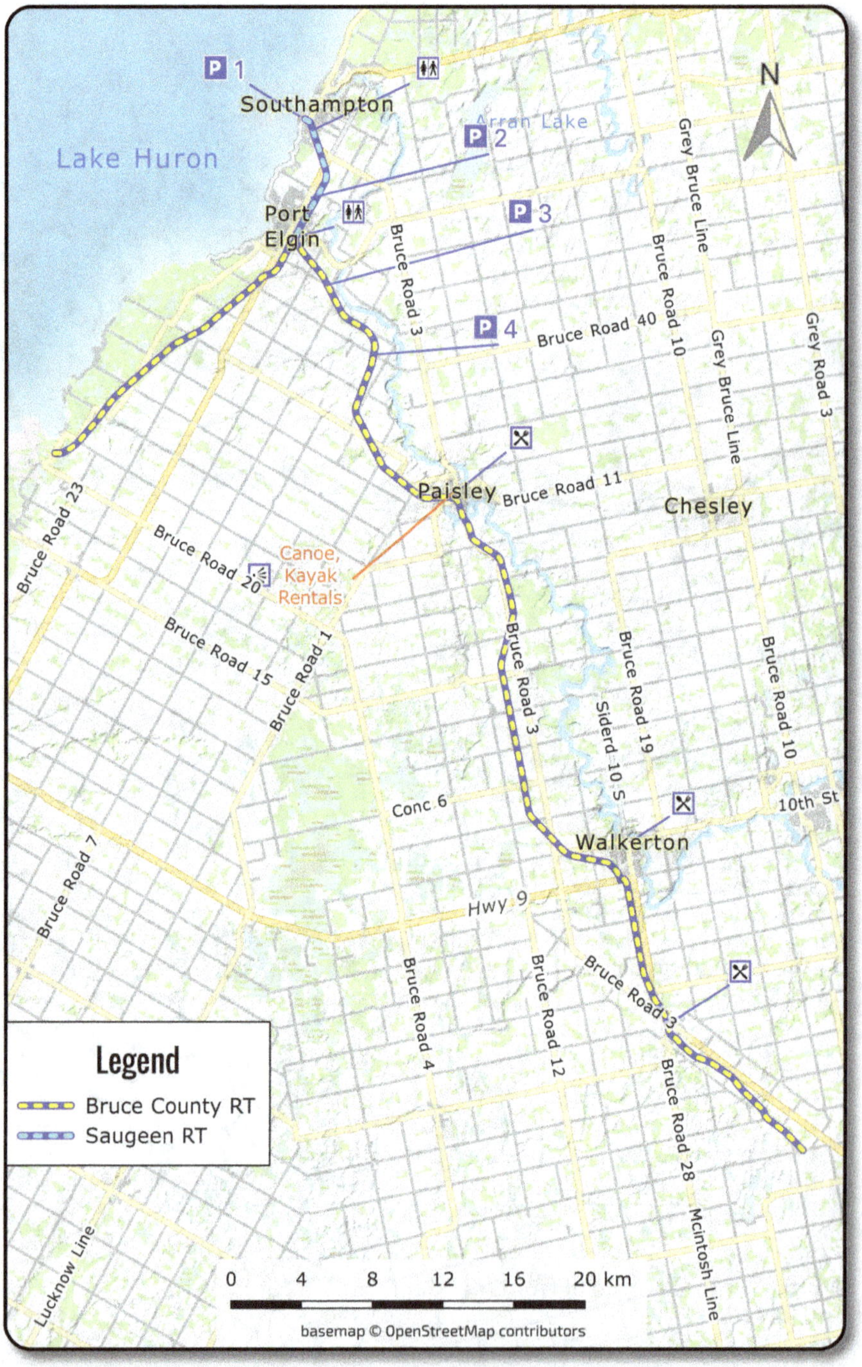

Review:

Make your way to **Lake Huron** via the **82 km Bruce County** and **8 km Saugeen Rail Trails** for your holidays. Cruise the **wide-open spaces**, spend time in **old farm towns**, walk **endless beaches,** and take in the **laid-back vibe** of this quiet part of **SW Ontario**.

I have combined two rail trails (RT) for this review as they do connect to give many options in planning your travels.

The short **8 km Saugeen RT** segment connects the two summer resort towns of **Port Elgin** and **Southampton**. This long-established path has **all the extras and amenities RT riders like** and expect.

It's a pleasure to cycle along, though it's a short outing: well marked and maintained, and, as with most RTs, no hills and no ATVs.

A favourite loopback is to cycle the **North Shore trail** along the water. Visiting these two towns and the shoreline is an **enjoyable way to spend the day.**

The other, much longer **82 km** route is almost finished **getting resurfaced and 90% ready** for you to consider venturing on. This adds the possibility of long day trips or doing a **multiday Bikepacking trek.** I think this **RT has potential** and with time will evolve into a popular destination.

What was five years ago once a hellish minefield of stones and washboarding that only an ATV or MTB could manage has been tamed. Only **one small 8 km segment** from the **Port Elgin junction to Hwy 40** is still rough and due to be resurfaced by mid-summer 2023. Hurray!

The **Bruce County RT** starts on **Huron Bruce Rd**, in the middle of Ontario farmlands, on the county boundary. Even though the tracks did at one time go much farther, the trail does not. (I think this is a classic case where one county kept the rail lands when the tracks were lifted and the neighbouring county let it be sold off (in the '80s). So much for forethought.)

Starting northwest of the village of **Clifford**, this RT heads in that direction towards **Lake Huron**, passing through **Mildmay, Walkerton,** and **Paisley** to **Port**

Elgin. Here the **RT splits at the junction**; the **Bruce RT goes left 18 km** farther SW, almost to **Inverhuron Provincial Park**. Going right is the **Saugeen RT**.

Your ride will have **farms** and **fields** with that **big-sky feel** (which means not much shade), interrupted by **sleepy towns** that once depended on the rails to bring goods to market. **ATVs use the route**, so expect a few and let them pass. I have never had a problem.

After the old trestle rail bridge near **Paisley** was set on fire by vandals in 2021, part of the trail was closed for some time, but repairs are now complete and the bridge is up and running again.

I have spent time in this area over the years. Back when I organized bike club weekend trips, we camped at **MacGregor Point Provincial Park**, or the **Saugeen Bluffs Conservation Area**. We even spent a day paddling down the mellow **Saugeen River** from **Paisley**. Look up **outfitters** in this town if you are keen to **rent a canoe or kayak** and get a shuttle.

May I also suggest visiting the warm waters of **Sauble Beach** further up the shoreline. And just off the **Bruce RT** is an easy mountain bike ride at **Brant Tract.**

One of the best things about coming out this way is the **lack of unbearable holiday traffic**. It is a **three-hour drive from the GTA,** so make it a weekend or longer. There is plenty here to see and do.

History - The **Wellington, Grey & Bruce Railway** (WG&B) rail line started in **Guelph** and two years later in **1872** the tracks reached **Southampton.** It was one of many railway start-ups to fill the **needs of pioneer farms** in this vast untapped area, of SW Ontario. Forests had been cleared and getting grain to markets on muddy roads was almost as laborious as growing it.

The **Northern Railway of Canada** (NRC) declined requests to build a line in this area noting that it would be a questionable money maker. The **WG&B** soon found this out and had difficulty paying expenses. The struggling **WG&B** was amalgamated into the **Grand Trunk in 1893** which in turn was absorbed by the **CNR in 1923.**

Never that profitable, this route did serve the area till the end of the rail era. A spur line was built from **Port Elgin** to the Bruce Nuclear plant at **Douglas Point** in **1970** to supply oil. It was recently resurfaced as part of this RT.

Cambridge - Paris – Rail Trail

Cambridge - Paris

Length - 18 km (one way)

98% rail trail path
2% road crossings, detours

Elevation - Flat with a very gradual 30 m slope south

Terrain - fine crushed stone, cut grass

Skill - Easy

Maps - Mapboards at trailheads, signage on the route

Traffic - Bicycles, hikers, joggers, Nordic skiers

Facilities - Three main parking, toilets (in Glen Morris), benches, amenities in Paris or Cambridge

Highlights - Ruins of mill and bridge, shaded woodlots, quiet

Trail Fee - Free

Phone - 519 621 2761

Website - Grand River Conservation Authority

Similar Trails - Grand River, LE&N RT, Hamilton Brantford RT

Local Clubs - Waterloo Cycling Club

Access - Parking lots at three locations:

⊕**P1** Cambridge - 210 Water Street S (Hwy 24)
P2 Glen Morris - End of Forbes St by the river canoe launch
⊕**P3** Paris - 166 Willow St at the north end of town

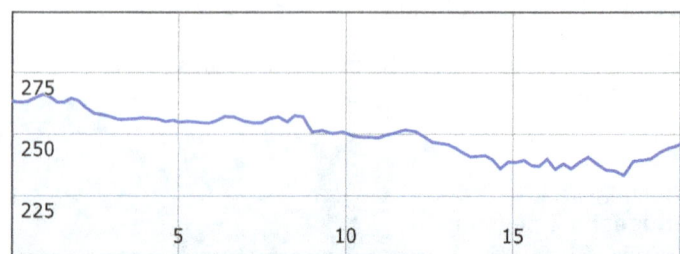

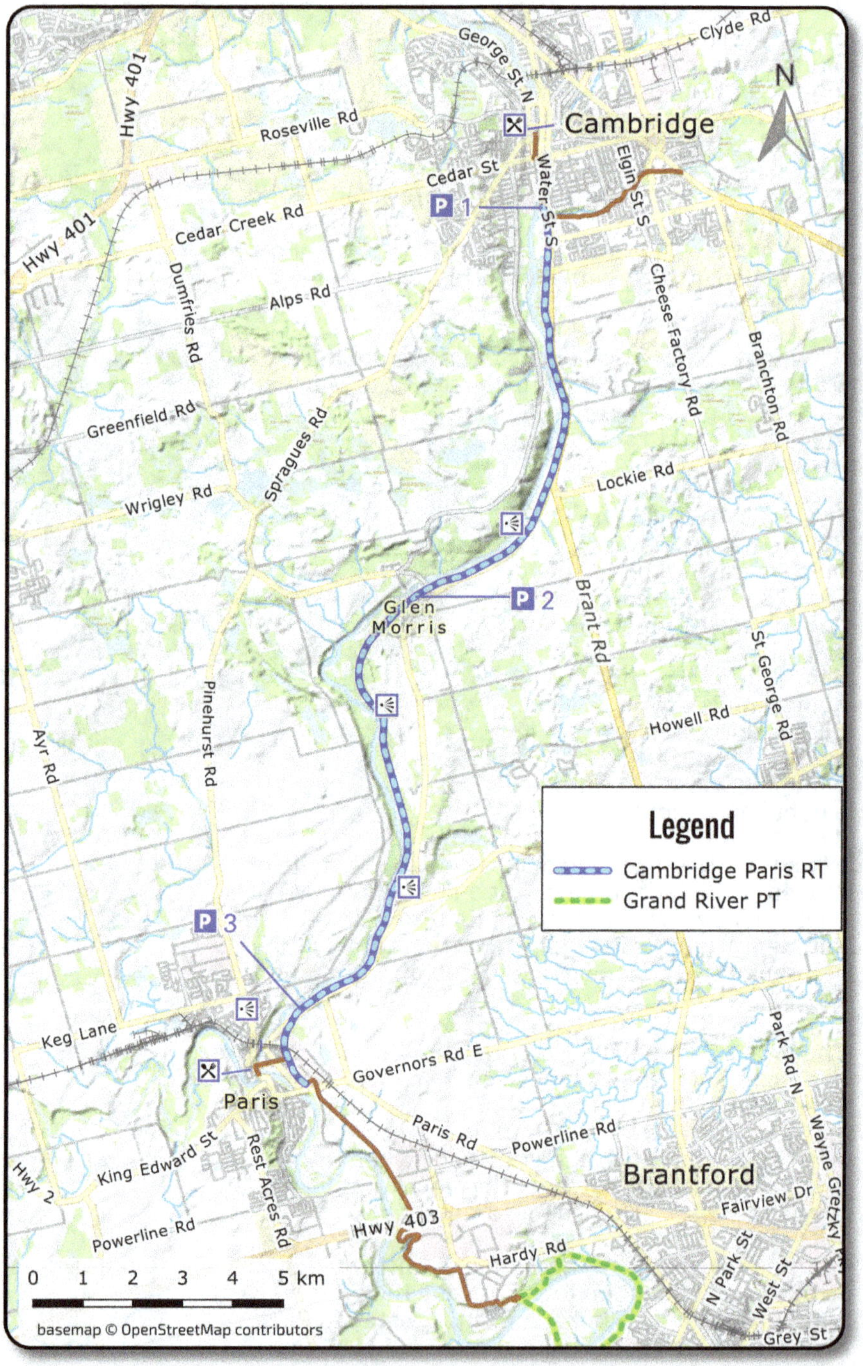

Review:

The **Cambridge** to **Paris Rail trail** follows the **Grand River** between the two cities of the same names. It's an enjoyable and popular bicycle ride that takes you along the east bank of the river for **18 km**.

You can start at either end or at the middle parking lot in the village of **Glen Morris**.

The trail winds through a quiet forest setting, with **rarely a sound of cars or any sign of homes or farms**. The river moves quickly below and the shore can be visited a few times from the **Cambridge** end as the route climbs up along the side of the river bank. By the time it gets to the south end near **Paris**, you are riding high up, far from the water's edge.

There are not that many **lookouts** to view the river and sit on a bench as this old rail

line **moves inland** a number of times. I saw **two interesting landmarks:** the stone ruins of the **German woollen mill built in 1867 (and later a hotel)**, fenced off and hidden in the trees; and the **stone pillars** of a metal truss rail bridge (now long gone) that once crossed the **Grand River** at **Murray Lookout.**

Beyond these few sights, it's a pleasant, easy ride through woodlots and clearings with not much else to see. With next to **no road crossings**, this is a super-safe route.

The finely crushed gravel **path is firm** after many years of use. I saw no puddles, though sections had grass growing down the middle, turning them into **doubletrack**. It was evident that a maintenance crew had mowed the grass shoulders and cut the brush back.

An assortment of signage was posted on the trail, some so old and sun-bleached they were just white placards. (Not that you need signs; the right path is evident.)

This is a very popular trail with a **long history of use** by many cyclists, hikers, and joggers. The parking lots may overflow with cars on sunny weekends, an odd but pleasant sight for a Rail trail. But no worries, there is **always plenty of space** for everyone to ride on a RT.

Cambridge, a good-size city, has an interesting town centre, with elegant heritage buildings and a pretty waterfront, that you can easily reach on a bike path leading north from the RT. Once you cross **Water St S**, follow the path north for **10 minutes**.

Paris is a quaint old town with **some nice waterfront eateries** where you can relax before cycling further (if you wish) beyond the **Paris** trailhead parking lot, by crossing **Hwy 51** heading farther south for about **2 km** to **Curtis Ave**. Following that road south for **400 m** connects you back onto this old rail line now called the **SC Johnson Trail**. The route continues on the rail bed for **11 more kilometres to Brantford** (with one detour around an industrial park).

You can even cycle all the way to **Hamilton** about **40 km** from here on trails, making it an overnight bike trip adventure, if you want. Or continue **46 km** on the old **LE&N** line south to **Port Dover** and all stops in between. All aboard!

History - This was once an important transportation railway corridor. Built between **1913** and **1916** as an **interurban electric railway**, with streetcar-like trains, the **Lake Erie and Northern Railway** (LE&N) track continued down from **Cambridge** to **Port Dover** on **Lake Erie**. While it was being built, the **CPR** purchased it.

Flooding in February 1916 on the **Grand River** damaged the competitor's tracks (Grand Valley Railways) north of **Paris** ending passenger service. Quickly the **LE&N** was pressed into service to replace it only days after the overhead lines were up and the first test run was done.

Other than one year during WW2, when employment spiked and more people took the train to work, ridership peaked at 600,000 in **1921**, when summer excursions to **Lake Erie** resort towns became popular with city dwellers. In the **1950s**, the CPR, focused on freight shipping, made little attempt to keep the number of riders up, and passenger service was ended in **1955**. The track was converted in **1961** to diesel locomotive use, but even freight gave way to truck deliveries five years later. The golden era of rail slowly faded away.

In **1989 CP Rail** abandoned the rail line, and today there is no public transport along here, not even a bus route. However, it was quickly redeveloped as a recreational path, becoming one of the earliest Rail Trails in **1994**.

CASO – Rail Trail

Windsor - Ridgetown - St. Thomas - Tillsonburg

Length - 104 km = 49 + 32 + 4 + 19 (one way) + more kms in the future

95% rail trail path
5% road crossings, detours

Elevation - Flat as she goes

Terrain - New crushed stone base (may be dusty), loose sand & gravel, asphalt sections

Skill - Easy

Maps - New map boards at gates, directional sign, interpretive plaques

Traffic - Bicycles, hikers, Nordic skiers

Facilities - Parking lots, outhouses, benches, many small communities along the way for food and lodging requirements

Highlights - Farms, bridges, wildlife, open spaces, train history in St. Thomas, Lake Erie is as close as a 9 km ride, warmest area in Ontario

Phone - Call regional county tourism #

Website - Essex Conservation, Chatham Kent Trails, Railway City Tourism, Oxford County

Similar Trails - Essex Greenway RT, G2G RT, Friendship RT

Local Clubs - East Side Riders, Railway City Cycling Club, Silver Spoke Cycling Club

Access - Essex County has yet to establish where car lots will be; the other three areas have these as possible start points:

P1 Large lot at 113 Erie St N, Ridgetown
P2 Spaces at trail gates along the path
P3 Elevated Park - 18 Centre St, St. Thomas
P4 335 Tillson Ave, Tillsonburg
P5 Zenda Line & Kellett Rd, Tillsonburg

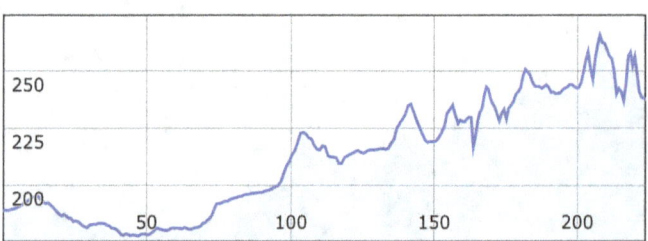

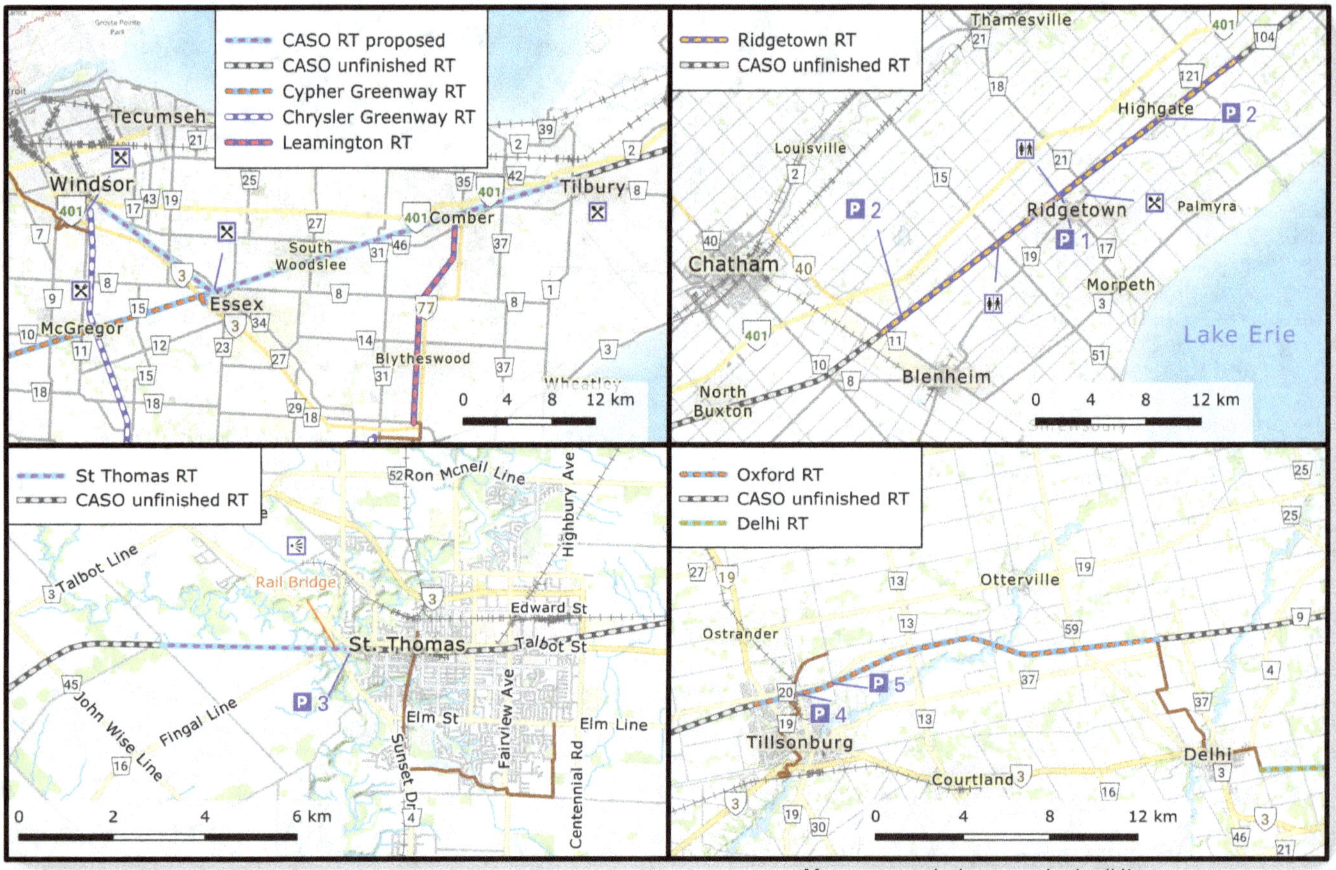

Map on page 4 shows orginal rail line.

Review:

The **CASO Rail Trail** is **in its infancy with great potential.** Sections of it are **ready to ride** and new parts are **being added yearly.** Towns and counties are starting to find the will and funds to turn this abandoned rail line that once ran from **Windsor to Fort Erie** into a long-distance, car-free ride.

I started to notice a few years ago rideable **snippets of RT** across the **north side of Lake Erie** and did a little sleuthing with maps, which revealed that these were sections of the **old CASO line.** There is not a lot of info out there yet to **piece it all together,** but let me try and sum it up.

Essex County announced in early 2023 that its section of the CASO line is now protected for public use; **plans are in the works to turn it into a 49 km RT** from **Windsor to Tilbury.** It took years of negotiations to get this far and now to plan, fund, and build will take a few more, I would think. The idea is to create a RT loop to **join the three other existing RT rides** of the **Essex Greenway.**

photo – Dudek Photography

Further east up the line, in **Chatham-Kent** county, the **Ridgetown section** has been expanding since 2019. In 2023, the trail will be extended 11 km from Communication Rd to MacPherson Line, making **32 km** in total. It may be a straight line, but a very well made linear path it is, with ample signage and places to park. **Ridgetown** can be your starting point or a lunch stop. Easily accessed from **Hwy 401 as it parallels the RT** a few kilometres north of the route.

Naturalists have posted that they have tallied more than 275 species of plants, 50 species of birds (46 with evidence of breeding), 28 types of butterflies, 8 species of reptiles & amphibians and 8 kinds of mammals in this area.

Another segment is in **St. Thomas**, another centre of railroad activity in a bygone era. You can visit the exceptionally **long historic train station** home of the **North America Railway Hall of Fame** and the **Elgin County Railway Museum** a short distance away. On the west side of town, a former rail bridge has been jazzed up for tourists and residents and named the

Elevated Park (fancy name). This conversion is quite impressive—it's worth a visit to check out the view.

There is no RT going east to the museum from here, and the westbound option is a **rather short affair at 4 km.** It should be longer for a place that calls itself **"The Railway City."** Locals agree; come on, **make it happen,** city hall!

Moving along east to **Oxford County**, you can ride a **19 km section of the CASO line** starting in **Tillsonburg**; it's part of the **Great Trail (aka the Trans Canada Trail).** You can continue east with a road detour south onto the **Delhi RT** that will lead to the longer **LE & N rail trail.** Oh, the possibilities!

photo – Essex Region Conservation

Actually, years ago when I was **gazing off the old iron bridge** on that RT in **Waterford,** I was sure the dirt path beneath the bridge was another forgotten RT. And now I know it's the **CASO coming through town.**

The more I look at **aerial photos**, the more future possibilities I see to reconnect by bike to other abandoned rail lines, like where the **CASO** crosses the **Grand River.**

Who knows how much of the CASO will be a **rideable trail in ten years?** Most of it is still a **rough MTB journey,** and parts of it are on private land. **It will take years** for all levels of government to sort out land-use agreements, do studies, find money, and build a path to welcome riders.

I know I am ahead of myself with this review for a RT that is not yet complete. But I **really wanted to kick-start-this initiative** and **represent SW Ontario** to encourage city dwellers to check out the area. You will enjoy the break from your hectic pace and the **slower, peaceful, agricultural vibe.**

You can look forward to plenty of sunshine in these **warmer lower latitudes of the province**. This is where your food comes from—acres of it, everywhere! Can you recognize what's growing?

With all the small towns and villages along the way, the **future growth of bikepacking** on this route looks inevitable. Right now, there is momentum to repurpose rail trails. Keep an eye on this one. **I like where it is going** and you will, too…on your bicycle.

History - continues on page 118

Essex Greenway – Rail Trail

Windsor - Leamington - Amherstburg - Essex

Length - 148 = 52 + 23 + 24 + 49 km (one way)

90% rail trail path
10% road crossings, detours

Elevation - Nearly none; it's the flattest part of Ontario

Terrain - Typical crushed stone base, where not resurfaced a coarse ATV track, town paths may be paved

Skill - Easy

Maps - Signed route, easy to follow, not sure about directions on the detours

Traffic - Bicycles, hikers, horses, ATVs, snowmobiles, Nordic skiers

Facilities - Parking lot, outhouses, benches

Highlights - Wineries, beaches, history, birding, greenhouses, Windsor, Leamington

Phone - 519 776 5209

Website - Essex Region Conservation

Similar Trails - CASO RT,   G2G RT,   LE&N RT

Local Clubs - None

Access - Parking lots can be found here, more are being built:

P1 Hwy 9 & Howard Ave, Windsor, take the Centennial Hub trails to get to the RT
P2 3184 Hwy 8
P3 15 Scott Lane, McGregor
⊕**P4** 457 Concession Rd 2 (Thomas Rd)
P5 357 Queen St, Harrow
P6 2057 Arner Townline, Arner
P7 Train Station/Restaurant - 162 Lansdowne Ave, Kingsville
P8 1995 Country Rd 34, Ruthven
P9 Edgar Side Rd 18
more parking bottom of next page...

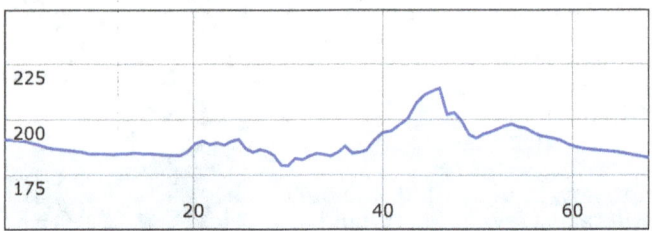

Review:

Down on the southern tip of Ontario, where the weather is the warmest and wine and ketchup are prized, you can find many hours of riding to your liking. Here in **Essex County**, farmland spreads out in all directions, and so do these rail trail networks. And I am pleased to add a new one to the mix.

I call it the **Essex Greenway RT** network. It comprises four RT routes that make about **150 km** of cycling, and a loop! The original **52 km Chrysler Greenway RT** route forms a cross with the **Cypher Systems Greenway, a 23 km RT** that takes you to wineries, birding areas, beach resorts, historical spots, or the ferry to **Pelee Island.**

Most of the paths are tree lined, with trees and brush that have grown over since the years of train traffic. This will obscure how **flat the farming landscape** is (which is very)!

photo – Essex Region Conservation

The trail base has been resurfaced with that crushed fine stone we are so familiar with and love (well, I do). Most road crossings are quiet and safe, except for the main **Highway #3.** Side roads have light traffic in these parts.

The first RT route leaves Windsor headed east, then jogs south down to **Harrow,** and does a 90-degree turn out of town to **Kingsville** on the shores of **Lake Erie**. Here, you can still see the old train station, now a restaurant, and visit a winery. Onward, a short **12 km rid**e and **40 m hill** to get over, you'll reach the larger town of **Leamington,** with a slight detour to the road at **Ruthven** for some reason.

By now you will have noticed all the **greenhouses— the highest concentration in North America** —part of the **Leamington tomatoes/ketchup industry**. You could spend the night here, then ride down to **Point Pelee National Park** to **bird watch** or simply walk out on the sand to the most **southerly point in Canada.**

Or take a **ferry to Pelee Island** for a day of wine tasting and do a traffic-free coastal loop cruising around the edge of the island. (Further south but technically not connected with the mainland.)

The third direction is the newly resurfaced **24 km Leamington RT** heading straight north from town at **Country Rd 18** to the town of **Comber**. Take **Erie St N** to get there and then follow the hydro towers.

photo – Essex Region Conservation

If you ever wondered what the **flat, open empty prairies** may look like, this area will give you a good idea. It's boring to some, **mesmerizing** to others. This RT offers **big sky panorama**s, wind turbines, and a less than shady path, so it could be a hot ride, and windy, I will assume.

The newly announced RT is the **49 km CASO** route leaving **Windso**r at the **8th Concession,** dropping down to the town of **Essex**, it does a 90 and continues up on to **Tilbury.** That's the plan, actually, the dream is to keep going to connect with the **Ridgetown RT** section, then on to **St. Thomas** one day like it did a hundred years ago...and beyond??

You may have thought there was little reason to visit down here. Well, now you have **more reasons to explore this corner of SW Ontario**, with its rich history. Visit **vineyards, enjoy fresh produce, relax on the beaches**, and take in the warmer weather some day soon.

History - The rail line from **Sandwich (Windsor)** to **Leamington**, partly financed by the **Hiram Walker & Sons distillery**, was completed in **1889**. Later, it was operated by an American midwest railroad out of Cleveland, the **Chesapeake and Ohio Railway (C&OR)**, and later still it was called the **CSX** till the late 1980s. Now it's called the **Chrysler Greenway RT.**

It connects to the **Essex to Amherstburg** line, a spur line off the **Canada Southern Railway (CASO or CSR)** mainline from **Windsor**. Service started in **1869** to **St. Thomas** and on to **Niagara Falls**. **CN Rail** donated the spur line in **1997**, but funds didn't become available until twenty years later. It first opened for recreational use in **2017** and is now called the **Cypher Systems Greenway RT.**

A spur line from **Comber to Leamington** was built in **1887** by the **Leamington & St. Clair Railway** (part of CASO) to serve the growing tomato and tobacco industry. A large **Heinz** ketchup & baby food plant was built in **1910**; the area was also a summer tourist destination. Many original railway buildings still exist.

...parking conitues from last page
P10 143 Keown St, Essex
P11 Seacliff Park - Forest Ave, Leamington
P12 Mersea Rd 8
P13 Mersea Rd 10
⊕ **P14** Hwy 46, Comber

G2G – Rail Trail

Goderich - Guelph

Length - 88 km (one way)

85% rail trail path
15% road crossings, detours

Elevation - Flat with a very gradual slope to Lake Huron

Terrain - Fine crushed stone, gravel, asphalt

Skill - Easy pedalling

Maps - Map boards, trail distance markers

Traffic - Bicycles, hikers, horses, Nordic skiers

Facilities - Parking, info kiosks, benches

Highlights - Open, big-sky country; large farms; Menesetung bridge; craft brewery in Blyth, Goderich sunsets

Phone - None

Website - G2G Trail

Similar Trails - Kissing Bridge RT, Bruce + Saugeen RT, Grey + Bluffs RT

Local Clubs - G2G Cycling Club

Access - Many entry points and parking lots along the route. Here is a sample, check the G2G website map for more choices.

⊕ **P1** Milbank - John St (bridge missing, detour around to pick up the trail)
P2 Milverton - Whaley Ave
P3 Monkton - at the arena, Nelson St & West St
P4 Walton - Brussels LineP5 Blyth - 856 Queen St
P6 Auburn Parking Lot
P7 Menesetung Bridge - 160 N Harbour St W, Goderich
⊕ **P8** Rotary Cove Beach - south end of Cove Rd, Goderich

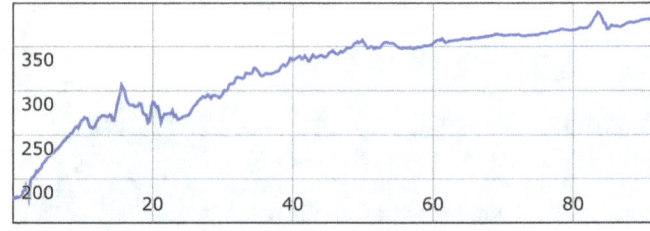

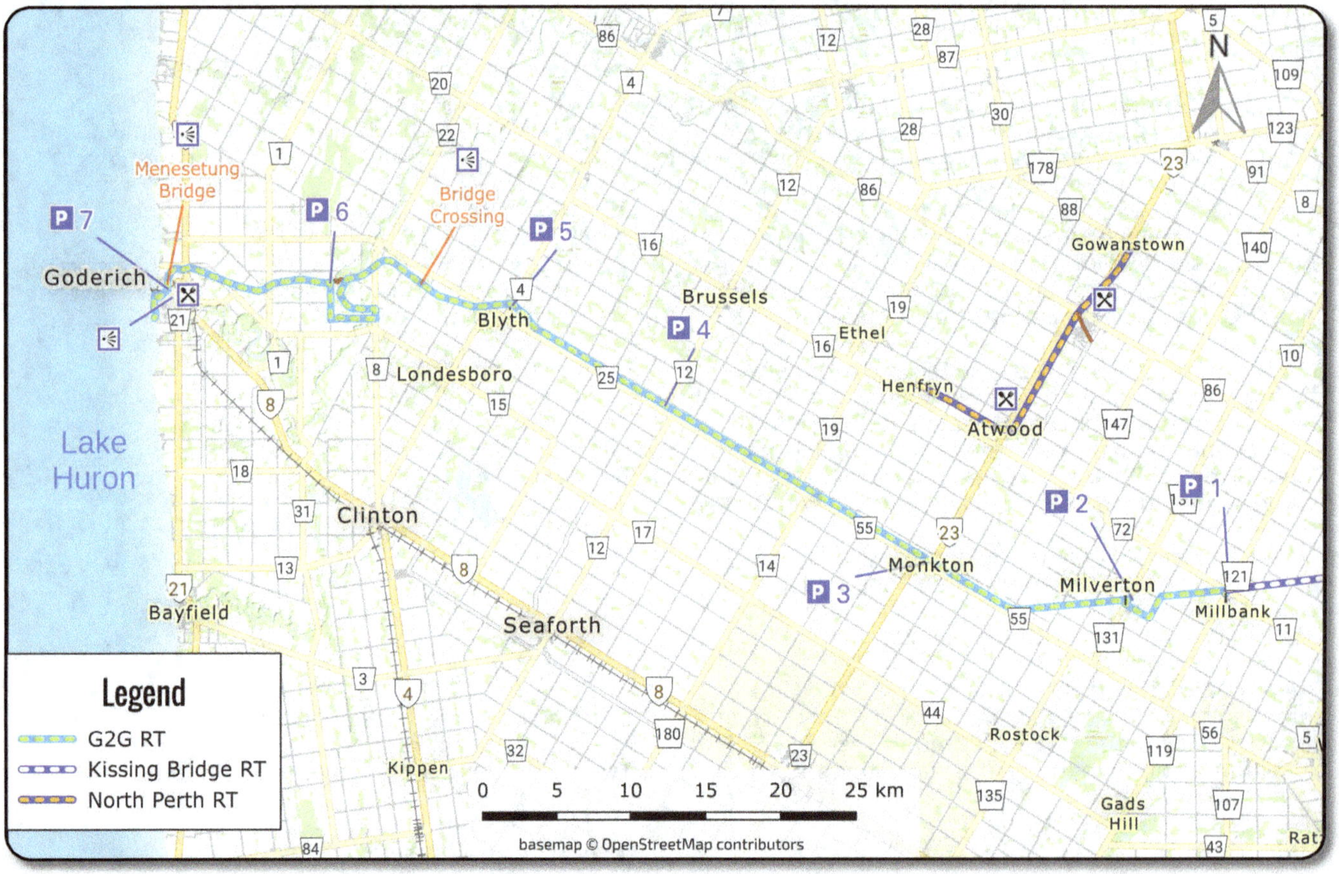

Review:

Cyclists can now ride the new **Perth Harvest Pathway** section of the **G2G (Guelph to Goderich) Rail Trail** to **Lake Huron**. Here it ends at **Goderich** after running west for **88 km** from **Millbank**, crossing through some scenic parts of Ontario's farming heartland.

I am pleased to be able to add this section to my new book, as it was resurfaced in **2020** and is now **ready for your enjoyment.**

A few years back, I cycled the **Kissing Bridge** section of the **G2G** that continues from outside **Guelph** to **Millbank**. Beyond this, it was not resurfaced, the terrain started to get **unfriendly** for casual road riders, but **not that interesting** for the mountain biking crowd. So it was **not really enjoyable for anyone**.

photo – Ed Daugavietis

Back then, I encountered an uneven grass/gravel path of tall weeds, mud, and gopher holes. Now, with **great effort, enthusiasm,** and cash, the dedicated group running the **G2G trail network** has made this route viable. (Please give them some financial support, as they need to build more bridges.)

photo – G2G RT – Bill

The trail base has been levelled using the **fine crushed stone** you will find on most rail trails. Many **new kiosks, map boards, distance markers,** and **benches** have been added.

The scenery on this route is **big-sky country:** in this flat part of Ontario, large farms and fields go on forever. About half of the route is in the **tree-lined shade** we all crave; the other parts are out in the hot sun and it could get **windy.**

Currently, there are a few places to eat, **campgrounds, and a B&B along the route,** but with mighty efforts underway to repurpose this railbed, it's already a great destination. And I think there are even more good things in store for its future.

From the town of **Millbank,** where my **Kissing Bridge** trail ends, there is a minor road detour. Unfortunately,

there are going to be a few along the way. When the tracks were removed and sold for scrap, **so went the bridges.** Rebuilding them for cycling has been an ongoing (expensive) goal by dedicated G2G volunteers.

The next town, **Milverton,** has a **5 km road detour,** but traffic is light in this region, so it should not be an issue.

This old rail line bends to the right and then goes linear for **37 km** through the villages of **Monkton, Walton,** and **Blyth**. It's likely the **longest straight cycle path** in the province.

Though there is a subtle descent of **250 m** to the lake, you won't notice it until the end. After **Blyth,** (which has a craft brewery) the trail starts to get interesting as it curves down to the **Maitland River**. Here, again, a large bridge is missing, resulting in a **10 km detour.**

This sucks, but until $1M in funding can restore the span with a suitable recreational bridge crossing, hit the road detour (BTW, friends have waded across, you decide...).

Fortunately, not all the original bridges are gone. As you reach **Goderich,** the **Menesetung Bridge** offers a spectacular view from high above the river.

The trail continues to a **Lake Huron** shoreline park trail with beaches for a little more meandering and an opportunity to rest, refuel, and dip your toes in.

Why not stay over in **Goderich**? **It's a beautiful town to explore,** and you might catch one of its famous sunsets.

Connecting the original **Kissing Bridge** section east of **Millbank** (in my first book) and with a planned bike path into downtown **Guelph,** the **G2G** has become a great addition and cycleway to see Ontario's farm country on a grand scale. If you're a cyclist who desires **wide-open scenery, and quiet long-distance rides,** bikepacking this route will give you **many delightful kilometres**.

History - This line was built in **1907** by **Canadian Pacific Railways** during the golden age of rail to service the transport of goods, produce, and people from the port in **Goderich to Guelph** and beyond.

The **CPR** ran the line until it was abandoned in **1988.** Tracks were later lifted and, unfortunately, bridges were dismantled. The Ontario government purchased the land and eventually it was resurfaced by local groups in **2020** for recreational use.

Grey + Bluff – Rail Trail

Owen Sound - Orangeville

Length - 112 + 20 km (one way)

90% rail trail path
10% road crossings, detours

Elevation - Flat on the south end with a very gradual 345 m slope from Dundalk down to the water = constant long climb back up from Owen Sound

Terrain - Rough parts; currently being resurfaced with crushed stone

Skill - Easy going, not rough like it used to be

Maps - New signage planned

Traffic - Bicycles, hikers, horses, limited access to ATVs, snowmobiles

Facilities - Parking lots, outhouses, benches, to be determined

Highlights - Small bridges, shaded woodlots, many small farm communities

Phone - 519 376 2205 & 519 941 2816

Website - Grey County Dufferin County

Similar Trails - Bruce + Saugeen RT , G2G RT, Georgian RT

Local Clubs - Owen Sound Cycling Club

Access - Side crossroads, park on the shoulder. New lots will be added when the trail is upgraded. Check websites.

⊕**P1** Bayshores Community Centre - 1900 3rd Ave E, Owen Sound
P2 Kelso Beach - 2nd Avenue West
P3 Concession 11, Owen Sound
P4 203 Main St W, Markdale
P5 405086 Grey Rd 4, Ceylon (Flesherton)
P6 to be determined, Shelburne
⊕**P7** Hwy 16 north of Broadway, Orangeville

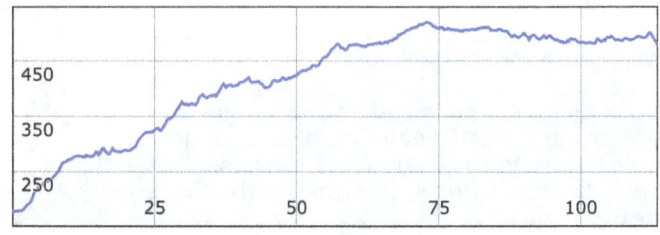

Review:

The **CP Grey & Dufferin County Rail Trail** is a long **112 km** ribbon that cuts diagonally across Ontario farm country. I've added the shorter **20 km Georgian Bluff RT** that continues from **Owen Sound** to this review as well.

I first hesitated to include this RT in the book, but I feel the trail will appeal to some riders looking for a more challenging, rugged adventure—and this review might also help inform others not to attempt it.

Then I came across a few local newspaper reports that the two counties had found the money and **the will to resurface** this **abused ATV track**. Well, that turned things around! The review had to be rewritten.

This is good news, and it has already been an ongoing transformation for a few years during Covid. Believe me, you would have needed a mountain bike to ride it or at least a gravel bike and a **lot of determination.** Not only can **bikepackers enjoy riding** the **Grey**, so can your kids for a Sunday stroll.

The route is a journey through **small-town agricultural Ontario**. The railway served farming communities along the way, as well as furniture and water-bottling enterprises. You might still **see signs of aging warehouses, feedstock silos, barns, and rusting machinery.**

It travels through or close to **quiet towns** like **Shelburne, Cobetton, Dundalk, Proton Station, Saugeen Junction, Flesherton, Markdale, Berkeley, Holland Centre,** and **Chatsworth** into **Owen Sound.** So many places you may have never heard of.

You will be well supported by those small communities when food and sleep overcome your will to go on. **This makes it a great route for bikepacking,** and perhaps a more interesting trek than the **G2G RT** to the south.

The scenery is farm fields with little shade from any trees lining the track bed. You will cross over many small bridges, but there are **no large river crossings** on this trek.

The landscape is flat farmland when you start from the south end outside **Orangeville**, becoming **hilly and more treed past Markdale.** As you get closer to **Owen Sound,** there's a gradual descent to the harbour, with views of **Georgian Bay.** (You will feel it coming back!) The train had to do a **wide switchback to get into town**, but you may opt for a direct shortcut on the road.

The trailbed continues on the other side of this **deep harbour,** up a **76 m climb** on the **Georgian Bluff RT.** The climb may seem daunting, but **if a train could do it, your bike legs certainly can.** And this RT is resurfaced for those who wish a less jarring journey.

Along the top it continues, through **woods and wetland areas,** ending at the **village of Park Head.** Based on my map perusals, **it could go farther in the future,** but I don't know if it will.

The ride can be done in **six to seven hours one way, nonstop,** but why would you? A two- to three-day return tour seems more agreeable.

And where are they at in terms of repaving the trail with crushed stone and adding new signs, car lots, and outhouses? This is what I was told: The path is resurfaced from **Owen Sound** to north of **Dundalk** as of spring 2023. The next county, **Dufferin**, is behind in upgrading its section of this trail to **Orangeville.** Give it another year to finish and for portable toilets and car lots to be placed at suitable locations in **Orangeville** and **Shelburne.**

Exciting stuff, kids: **from dubious to a definite addition** to your RT "to ride" list. This new bikepacking destination has the **potential to become something grand** in the next decade.

Note: there will still be ATVs and snowmobiles on this trail, but not as freewheeling as before. And the dust will be there till the base firms up over a few winters. Last I heard, the segment from **Owen Sound** south to **Grey Rd 18 is ATV free.** That may change over time. So check up on Grey and Dufferin county websites to see how this trail pans out.

History - continues on page 119

Guelph Royal – Park Trail

Guelph

Length - 20 km loop

70% park path
20% hiking trail
10% road riding, crossings

Elevation - Flat along river's edge, short hills

Terrain - Path alternates from paved to crushed stone , bridges, boardwalks, (optional singletrack trail has rocks, roots, and muddy parts, best on a hybrid bike)

Skill - Easy to Advanced

Maps - Map boards (some missing), old trail posts, needs more and better signage

Traffic - Cyclists, hikers, strollers, kids, dogs, (cars)

Facilities - Lots of free parking lots, toilets, benches, picnic tables, shopping mall

Highlights - Eramosa River, covered bridge, dam, university campus, arboretum, rail trail, many boardwalks

Phone - 519 822 1260

Website - City of Guelph, Visit Guelph

Similar Trails - Grand River Loop (Brantford), Thames Valley (London)

Local Clubs - Guelph Cycling Club

Access - Plenty of parking can be found in Guelph, here are a few choices:

P1 Eramosa River Park - 259 Victoria Rd S
P2 Lyon Park - 25 Waterworks Place
P3 York Road Park - 85 York Rd
P4 Covered Bridge - 110 Gordon St
P5 148 Edinburgh Rd S
P6 Centennial Park - NW end of Centennial Rd
P7 Hanlon Creek Park - 505 Kortright Rd W
P8 RT trailhead - 735 Stone Rd E

Graph starts at P4 on the map

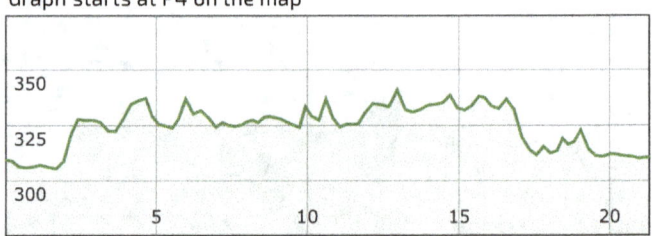

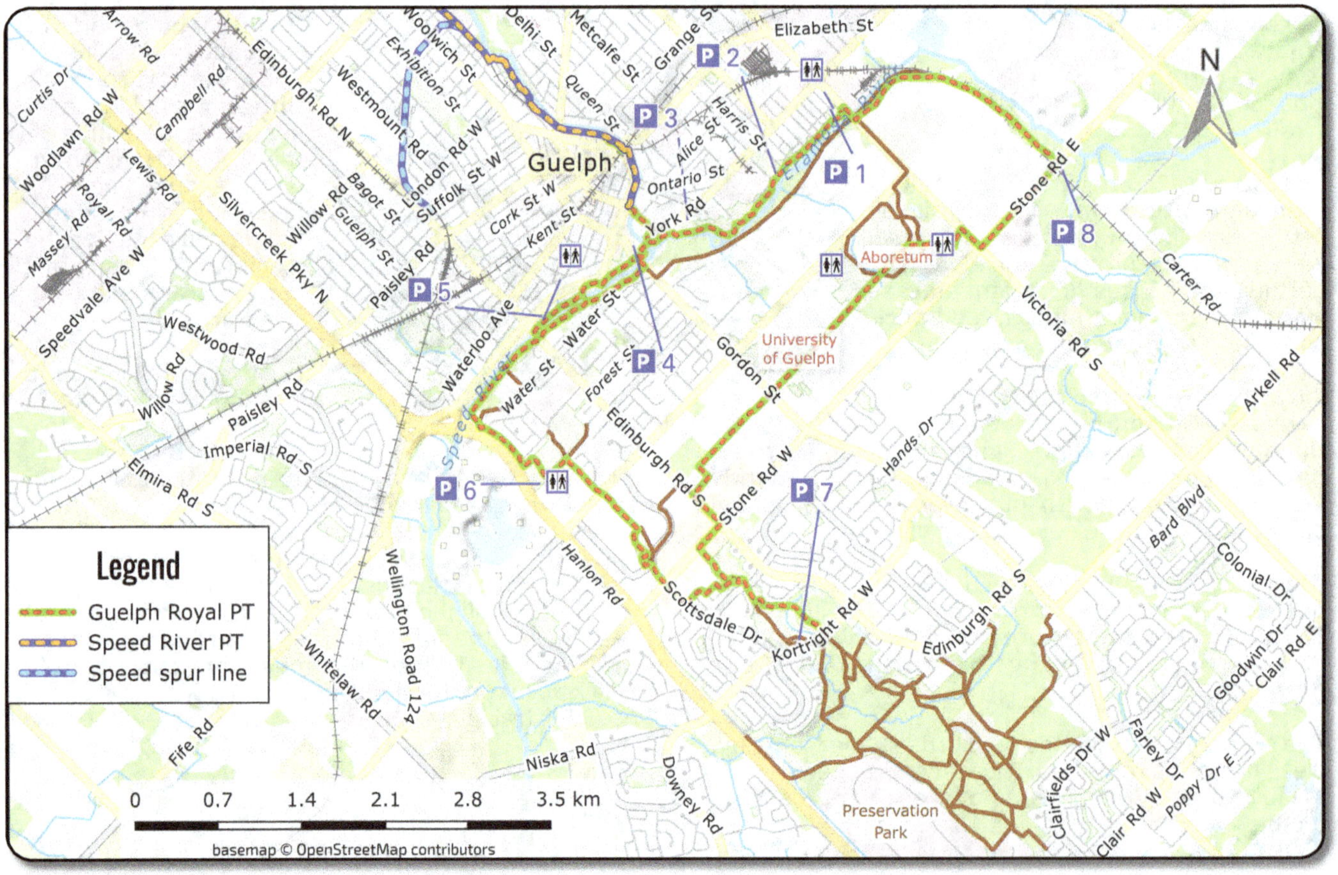

![Map of Guelph Royal Park Trail]

Legend

- Guelph Royal PT
- Speed River PT
- Speed spur line

0   0.7   1.4   2.1   2.8   3.5 km

basemap © OpenStreetMap contributors

Review:

The **Guelph Royal Recreational** trail is part of a loop I designed to give you about **20 km** of cycling time in the saddle. The route covers a mixture of **treed riverside** and **open parkland** settings and goes into forests, winds through the **university campus** and **arboretum**, and comes back using an **old railway trail.**

I rated this loop **Easy** to **Advanced** because it not only varies in **terrain competence,** you also have to **self-navigate** more than on most trails in this guide. Also, the only way to bridge paths together is with a few short road connections. (Most have **bike lanes**—this is a **bike-friendly town**.)

A good start is in the **centre of town**, by the **covered bridge** where the **Speed River** meets the **Eramosa River**.

Heading SW the trail on the north side of the river has manicured parkland while the south trail is more natural. Posts marked **RRT (Royal Recreation Trail)** show the way; they are old and there are just not enough of them. You may need to **use a map app.**

Cross one of the **four bridges** to the south trail to carry on. Perhaps at the **dam** you will see fishermen. This side takes you farther, to the highway and the next section of adventure.

The path turns away from the river up a hill to **Municipal St** with its raised bike lane. This brief road connection takes you back onto parkland paths beside neighbourhood sports fields and school yards. **Signage is missing here,** so stick to the gravel path and go left at the parking lot, then SE behind the school.

All should be pleasant and easy going 'til **Scottsdale Drive,** a mall district (with restaurant options). Here, you can decide to **take on an extra 6 km** of forested side trail loops. A wonderful ride in the woods, with the scents of evergreens. I have never seen **so many long boardwalks!**

If you chose this side trail, **continue down Scottsdale** and take a **left on Cole Rd.** You will find park access at the end leading to the gravel path along **Hanlon Creek.** When you **cross Ironwood Rd,** the trail splits. I want you to cycle the longer path on the left that goes to **Preservation Park.** Once you pass the wetlands, take the light at **Kortwright Rd;** you are now in the forest.

There were few signs, so **we went happily in circles exploring** the dirt trails 'til it was time to **reference our GPS tracks** and get back up to the main loop.

Watch out for the roots, the odd boulder, and muddy patches...and **dogs off their leashes.**

Head back the same way, this time to further to the **Stone Rd exit.** A short **800 m** stretch of busy **road riding is required.** Go NE on **Stone Rd,** left on Edinburgh Rd S, and right on **Chancellor Way.** Now you are back on the main loop.

If you skip the forest trails, take this **1.5 km road connection** to get to the university "cow path" bike trail. From the park, **ride NE on Scottsdale** behind the mall, turn on **Wilsonview Ave** to meet **Edinburgh Rd S.** Here, go one block SW onto **Chancellors Way.** Once past the student dorm brick buildings, on the left is the **Cow Path,** marked only by a yellow emergency pole (no sign).

This gravel bike path takes you past **barns, horses, and the smell of manure** (this university is well known for its agricultural and veterinary studies). Onward it goes through the **heart of the campus** full of unique architecture onto the grounds of a **large arboretum** (a botanical collection of trees).

This relaxing treed oasis ends at **Victoria St S,** where you can shorten the ride. If so, use the **Victoria bike lane** and go 750 m NW over the river bridge and cross the road. Use the scenic park path back along the **Eramosa River** to the covered bridge. I am not quick to suggest posting lights, but we found it **hard to cross Victoria St.**

Or for the full tour, head NE on **Stone R.** over the hill and take the **dirt trail at the parking lot** right after **crossing the tracks.** You will need to carry your bike over the tracks midway; do be careful, as there is train traffic. Note the layers of **limestone on the rock cuts.**

Onward **the trail splits, left takes you up** on a gravel path to **Victoria Rd.** Cross the bridge and then the road on the other side to connect with the park trail. Ride the path back to the covered bridge along the river.

The right fork is a little more challenging, rocky and **prettier too.** It stays low, meets the river, and **goes under the bridge.** The path widens into a **long forest corridor** with more **grey stone cliffs.** This old rail trail section ends at **James St E.** Take the road back out to cross the river at **Gordon St** to find your car.

If you stay the weekend, ride the **Speed River** trail to **Guelph Lake** for more adventures.

Guelph has stated that in the last twenty years, it has increased its cycling infrastructure **per capita more than most cities in Canada.** See for yourself if its claims are to your liking. (And, svp, let's see some more signs so my review does not need to be so wordy, lol!)

Iron Horse – Rail Trail

Kitchener/Waterloo

Length - 11.5 km (one way)

80% rail trail path
20% road crossings, detours

Elevation - Mostly flat with a gradual slope north

Terrain - Paved asphalt, like a Park path; cleared in the winter

Skill - Easy

Maps - Well-marked trail signage, some newly painted lines

Traffic - Cyclists, walkers, joggers, rollerbladers, dogs, kids and strollers; a busy place on weekends

Facilities - Parking, toilets, benches, fancy bike racks, playgrounds, close to food and lodging

Highlights - Modern inner city and buildings, parks, LRT trains, downtown galleries

Phone - 519 741 2345

Website - City of Kitchener

Similar Trails - Beltline RT, Speed River, Greenway

Local Clubs - Waterloo Cycling Club

Access - Parking/start point suggestions along the trail:

⬦**P1** Nyberg St (street parking)
P2 Victoria Park - 32 Dill St
P3 Waterloo Park - 50 Young St W
P4 Train Station Museum - 83 Erb St W
P5 U of W lots, many choices (metered)
⬦Wes Graham Way & Bearinger Rd

⬦Spur Line starts at Brethaupt St & Ahrens St W

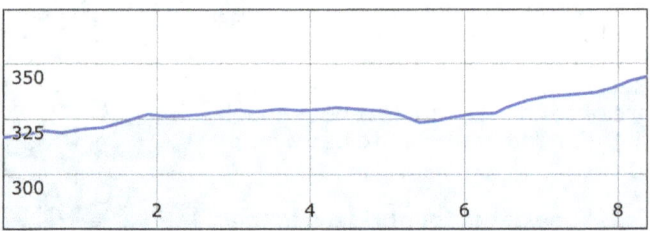

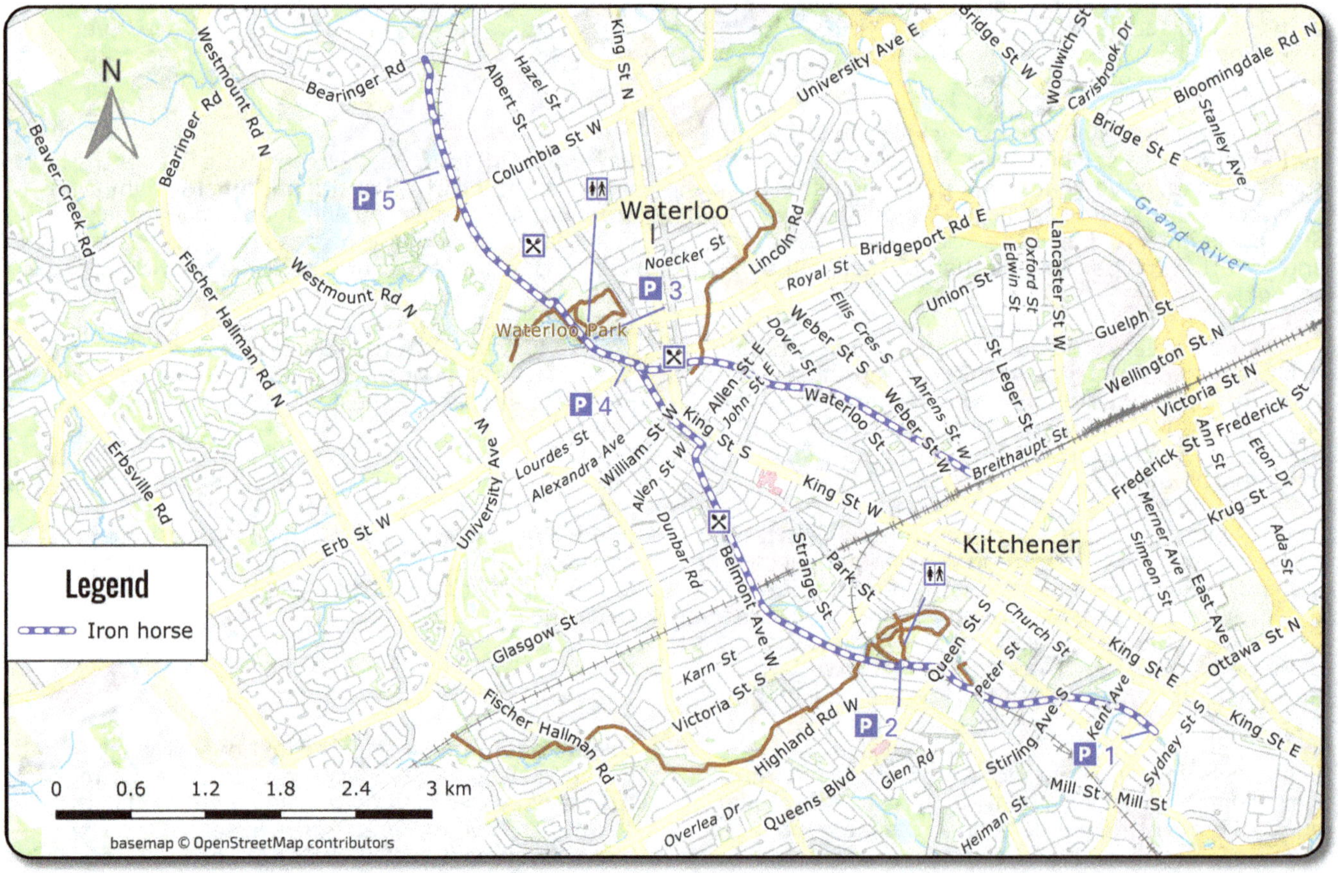

Review:

In the centre of **Kitchener-Waterloo** runs a **11.5 km** urban Rail Trail network that is a pleasure to pedal. The **Iron Horse + Spur + Laurel Trails** all run on or beside train tracks, old and new. I highly recommend continuing further, along at least part of the **Laurel Trail**, to continue your ride a little longer. It, too, seems likely to have been a rail line years ago, and the two flow into each other nicely.

There is a **train theme** to this route that echoes the days when older trains passed by. Today, **electric LRT streetcars** run commuters about town on new tracks to new stations.

The city of **Kitchener-Waterloo** is a **bike-friendly town**, with many routes cyclists can take. Alas, none of the paths here is of any great length. (I usually look for 10 km or more of riding to recommend.) Wishing to include something representative, I have connected these two paths for an **8 km cycle**. And a popular, family-friendly ride it is.

We started on a fine day at the **south end,** starting off of **Ottawa St** in an industrial area. Not the prettiest of sights, nor is the waterway we followed, **Schneider Creek,** which is all encased in concrete!

Eventually, this becomes a **more green** and **shady ride** as you pass **Victoria Park.** At this beautiful park, you can explore paths around the large pond. By the **5th km**, at **Caroline St S**, the **Iron Horse** appears to end**.**

Fear not! It continues northwest along the sidewalk as a designated path for **800 m (8 blocks)**. One street over is **King Street**, a hub of activity, **stores, and eateries.**

Upon reaching the busy intersection at **Erb St W,** you can go west on the **Laurel Trail** for **4 km** alongside the LRT tracks to **West Graham Way & Bearinger Rd.** Also, glance to your left to spot the **old train station**, now a museum.

Immediately you will be struck by the modern architecture of the **Canadian Clay and Glass Gallery** and

the **University of Waterloo** campus buildings. Along either side of this path lie the expansive sports grounds and parklands of **Waterloo Park** and **Silver Lake**, another stop to rest, explore, or let the kids go wild at the playgrounds.

The optional side Rail Trail running east from the **Erb St** junction is the short **Spur Line Trail**, a mere **2.6 km** long.

Unlike most Rail Trails, these ones are urban, with much to see and hear. These railbeds have been tamed into actual **Park-style paths**, and the city has **paved** them and added **directional signs, info boards, benches,** and intriguing **sculptures** of old machinery parts on the route.

Being in the city, the **road crossings are many** and **at times busy**, so keep an eye on the kids. Crossings are well marked, with lights and islands to aid cyclists and keep them safe.

Head out here one day and ride the **Iron Horse, Laurel, Spur,** and many others. This is a great starting point for exploring and discovering the modern metropolis of **Kitchener/ Waterloo.**

History - The **Waterloo Junction Railway** (WJR) was a short line built in **1890** to connect **Kitchener** (then called Berlin) to **Waterloo** and later to **Elmira.** Operated for decades by the **Grand Trunk Railway** (GTR), it became **Canadian National Railway** property in **1923.** CN trains still run on these tracks, called the **Waterloo Spur.** The Laurel and Spur bike trails run beside them.

The Iron Horse RT was the northern section of the **Grand River Railway's (GRR)** main line that travelled down to **Cambridge** (Galt). It was built as an inter-urban **electric railway with streetcars**, which was typical for its heyday in the **1920s.** But car traffic killed it by **1955** with less commuter use and too many dangerous urban at-grade crossings. It's been a bicycle trail since **1997.**

If you want to ride a real steamer, the **Waterloo Central Railway** runs a 12 km **heritage tourist train** to Elmira on the Waterloo Spur.

Mill Run – Park Trail

(Preston - Hespeler) Cambridge

Length - 13 km (one way)

40% park path
55% double track
5% road crossings, detours

Elevation - Mainly very flat along water's edge, a few short climbs

Terrain - Dirt/limestone screening base, muddy patches, some paved sections, large bridges, board-walks

Skill - Intermediate

Maps - Map boards; trail markers are old and sparse

Traffic - Typical path users, no motorized traffic

Facilities - Parking lots, toilets, benches, picnic tables, rain shelter and food at either end - not much in the middle

Highlights - Relatively shady route, three dams, falls, bridges, old stone buildings

Phone - 519 623 1340

Website - City of Cambridge

Similar Trails - Greenway, Speed River, Etobicoke Creek

Local Clubs - Waterloo Cycling Club

Access - Reach Cambridge from Highway 401, which passes through the area. Park at any of these spots:

⊕ 69 Apple Dr, Hespeler
P1 Sheffield St, Hespeler
P2 578 Beaverdale Rd, Cambridge
P3 Russ St north end, Preston
P4 Riverside Park, Preston
P5 Hamilton St & Chopin Dr, Preston
⊕ **P6** Hamilton St & Bishop St S, Preston

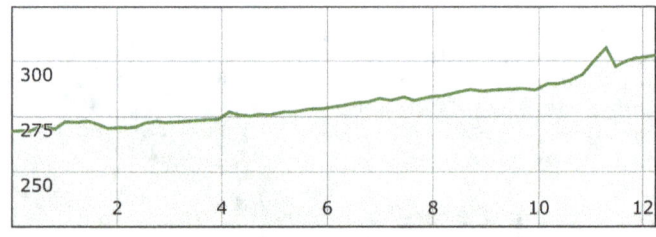

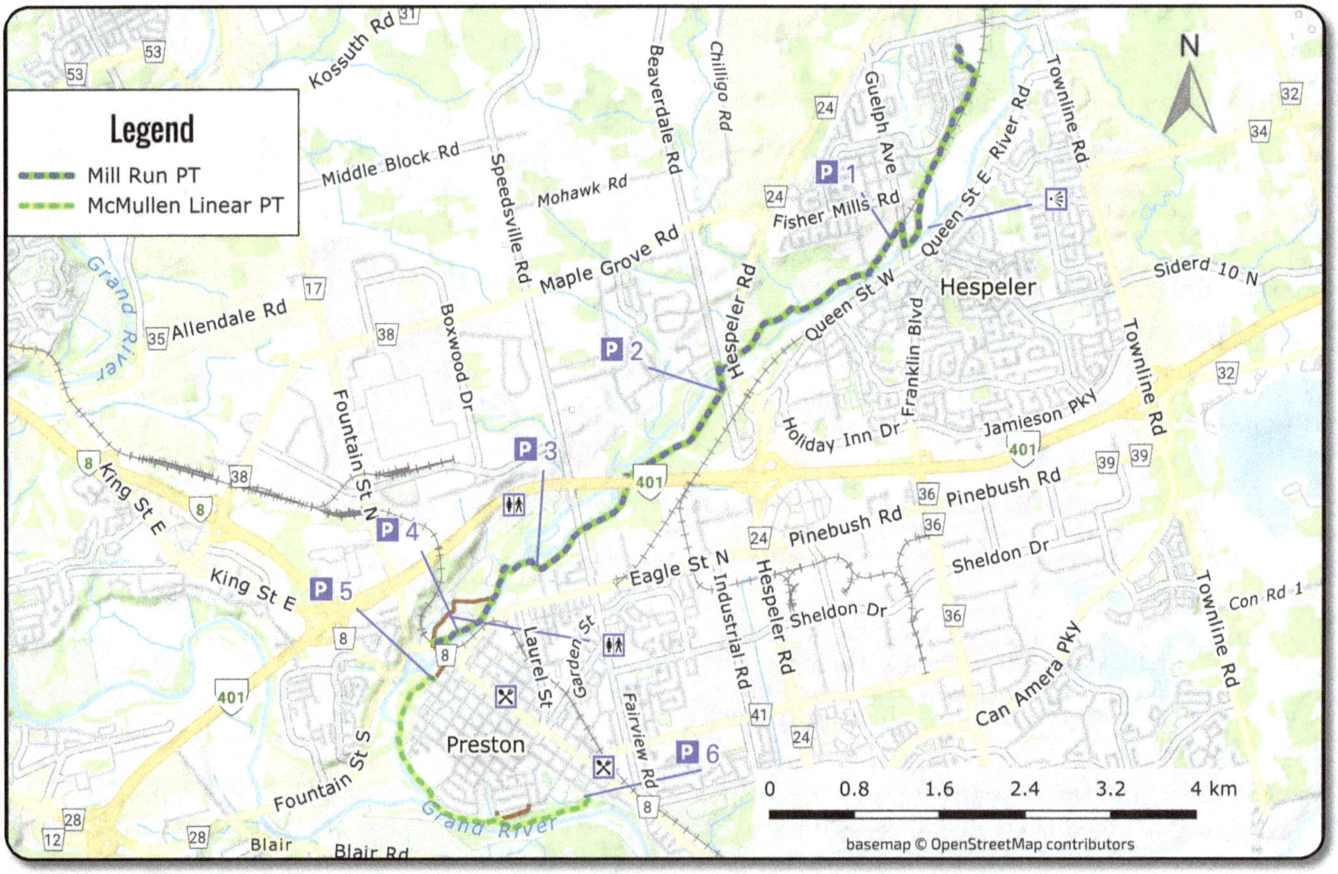

Review:

Cycle **13 km** of wooded Park paths north of **Cambridge** for a tranquil **cruise into history**. Following the shores of the **Speed River**, the **9 km Mill Run Trail** goes from the old settlements of **Hespeler** to **Preston**.

As well, to make this ride more appealing, I tacked on an **extra 4 km**. This is the continuation of the bike path, now being called the **McMullen Linear Trail.**

In **western Ontario**, you can find many short fragments of trail along the **Speed and Grand rivers**. The well-established **Mill Run** is longer and offers **varied scenery and terrain** the way I like it, not mundane spinning.

This bicycle route has **plenty of shade** as it cuts through cedar groves and hardwood stands, and it's mostly flat, as it stays in sight of the water. It crosses the **Speed River** a few times on **large pedestrian bridges** and once on a narrow road bridge at **Beaverdale Rd**. With little traffic, this should be a quick, safe bypass.

The path is mainly a **dirt or crushed limestone base** with a few paved sections. Some low-lying areas probably get flooded in the spring, as the water appeared to me at times almost level with the path.

Signage is old and spotty to follow, and maintenance to trim brush and fill in puddles would be nice, but I am not really complaining. It's a lovely outing on a **gently flowing river.**

Considering these points, I rate this trail at a slightly **more challenging Intermediate** level.

Maybe they got the "speed" out of the river when they put in the **three dams.** The water powered grist mills and textile and furniture enterprises over a century ago. Plaques at these points inform how **industrious settlers** were, even back then.

At **Riverside Park** in **Preston**, you can end your two-wheeled jaunt or cross the **King St E bridge** and take **Chopin Dr** briefly to reach the **McMullen Linear Trail** entrance. This trail is more of an **open parkland** experience as it meets the forks of the **Grand River** ending at **Hamilton and Bishop Street S.**

Starting from either **Hespeler** or **Preston villages** works out well if you wish to lunch at the other end or when you get back. Many of the **old towns' buildings** and features are still there if you fancy wandering. And I saw **ice cream** vendors and a **craft brewery**, so that's covered. ;^)

Highway 401 passes through this area, making it easy to get to. As you approach the highway underpass when cycling, you will briefly hear it cut the silence before you see it.

In **Hespeler**, some of you may not go east beyond the dam to the end at **Apple Dr**, but I encourage you to at least ride to the rail crossing, where the earthen dikes offer some **beautiful views** of a large, marshy pond.

Speaking of tracks, the **Mill Run** was the original **1886 railbed** for steam and electric trains. (So they say—I saw no evidence left of those days.)

I was there in the middle of a hot July day and the bugs were few, but I suspect they are an issue in spring. This is definitely a **worthwhile destination** in the fall when the autumn colours are out.

History - The trail follows the **Galt, Preston, and Hespeler** (now all part of Cambridge) Electric Railway Line. The Galt to Preston line was extended to Hespeler in **1896**, which is the Mill Trail part you ride on.

Towns and merchants were always in competition to attract business and shoppers to their communities. So this **electric line** was built during the **1890s** rail boom when everyone wanted this new form of transport.

This was a single track at first, that ran a simple **electric streetcar** that pulled two rail cars to move locals and goods just a short interurban distance. Eventually a larger steam train was added as the track was again extended to **Guelph**, a rail hub at the time.

The trail, from Russ Street to the Beaverdale Rd bridge you cross, is on a portion of the original **1895** right-of-way. Because spring flooding was a problem a new set of tracks further up the bank was put into service in **1918**. You can see the overgrown iron rails as you enter parking lot **P3**.

Ownership changed many hands with expansion and the advent of car traffic reducing use over the years. In **1998** this line was turned into a recreational trail.

K&P – Rail Trail

Kingston - Renfrew

Length - 180 km (one way)

95% rail trail path
5% road crossings, detours

Elevation - Flat with a very gradual northerly slope

Terrain - Paved in Kingston, fine crushed stone to Clarendon Station, rougher ATV track to Renfrew

Skill - Easy to Clarendon Station, Intermediate to Renfrew

Maps - Good signage (a few missing), map boards, trail milestones/markers, historic posting

Traffic - Bicycles, hikers, horses, snowmobiles, X-country skiers; ATVs and dirt bikes permitted north of Verona

Facilities - Parking lots, a few outhouses, benches, enough amenities can be found on the route in villages to bridge the journey

Highlights - Rock cuts, old train stops, Sharbot Lake Rail Heritage Park, Kingston train & station on the waterfront

Phone - 613 548 9400

Website - County of Frontenac, City of Kingston

Similar Trails - Victoria RT, Cataraqui RT, Ottawa Valley RT

Local Clubs - Kingston Cycling Club

Access - Suggested start points:

⊕**P1** Fluhrer Park - 350 Wellington St, Kingston
P2 West end of Dalton Ave, Kingston
P3 Sydenham Rd Hwy 401, Kingston
P4 2602 McIvor Rd, N side of Hwy 401
P5 4740 Hwy 38, S of Harrowsmith
P6 Verona St, Verona
P7 Road 38, Tichborne
P8 Sharbot Lake
P9 Clarendon Station - Hwy 509 to Clarendon Rd
P10 By bridge Lanark Rd Hwy 511, Calabogie
⊕**P11** Renfrew

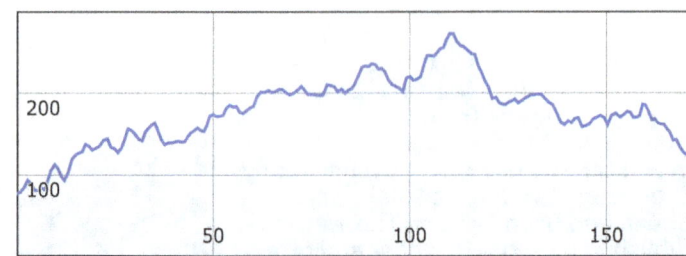

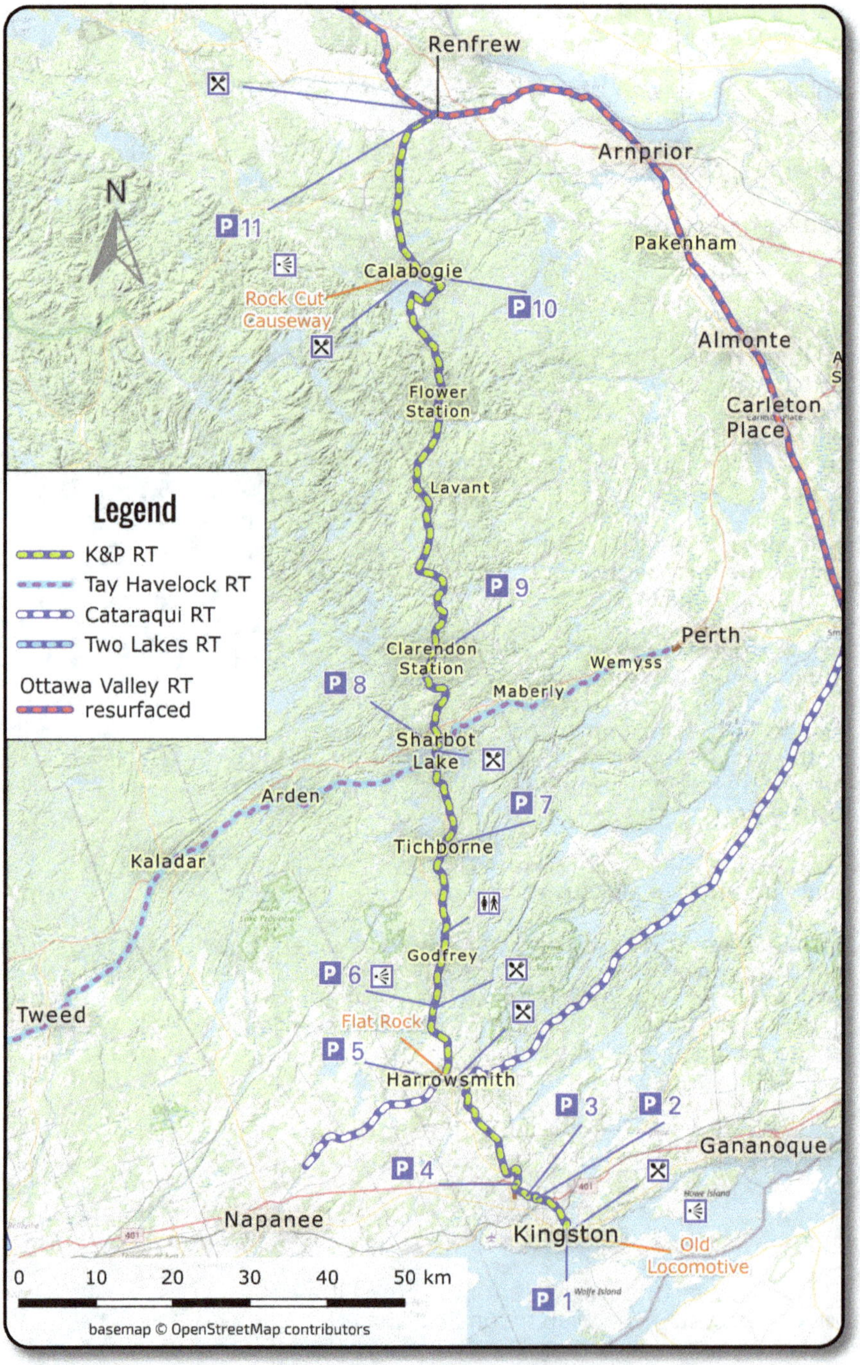

Legend

〰	K&P RT
〰	Tay Havelock RT
〰	Cataraqui RT
〰	Two Lakes RT
Ottawa Valley RT	
〰	resurfaced

Review:

Coming out of **Kingston** is the **K&P Rail Trail**, built over a century ago, winding its way northward into the **Ontario hinterland**. At approximately **180 km,** it is the **second longest RT in the province.**

This established recreational trail passes through many villages and abandoned train stops on its way through **Harrowsmith** at the **30 km** marker, **Sharbot Lake** at **75 km,** and **Calabogie** at **159 km,** ending after **180 km** in **Renfrew**.

The southern half from Kingston to **Clarendon Station**, at the **90 km mark**, has been nicely resurfaced for **hybrid/ gravel bikes**. Beyond this, expect a rougher ride where you have to pick your line to avoid a spill and rattling your molars. A MTB or Fatbike is suggested for this portion.

I finally had a chance to ride the **K&P** for a few days this summer with my cycling mate Bernie. It was **thoroughly enjoyable**, with few bugs, if not a bit TOO hot and humid.

Starting in **downtown Kingston**, we picked up what little was left of this railway at **Bay St & Wellington St.** It soon became a convoluted patchwork of RT paths and boring road bypasses.

Basically, leaving **Kingston** is messy and it would be best for you to pick up the trail at the edge of town, on the west end of **Dalton Ave** or off **Sydenham Rd**. From here, the cycling is pleasant, as it should be—and on the actual old train route!

Once you've gone through the **tunnel**, under the 401, and up and around the railbed **switch-back**, you're into farm country. Overgrown bushes and trees obscure many of the views. There are a few interesting **limestone rock cuts** as this path makes its way to **Harrowsmith**, which was a good point to end our first day.

We both thought the **second day was a better ride**. North of **Harrowsmith**, the scenery changes frequently from **field to forest to wetlands** and back. We crossed a few bridges, but none seemed original or large. We encountered farms, homes, and hamlets, likely built because of the train traffic, but now seeming a little lost in these quiet, trainless surroundings.

As can happen, the path at times becomes part of the county road. **Short detours** got us around. Generally, directional signs worked well, but there were a few occasions where we had to sort out the way (with our phone map).

For me, the highlights of the entire rail trail are the **geological features** we encountered, from **sedimentary layered rock cuts** in the south to large **granite boulder** passageways in the northern Canadian Shield. These make the route none too straight, which is fine by me. But it was an expensive line to build through this rocky, boggy wilderness.

The most stunning spot on the K&P is near Calabogie, where a long causeway across the lake was built (it's now closed) and a 900 m long, 14 m high, narrow 7 m wide cut was blasted out for passage.

I think if any Rail Trail could support **cyclo tourism** with a string of diners, cafes and places to stay, it would be the K&P. I saw a few convenience stores, and there are some places to lodge on the way. Our host at the B&B in **Sharbot Lake**, a RT cycling advocate, was working on it.

ATVs are permitted above **Verona,** but were never a worry. We would usually stop to let them slowly pass, then carry on.

Other Rail Trails intersect the **K&P** to give **bikepacking route options** for longer treks. The **Cataraqui RT** comes through at **Harrow-smith**, and **Sharbot Lake** connects with the **Tay Havelock RT**. In **Renfrew,** you can continue back down the newly resurfaced **Ottawa Valley RT** to make a week-long mega loop.

The **K&P - Kingston & Pembroke Railway** is a **mature, popular Rail Trail** with the potential to be similar to established, well-supported RT routes elsewhere like **Quebec's Le P'tit Train du Nord.** (If we come, they will build it.)

Sadly, there are no long bike paths to cycle on in **Kingston**, but do find time to **play the tourist.** Walk among the **old stone buildings** downtown. There is a **steam locomotive** on display by the old train station on the waterfront, and plenty else to keep you happy.

History - continues on Page 119

Lang Hastings – Rail Trail

Peterborough - Hastings

Length - 33 km (one way)

90% rail trail path
5% road crossings, detours

Elevation - Flat, with a very gradual slope

Terrain - Fine crushed stone, gravel, asphalt at either end, ideal for a hybrid or gravel bike

Skill - Easy

Maps - Well marked, new map boards and posted signs

Traffic - Cycling, hiking/jogging, horseback riding, cross-country skiing and snowmobiling

Facilities - Parking lots, outhouse, benches, rain shelter, food and lodging at either end with not much in between (yet)

Highlights - Large road underpass tunnel, old rail bridges, waterfront views, locks

Phone - None

Website - Lang Hastings Trail

Similar Trails - Omemee RT , Victoria RT, Lower Trent RT

Local Clubs - Peterborough Cycling Club

Access - Suggested parking lots

⊕**P1** Rogers Cove Park - 123 Maria St, Peterborough
P2 Beavermead Park - 1880 Ashburnham Dr, Peterborough
P3 2100 Technology Dr, Peterborough
P4 3289 Base Line Rd east of Heritage Line
P5 Trent Street, Hastings
⊕**P6** Homewood Ave & Bridge St N, Hastings

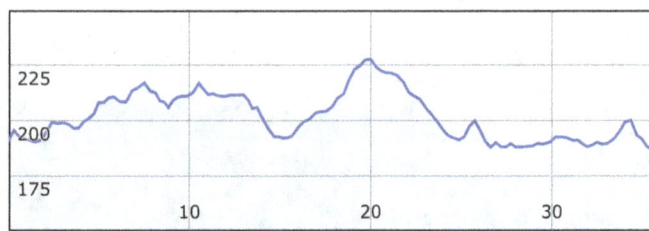

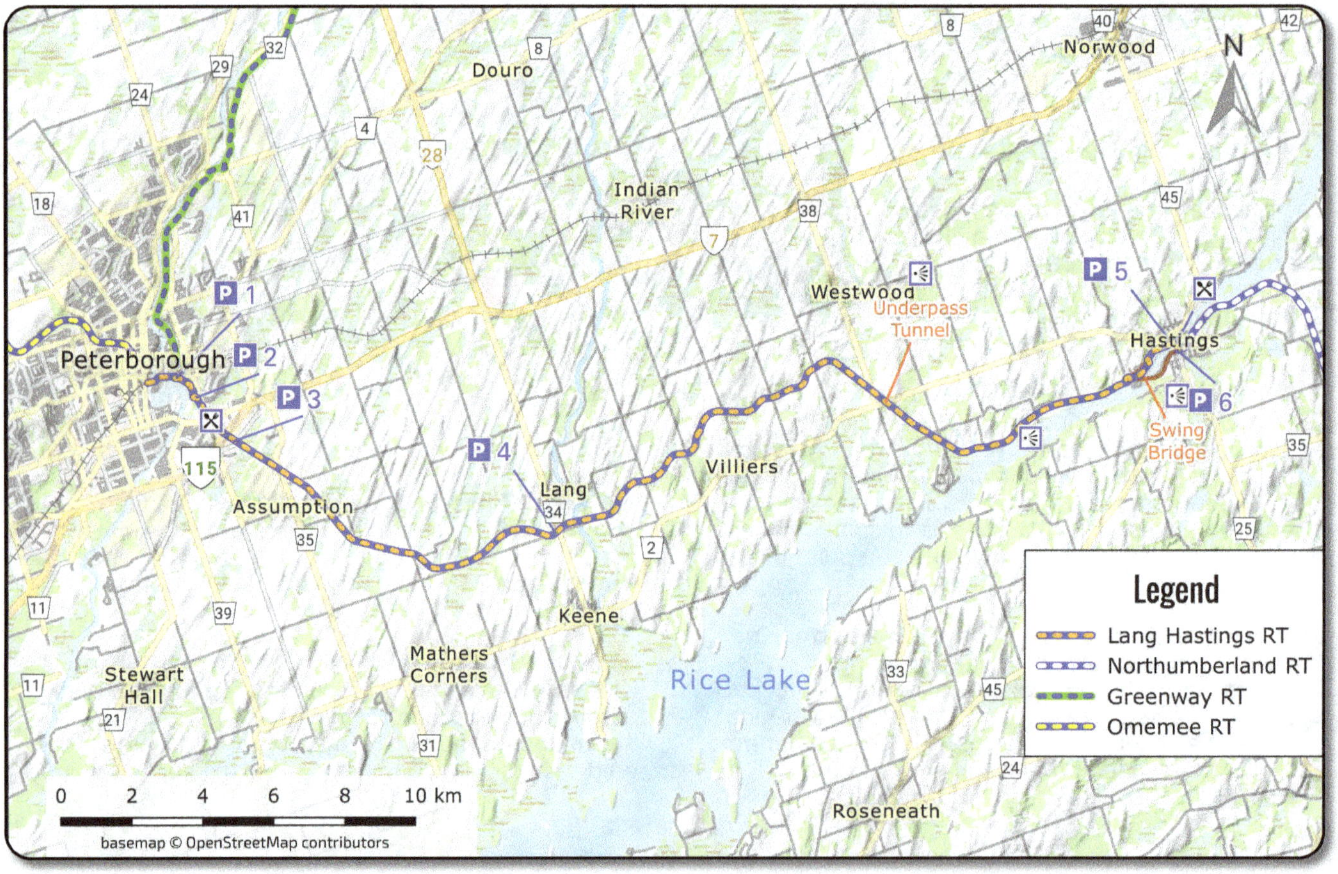

Review:

Enjoy a **33 km country cruise**, car-free, on the **Lang Hastings Rail Trail** this summer. Find your way out to **Peterborough** and cycle through the Ontario countryside to **Hastings.**

I recently rode the length of this trail with my friend Michael on a sunny day to scout the conditions of the path. I am pleased to say the **route is in excellent shape,** with new signs and benches, and is resurfaced with a fine crushed-gravel base.

We started in **Peterborough** at **Rogers Cove Park**, a perfect start point **1.5 km** back from the official trailhead. This was done for two reasons: no parking lot at the trailhead and extra sights to see by the **Otonabee River**.

First thing, everyone loves **iron bridges**. So it's worth going the opposite way west down **Maria St** for a minute; this will take you over a **long rail bridge** into town.

Then double back to start your journey heading SE on the park trail that crosses over the **Trent - Severn Canal at Lock 20.** You have to walk your bike over the top of the old wooden locks, rather novel.

A short jaunt down a paved path alongside **Ashburnham Dr** takes you to **Lansdowne St**. On the opposite side of this busy (take care) intersection is the **Lang Hastings trailhead.** That was the hardest part to navigate (lol, not hard at all); the rest of the way is easy sailing on two wheels.

This part of **Ontario** is full of **short hills (eskers)** that you do not have to manage. Track builders years ago found a way around these many **mounds of glacial deposits** to make a level route for trains. This in effect gives riders less of a straight, boring direct route and more of **an interesting, winding path to follow.**

The trip is a **quiet venture into Ontario farm country** with a few barns in the distance and the odd woodlot and marsh to pass through. We both agreed that sunscreen would help, as it was **not that shady a trip.**

I do not recall many road crossings on this trek. Most are underpasses with likely the **largest road "tunnel"** for bikes in Ontario going under **County Rd 2.**

As you near the tourist town of **Hastings,** the path swings down to the end of **Rice Lake** to give refreshing views over the water dotted with boats.

The odd part of this Rail Trail is that maps show the route crossing over to the other side via the **old train bridge**.

But in actual fact, cyclists can not partake in this crossing from mid-May to Thanksgiving, as the swing bridge is open (so sailboats can pass, I assume). It closes in the winter, so snowmobilers do get to use it. (The same thing happens on the **Victoria RT in Fenelon Falls**.)

I would still encourage you to ride to the end of the bridge for a grand view of the river, and take a few pictures.

So plan to ride around it on the road. When you meet **Asphodel 7th Line,** head north, then east onto **River Rd** and take **Park Lane** to avoid the large hill. Continue west on **Front St W.**

Soon you will see the town of **Hastings,** which has an excellent waterfront pub/patio and a coffee shop scene to relax and indulge. Check out the **dam/falls and locks,** then ride back or as we did, set up a car, left there, to **shuttle back** with the bikes.

For more mileage, this trail continues on the other side of the town locks and bridge, where it's known as the **Northumberland Rail Trail**. Another **34 kilometres** gets you to **Campbellford** on what they say is a little rougher route (ATVs are permitted).

And **Peterborough** has many options to continue cycling and refuel if you ride this trail in the other direction. Within reach from **Toronto** for a day trip or a longer getaway, it's yours to discover!

History - continues on Page 119

Lower Trent – Rail Trail

Trenton - Trent River lock 7

Length - 17 km (one way)

*95% rail trail path
5% road crossings, road detours*

Elevation - Pancake flat

Terrain - Crushed gravel; pockets of loose grit; wide tires needed; width of path varies, narrowing to singletrack at times

Skill - Easy

Maps - Map board at the gate, route signs

Traffic - Bicycles, eBikes, hikers, snowmobiles and X-country skiers in winter

Facilities - Parking, benches, amenities in Frankford and at locks

Highlights - Town of Frankford, six dam/locks, swing bridges, Bleasdell Boulder

Trail Fee - Free

Phone - 613 394 4829

Website - Quinte West, Lower Trent Conservation

Similar Trails - Caledon RT, Millennium RT, LE&N Rail Trail

Local Clubs - None

Access - Here are my parking suggestions, starting from the south end:

⊕**P1** Lock Rd east of Stockdale Rd
P2 Bleasdell Boulder - 762 Trenton Frankford Rd
P3 Batawa Community Centre - 81 Plant St, Batawa
P4 Perry Dr, Batawa
P5 Mill St & N Wellington St, Frankford
⊕**P6** Lock 7 Glen Ross, Trent-Severn Waterway - 1306 Glen Ross Rd

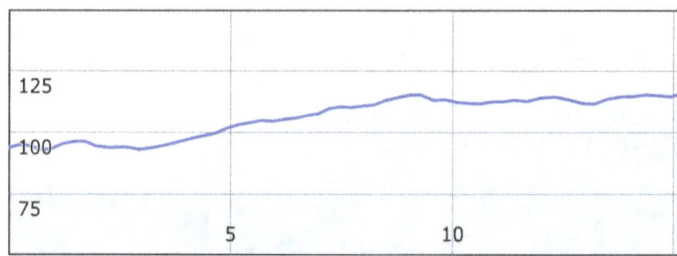

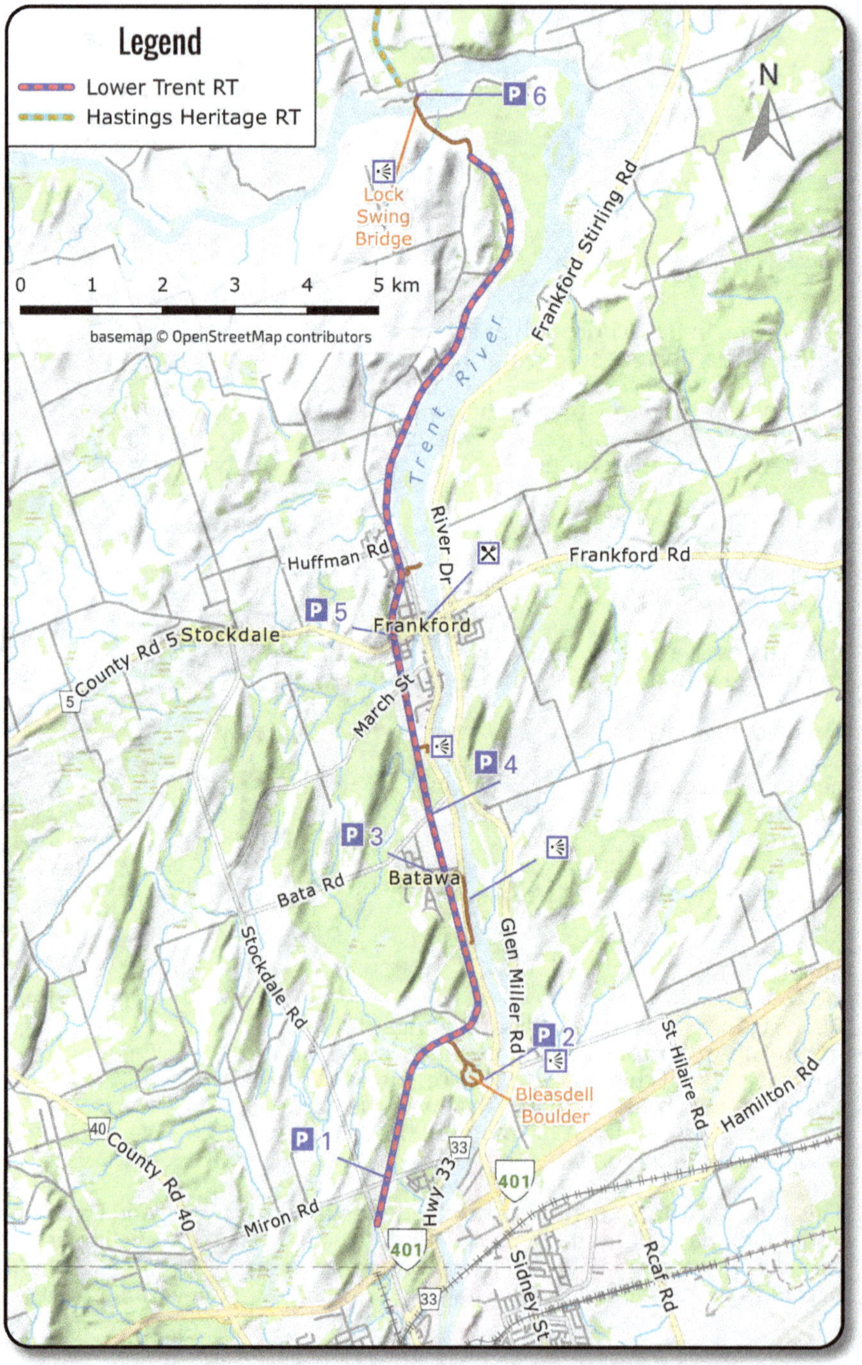

Review:

Discover the **Lower Trent Rail Trail** running north from **Trenton**, as I did one summer. It's a great find and an enjoyable **17 km** path to cycle. In my opinion, this under-publicized Rail Trail truly **deserves more attention.**

What makes this Rail Trail so pleasing is the **variety of scenery** along the way. Onward one rides, through quiet fields and small wooded enclaves. We encountered a multitude of small butterflies en route.

Because there was little info online to indicate we could ride it or even make it the whole way, we were pleasantly surprised to find the path resurfaced with the usual crushed-gravel base and well signed.

This length of the trail is also **free of any motorized traffic** (ATV, motocross bikes), though eBikes are permitted, as are snowmobiles in the winter.

At the south end, take a **300 m** side trail to visit the **Bleasdell Boulder Conservation Area, where** you can see one of the largest boulders left behind from the ice age, pushed down from the town of Madoc. Nearby you can try riding another small, wooded **1 km loop**.

We passed by the village of **Batawa**, which has a **ski hill** with a few simple **MTB trails**. The more interesting backyards of the larger town of **Frankford** were an unexpected highlight and a nice **change of scenery.**

The large hills you will see in the area are actually **eskers:** mounds of sand and gravel deposits left behind by **receding glaciers.** Though the route follows the **Trent River** with its **many dams and locks,** we only saw glimpses of it in the distance. A quick jaunt east on any side road will take you there.

The last section is rural countryside, ending abruptly at **Glen Ross Rd.** The trail continues past here to the train bridge, but this section allows **ATV action** and

it's a rough ride. Better to **take the road** around the bend to cross the **Trent River**, where this trail review ends at **Trent-Severn Waterway Lock 7 - Glen Ross.**

It would be novel to actually cross the old trail bridges, but they are closed.

The next segment of this Rail Trail does continue north beyond the locks off **Rosebush Rd** as the **Hastings Heritage Trail**. The **Trans Canada Trail** uses the south part to connect on more of a lumpy, bumpy trek best done on a MTB. Then it get worse going way up past **Bancroft** for **150+ km** on a route ATVs abuse.

Riding along this path, I have the feeling that an initial effort was made to establish this recreational trail and then the money/interest ran out. The **path narrows at times** to **singletrack**, and the brush is starting to grow in. The base could use a little grading and there is **a fair bit of loose grit** that may need a few years to pack down.

None of this should discourage you from venturing on to this new find. A **hybrid/gravel bike** with wider tires will manage nicely. And this review, plus your visit, will **spread the word.**

Afterwards, find a riverside patio in **Trenton** for a bite, or even stay over to explore the **Quinte area** and ride the Millennium RT, too.

History - In **1884,** the **Central Ontario Railway** (COR) built this branch line to bypass boats navigating risky river rapids. It ran from **Trenton Junction** to Coe Hill with a station in **Frankford**. Moving farm goods and lumber down the **Trent River** was difficult by boat until locks were built in **1920** to tame the seven sets of rapids

By **1923,** the line belonged to the **Canadian National Railway** (CNR), which operated it until the rails were removed in the late **1980**s. By **2005,** the railbed had been turned into a recreational path.

Northumberland – Rail Trail

Hastings - east of Stirling

Length - 51 = 40 + 11 km (one way)

90% rail trail path
10% road crossings, detours

Elevation - Flat, gradually descending eastward

Terrain - Rougher ATV ruts worn in, gravel, loose aggregate, ruts, stones, puddles

Skill - Intermediate

Maps - Signs for ATVs and snowmobiles mark the distances

Traffic - Cyclists, walkers/hikers, horseback riders, ATVs, snowmobiles

Facilities - Parking lots, washrooms,

Highlights - Ranney Falls and long suspension bridge, Trent River locks, rolling scenic hills, Hastings, Stirling

Phone - 905 372 3329

Website - Northumberland Tourism, Trans Canada Trail

Similar Trails - Trail of Two Lakes RT, Tay Havelock RT,   Victoria South RT

Local Clubs - None

Access - At rail crossing on side roads and these suggested lots:

P1 North end of Station St, Stirling
P2 1350 Burnbrae Rd E, Campbellford
P3 Ferris Provincial Park, Campbellford
P5 Trent Street, Hastings
⊕**P6** Bridge St & Dit Clapper Dr, Hastings

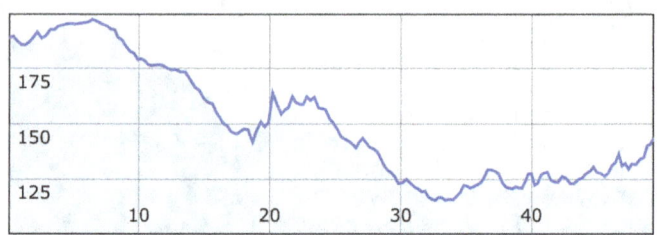

 comment removed

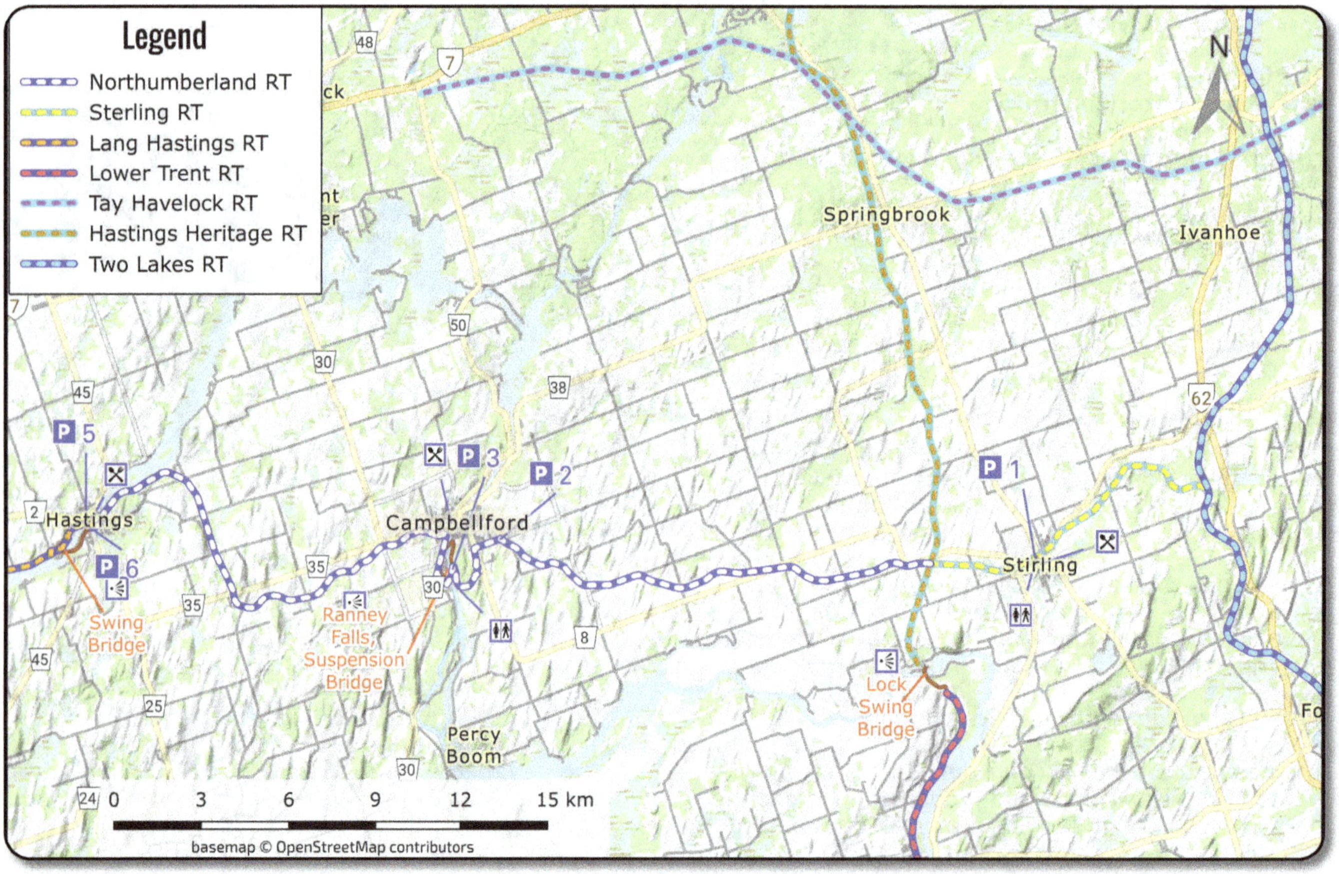

Legend
- Northumberland RT
- Sterling RT
- Lang Hastings RT
- Lower Trent RT
- Tay Havelock RT
- Hastings Heritage RT
- Two Lakes RT

basemap © OpenStreetMap contributors

Review:

For this review, I'm combining the **40 km Northumberland Rail Trail** with the next **11 km** short segment that goes through **Stirling** to meet the **Trail of Two Lakes RT.**

This was all part of the **Grand Junction Railway** back in the day. I'll start on the west side of the RT, heading out of **Hastings**, where the scenery continues to be beautiful just like the **Lang Hastings RT,** but the path does get rougher.

On this RT, motorized ATVs and snowmobiles are allowed, so you will find larger stones and loose gravel on a somewhat rutted double-tracked path. I don't want to make it sound impassable, but just make you aware that you need a sturdy **gravel/hybrid contraption** or **MTB** for this **Intermediate RT ride**. Wider tires and preferably shocks or a spring loaded seat post will help to soften the rough patches.

This Rail trail winds through hundreds of **ancient hilly glacial deposits** from when the ice sheet was over **2 km thick 20,000 years ago**—can you picture that? It makes for a less than straight route (all the better, if you ask me).

You probably won't need any bug spray, but do pull out the sunscreen, as this farm country tour has **little shade.**

This **idyllic country ride** passes many wetlands and rolling farm fields, with **cattle and sheep staring at you** and your odd wheeled contraption. After an hour or so, you'll be closing in on **Campbellford**, which sits on the **Trent River**. Here you will cross over the locks and an impressive **suspension bridge** to view **Ranney Falls,** the highlight of this RT.

The bridge takes you to **Ferris Provincial Park,** where you could camp. It also takes you around on a detour out of town to meet the continuation of the RT. The connection is a little disjointed, but I'm sure you'll figure it out.

You could also go north when you see the water to visit **Campbellford**, a medium-size community where you can have a meal, play the tourist by doing the river walk, or stay over. The bike path on **Trent Dr** by the water's edge is lovely.

Over the distance of this RT, you will notice a gradual descent eastward. I was surprised to find a few **steeper inclines**, greater than the usual train grades of a few percent. I recall enjoying the views of the **rolling hills and farms,** offering some good photo ops if the lighting is right.

When you get to the tiny community of **Anson**, the RT crosses the **Hastings Heritage RT** that goes north to the **Bancroft** area. I have yet to venture up that way, but I hear this **ATV trail is nasty**, not MTB friendly. Going south, it does mellow out and become a resurfaced RT below the **Trent River.**

Seventy-five minutes later, you'll be arriving at **Stirling**, an charming old agricultural town where you can stay a while, feed yourself, and check out the **old train station museum.**

If you continue up and around through the forested area, this RT ends when it meets up with the **Trail of Two Lakes RT** at **Madoc Junction** in about thirty minutes.

With enough support along the trip to eat and lodge, this is a good choice for a **bikepacking adventure**. You can head south on the original train route to **Belleville** or north towards the mining town of **Madoc** on more of the same terrain. See? I told you that **a MTB or Fatbike** was your ticket to ride.

History - The **Grand Junction Railway** (GJR) was a short line that ran from **Belleville to Stirling** by **1877** and on past **Peterborough** three years later. It was also a short-lived company, becoming part of the **Midland Railway of Canada** (MRC) in **1882** and acquired by the **Grand Trunk Railway** (GTR) two years later.

While passenger traffic ceased in the **1960s**, the line was used for freight until **1980**. when sections of the route began being abandoned one by one. By **1990** all the tracks had been lifted.

Ottawa River Pathway – Park Trail

Ottawa - Orléans

Length - 20 km

90% park path
10% road crossings, detours

Elevation - Flat along the water's edge, short steep climb to get to the roadway above (also a level route).

Terrain - Paved path, fine crushed stone on the 9 km lower river route

Skill - Easy - Intermediate

Maps - Ample map boards and trail markers

Traffic - Not busy, typical path users - hikers, joggers - parts of this trail are used for Nordic skiing in the winter

Facilities - Many parking lots, toilets (not many), benches, picnic tables, rain shelters, repair stations. Surprisingly, not very close to any food or drink.

Highlights - Views of the Ottawa River and Quebec shoreline, solitude, nature, lookouts

Phone - 1 800 465 1867

Website - National Capital Commission

Similar Trails - Upper Ottawa River, Cornwall Waterfront,   Greenway

Local Clubs - Ottawa Bike Club

Access - Lots of parking lots at:

⊕**P1** Rideau Falls - 115 Sussex Dr
P2 Rockcliffe Park - 53 Rockcliffe Park
P3 - P8 lots along Sir George Etienne Cartier Pkwy
P9 François Dupont Park - North end of Willow Ave, Orleans
⊕**P10** Petrie Island Beach - North end of Tweddle Rd, Orleans

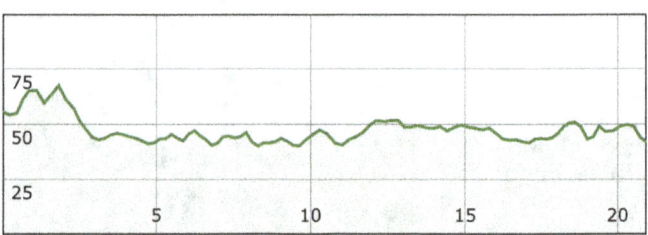

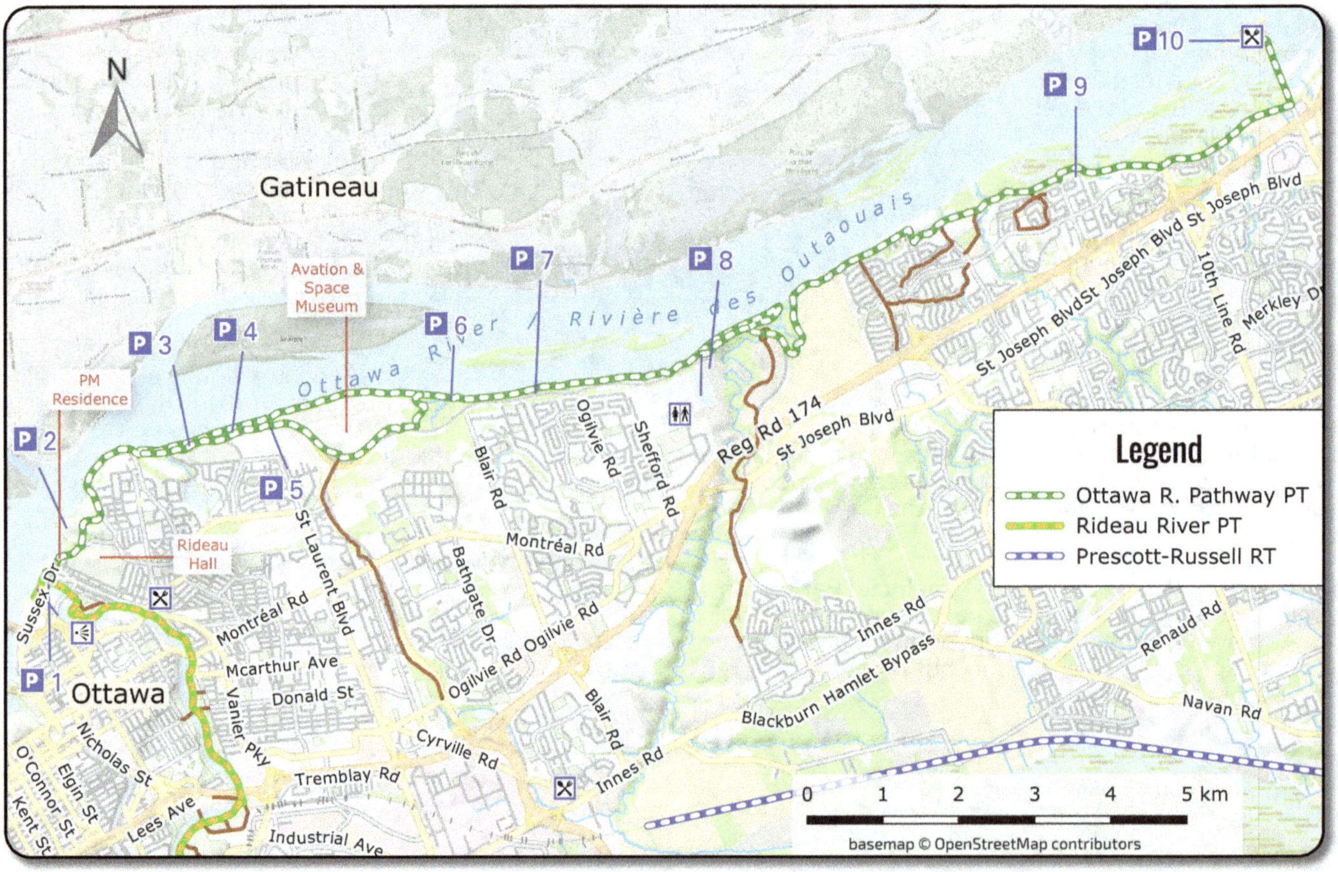

Review:

The lower **Ottawa River Pathway** heading east out of the town of **Ottawa** is a long **20 km** bicycle ride with many options along the route. This **scenic** and **tranquil** journey is a **completely different** cycling experience from the Upper Ottawa River route I reviewed in the first book.

Unlike that ride, this one is a more rustic, **natural setting** and hilly (for some) with fewer manicured parks or crowds. And much of it is **not paved.**

The section that is **crushed fine gravel** is the **9 km** length running down along the water's edge. It's an **easy** spin on level ground if you have a **hybrid** or **gravel bike** with medium-width tires.

For the skinny-tire set, fear not, there is a way to ride it all on the pavement, you just have to do **5 kms** on the **Sir George Etienne Cartier Parkway**. There seems to be enough space on the paved shoulders and traffic is light on this road.

I started my ride, as many may, to sightsee from the centre of town just a mere kilometre sooner where the **Rideau River** bike path ends (another fine trail to try) by the **Rideau Falls**.

Take a few pictures of the falls then ride this short extra bit of road on the bike lane past the **Prime Minister's Residence** on **Sussex Dr** on to **Princess Ave** to connect to the **Ottawa R. Pathway.**

Officially this off-road route starts on the west side on the **Cartier Parkway** at the roundabout meeting **Rockcliffe & Princess**. The road has a paved path running on both sides. Take either one, but eventually, it moves to the right side as a single path...then to the left.

You will pass **Rockcliffe Park**, lookout, and marina, then ride around the bend where the route turns into the **Aviation Pathway.** When you see signs for the **New Edinburgh Club marina,** take the steep road down to start the gravel waterfront route.

This is the best part, as it offers serene cycling with many **views across the grand Ottawa River** and opportunities to stop and sit awhile.

If you're not so inclined, opt to stay by the roadway for the easier paved ride. As you may suspect, this trail will lead you to the **Aviation and Space Museum** (a worthy side trip, or your destination).

Beyond the open fields for the runways, eventually, this route heads down to the water. So at this point, road riders need to hit the road and ride **5 km** to the **Green's Creek bridge**.

Those on the river route will also need to swing back up to cross this bridge. After which you are back onto **paved paths 'til the end**. Smooth sailing, ahhh! This part of the route, the **Heritage East Trail,** moves further away from the river's edge, into the woods, though you will still get plenty of glimpses of the river.

Subdivisions start appearing for the first time and there is a short neighbourhood street detour on **Radisson Way,** then **Hiawatha Park Rd** to connect back with the trail.

Eventually, the trail ends at **Jeanne D'Arc Blvd N** and **Tweddle Rd**, where **Petrie Island Beach** is. Hmm, care to soak your feet or do a lunch stop here? There are not many food choices on this route; you may be better off bringing a picnic.

For more riding, the **Aviation Pathway** is a pleasant off-road route that branches out in a southerly direction for **4 km** to **Ogilvie Rd.** Another ride option is taking the **Greenbelt Pathway E** at **Green's Creek** to follow the creek south.

It's not an overly shady trail - I would put on a coat of that sunblock goo.

I fully enjoyed the ride on my hybrid bike and saw **plenty of parking lots** and access paths down to the gravel trail. This will help you plan where to start and when to turn around and head back when you make it out here one sunny weekend.

Ottawa Valley – Rail Trail

Smith Falls - Mattawa

Length - 296 km (one way)

95% rail trail path
5% road crossings, detours

Elevation - Flat, gradually sloping northward

Terrain - Fine crushed stone, larger gravel patches, asphalt sections in towns

Skill - Easy

Maps - Map boards and new signage

Traffic - Cyclists, hikers, ATVs, snowmobiles

Facilities - Parking lots, benches

Highlights - Bridges, shoreline views, old historic towns, railway museum in Smith Falls

Phone - 613 735 7288

Website - Ottawa Valley Recreational Trail, FB page

Similar Trails - K&P RT,   G2G RT,   North Simcoe RT

Local Clubs - Ottawa Bicycle Club, Ottawa Valley Cycling & ATA

Access - Parking lots exist on these roads:

⊕558 Sturgess Rd, Smiths Falls
P1 510 Perth Road (County Rd 10), Franktown Station
P2 17 Coleman Street, Carlton Place
P3 Reserve St, Almonte
P4 171 Waba Road (Hwy 20), Pakenham
P5 John St N & Meehan St, Arnprior
P6 Hwy 132 at K&P RT, outside Renfrew
P7 Nelson St & Mackay St or Waterfront Park, Pembroke
P8 15 Norman St, Petawawa

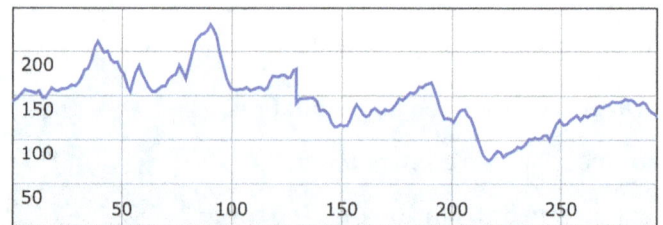

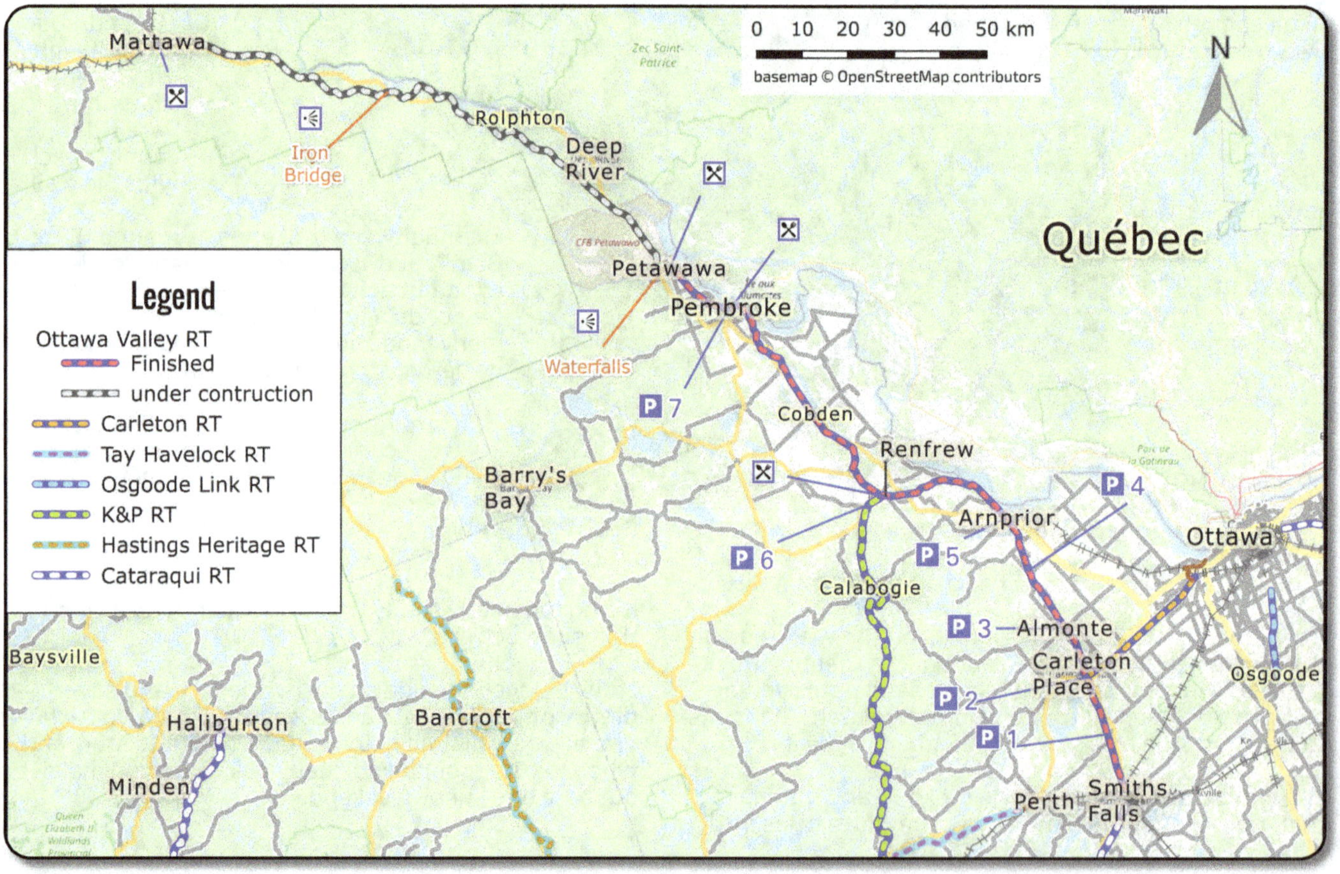

Review:

The new **296 km Ottawa Valley Rail Trail** (OVRT) will be the **longest rail trail in Ontario** when finished. What was once a **CP rail line** running up the **Ottawa Valley** and river is now being resurfaced as a **very long** recreational trail.

It starts just above **Smiths Falls** at the south end and runs northward through many old towns in the **Ottawa Valley** to **Arnprior,** where it meets the **Ottawa River**. Then this rail trail follows this mighty waterway NW all the way to **Mattawa**. Wow, that is almost to **North Bay!**

I am happy to announce that the **southern half of this trail is ready** for you to explore this summer. The northern half, from **Petawawa** to **Mattawa,** is still being resurfaced and mani-cured, to be finished by 2025, they say.

We had a chance to ride two sections. First, we sampled the **Pembroke** to **Petawawa** section (called the **Algonquin Trail**). High-lights are the **old bridge crossings** in town and the shoreline views in **Pembroke.**

The trail continues south through **Cobden** and **Renfrew** before meeting the **Ottawa River** again near **Arnprior.**

Then, further south in farm country, we rode the **Lanark County** section through the towns of **Pakenham, Almonte/Mississippi Mills,** and **Carleton Place.** These are old milling rail stops along the **Mississippi River** (yes, another one).

Quaint, **historic downtown streets** with antique shops and **ice cream vendors** can give you a reason to stop for a while and are the **most interesting part of this trek.**

The countryside in this very wide valley is **flat farmland.** As such, sections of the track run **relatively straight** between towns. Views are of crops in farm fields and wetlands (when not obscured by trees and tall shrubs). We had little shade on our midday ride.

This rail trail path has a new base of **fine crushed gravel,** which will still be **dusty** for a few years until it compacts. I noticed crews had used larger gravel for pothole repairs (why this large?). You have to watch out for these rocky patches. Otherwise, **the going is easy** for a gravel bike or MTB.

This path allows **ATVs;** we saw a few pass us slowly with no issues, then we waited for the dust to settle. **Snowmobiles** are also allowed but were not much of an issue on our sunny July weekend.

I am glad to see this trail open up to enable **long-distance trail riders** and **bikepackers** to connect with other rail trails. You can now reach **Ottawa** via the **Carleton RT** from **Carleton Place** or get to the **K&P RT** at **Renfrew** or continue onto the Cataraqui RT at **Smiths Falls**. This really opens up route possibilities.

When finished, the **120 km** stretch from north of **Petawawa** heads back into the bush for a long and solitary ride before emerging near **Driftwood Prov. Park**, where one could camp. (**Chalk River** is the last good supply stop 'til the proposed end of the line.)

After **Driftwood,** the RT will meet the river again, offering views of the more hilly **Quebec** side and **Hwy 17** a few times. Then it will go inland through a narrow valley after crossing the **iron bridge at Bissett Creek.** By **Deux-Rivières,** the RT will hug the river again for **20 km.** That should make the sights better than a corridor of endless trees.

You will be happy to find a good meal and a bed when you reach **Mattawa.** And it will be well deserved! You will have survived the wilderness of Ontario (and its biting bugs)—**congrats!** A **journey like the voyageurs** took paddling centuries ago up the mighty Ottawa to rest in Mattawa before moving on to **North Bay.**

This cycling trailway is **certain to become popular,** as it has enough town stops with **meals and lodging** to **service riders' needs** in the south. And the northern half will give those bikepackers desiring a **dose of wilderness** plenty to take in.

When crews get finished resurfacing the railbed and adding new parking lots, signs, benches, and other frills, it will be a joy to tour...and a **long way to crank.**

History - continues on page 119

Pinecrest Xfarm - Park Trail

Ottawa

Length - 13.5 km = 3.5 + 8 + 2 km (one way)

95% park paths
5% road crossings

Elevation - Gradual climb away from the river, inland continuing flat across

Terrain - Paved, some gravel and sandy spots

Skill - Easy going

Maps - Map boards, trail post markers

Traffic - Typical city path users, light traffic

Facilities - Parking lots, toilets, but few services till you get to the gardens

Highlights - Arboretum and ornamental gardens, museum, Dow's Lake, open spaces, inner-city solitude, not busy, makes a loop (we all like that)

Phone - 1 833 864 7839

Website - NCC - Capital Pathway

Similar Trails - Lower Ottawa R, Prescott Russell RT

Local Clubs - Ottawa Bike Club

Access - Pick up the trail from the Ottawa River Pathway at either end or from the Rideau Canal Trail at Dow's Lake. There are not many car lots adjacent to the trail; here are a few suggestions:

⊕ Britannia Conservation Area
P1 16 Constellation Dr, fee
P2 Carlington Park - west end of Morisset Ave
P3 Agriculture and Food Museum, 901 Prince of Wales Dr, fee
P4 Dows Lake Pavilion - 1001 QE Driveway, Hwy 73, fee
⊕ Ottawa R & Trillium Pathway

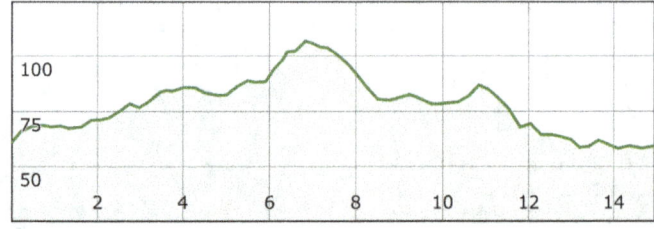

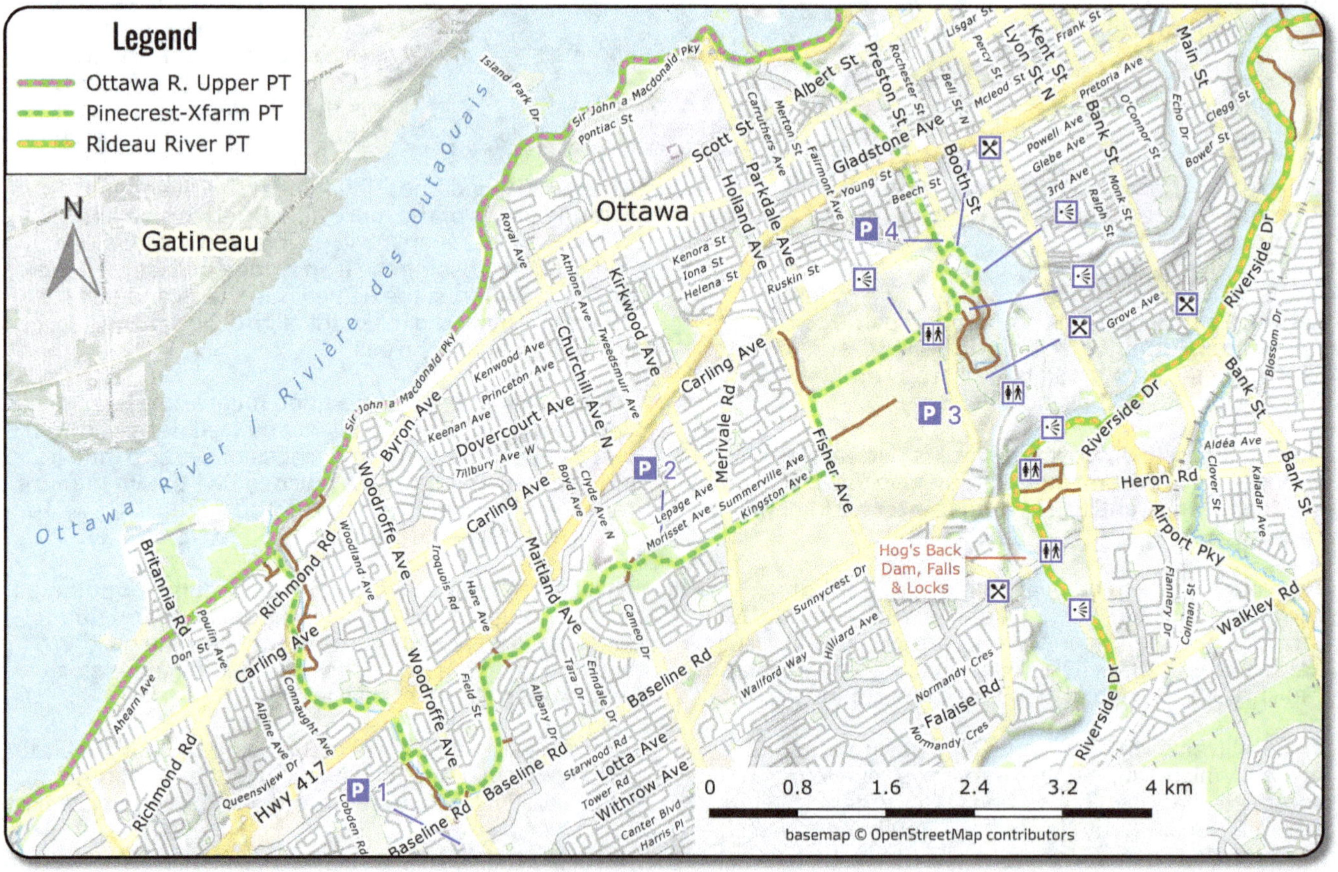

Review:

Ottawa is a bike-friendly city with an abundance of good trail riding destinations. I call this one the **Pinecrest-XFarm** Park Trail, **a combination of three routes** that will help you make a loop for an enjoyable **meditative inner-city day ride** on your two-wheeler.

This cycling excursion is what I call a **calming zen-like journey**; you are somewhat removed from the city's influences and distractions. **Time to reflect on your inner thoughts,** or none at all, as your pedals go round and wheels turn…- like the circle of life.

My proposed route starts from the very popular **Upper Ottawa River** pathway by the Britannia Conservation Area. Signs posted will point you inland onto the **3.5 km Pinecrest Creek pathway.**

Wind your way up this paved path beside the **Transitway** road; it's all green grass parkland, void of storefronts and people in a rush.There are brief moments when you're in the woods and then out again. The road is at a distance and soon to be left behind.

The path splits at **Iris St** and it should be well marked enough for you to continue on the **east side** of the **Transitway** to send you **SE to Woodroffe Ave.**

Once you cross the road at the fire station, you'll be on the **Experimental Farm Pathway.** Say goodbye to traffic. This **8 km** paved path meanders through fields between neighbourhoods for **3 km,** then straightens out to meet **Merivale Rd.** And straighten it does, for now you are entering the farm fields of the government's experimental farming property. (Why does that sound sinister? It's not.)

I find these open farm fields, surrounded by homes and traffic, such an **oddity in the middle of a large metropolitan city.** Here is this valuable land still used to grow seedlings. It must drive land developers crazy!

Cyclists' goals differ: **we seek out a peaceful, worry-free spin.** And these straight trail lines down evenly spaced fence posts can **mesmerize or bore you.**

Once you make your way across this expanse (hopefully not on a windy day) you will be entering the **botanical** and **arboretum grounds** by **Dows Lake.** Here you can **wander around on quiet paths, carefree.** Check out the **rose gardens, smell the lilac bushes,** and visit the **Agriculture and Food Museum.**

There are **places to eat and rest** while you take in **views from the hill,** as you live out these **contemplative moments with nature.** Find your way down to the lake and perhaps enjoy a **waterfront patio beverage.**

When you are ready for more time in the saddle, no rush…today's route heads back to the **Ottawa River.** Look for signs to the **2 km Trillium pathway,** which starts by the **Carling LR Transit stop** at **855 Carling Ave** and runs along the tracks behind a row of trees. Consider it a bike commuter path—not too pretty, but functional. You'll only encounter traffic at one street crossing before you reach the **long trestle rail bridge to Quebec.** (Abandoned, could it one day serve cyclists? That would be so cool.)

Now you are back again on the **Ottawa River Pathway,** ready to re-engage with the city flow. Either loop back or go east downtown the other way.

Another alternate direction from the gardens can take you along the **Rideau Canal** on either side for more **contemplative circular rotations**…and to ponder the science of how we can possibly balance ourselves on two wheels.

Prescott- Russell – Rail Trail

Ottawa - St-Eugène

Length - 72 km (one way)

*95% rail trail path
5% road crossings, detours*

Elevation - Fairly flat, mellow hills

Terrain - Fine crushed stone, gravel, paved asphalt in towns

Skill - Easy

Maps - Map board at parking lots, with plenty of signage on the route.

Traffic - Very light use by cyclists, hikers, horseback riders, and snowmobilers in winter

Facilities - Large parking lots, outhouses, picnic benches, bike racks, benches on the route

Highlights - Some farms, bridge at Plantagenet, train station in Bourget

Phone - 1 800 361 7439

Website - Prescott Russell County

Similar Trails - G2G RT, Elora Cataract RT, Bruce RT

Local Clubs - Ottawa Bicycle Club

Access - Parking lots at the Rail Trail Pavilions:

P1 S of Renaud Rd on Anderson Rd Hwy 27, Ottawa
P2 937 Smith Rd, Navan
P3 3275 Grendon Rd (Hwy 21), Hammond
P4 178 Levis St & Etienne St, Bourget
P5 647 Hwy 9, Plantagenet
P6 Station Road (southwest of Alfred)
P7 Caledonia Spring Road (east of Alfred)
P8 51 49 Hwy 34, Vankleek Hill
P9 top of Mill St, St Eugène
P10 old Rigaud train station - 131 Rue Saint-Viateur, Rigaud

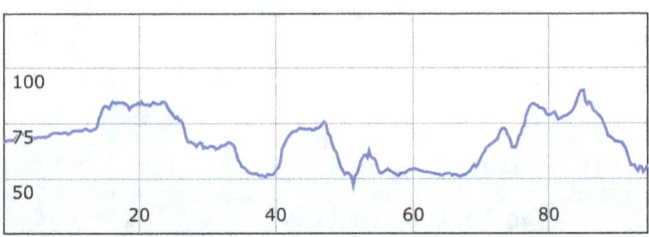

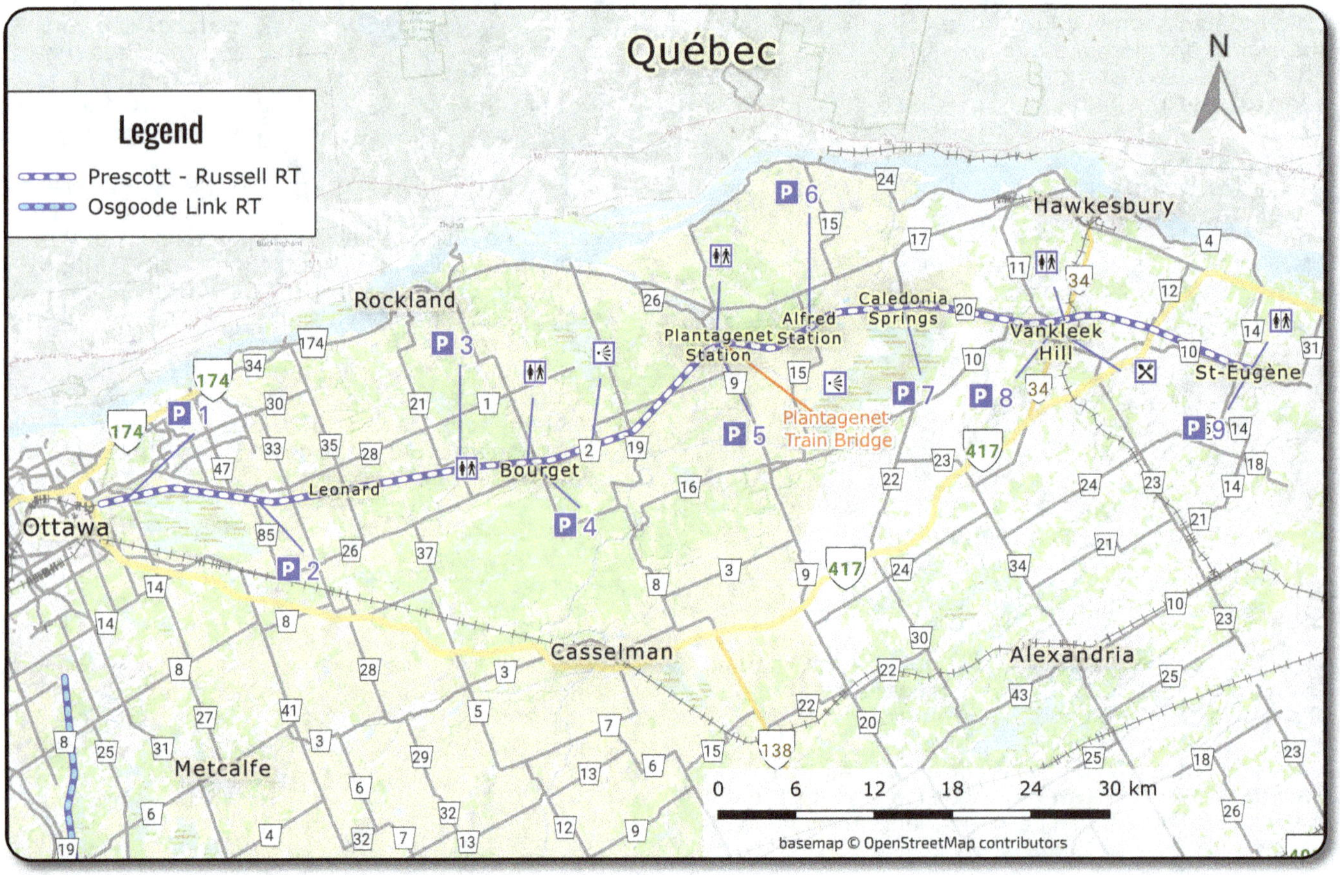

Review:

Out by the eastern end of Ontario, the **72 km Prescott - Russell Rail Trail** runs from outside **Ottawa** to **Rigaud** in **Quebec.**

A once busy train line running through farm country, this is now a "bike highway" to connect with other road touring loops. It's a great way to get to **Montreal** or **Ottawa**.

This Rail Trail is relatively new and **well maintained** by the county. The path base is the crushed limestone gravel riders are used to. Only the thinnest of tires would have a possible handling problem. Some sections in towns are paved. (I don't know why...)

There's plenty of signage on the route, which is built better than most RT conversions. It has many parking kiosks with simple comforts like outhouses and picnic benches that make the **trail welcoming.**

Perhaps one can attribute the low traffic to its newness, lack of stellar landmarks, and location. Yes, this is a corner of eastern Ontario by the **Ottawa River** few of us venture to.

What you will find different are wide-open spaces and a peaceful ride. No hum of highways, airports, or industry. Just **pure country**, with crickets and BIG views of farms, fields, and sky.

The **Prescott - Russell Trail** does not traverse many woodlots. There is **little shade**, so expect to get plenty of sun on your neck.

This part of Ontario is pretty flat, so when they laid the track the cheapest way, they naturally made it **straight with few curves to it.**

The route passes by **many small towns and villages**, so you are never too remote, though it may feel that way. You will likely be able to find food and lodging somewhere along the way.

You may want (need?) to stop in **Vankleek Hill** for some craft beer samples.

This area is close to **Quebec** and has a distinct **French-Canadian feel,** as French signage and communities are evident.

Starting just **SE of Ottawa**, you can ride this path till **St. Eugène;** then it gets rough and peters out on the **Quebec** side, ending at the bridge in **Rigaud**. I think the trail could be developed further, as the rail line looks abandoned; the only things missing are time and funds. If it did continue, it could take you down to the **Hudson ferry** on the **Ottawa River**, extending your adventure.

In summary, this is an excellent car-free route for **bikepackers** that connects two great cities - **Montreal & Ottawa**. Both have extensive city bicycle trails worth a week of exploring when you get there. Start planning...

History – The Prescott Russell RT began in 1872 as the **Montreal & City of Ottawa Junction Railway (M&OJ)**, which was planned to run from Ottawa to **Coteau, QC,** just west of **Montreal**. However, no track was laid until after the M&OJ was purchased by lumber tycoon **J.R. Booth** in **1879**, becoming part of his **Canada Atlantic Railway (CAR)** line.

The CAR would eventually send trains southeast into **Vermont**, loaded with grain and wood products destined for **eastern seaboard port cities** and beyond. But first, there had to be a bridge built across the mighty St. Lawrence—and that was a challenge. The bridge construction, which took almost three years, was completed in **1890**.

In **1905**, the CAR was purchased by the **Grand Trunk Railroad**, which itself was eventually rolled into **CN Rail.**

The **City of Ottawa** signed an agreement with **VIA Rail** to build this recreational trail in **2011**. (VIA can claim it back at any time for rail service if needed.) In **2021** an agreement in principle was signed that would see the trail continue with maintenance funding in place for the next ten years.

Rideau River – Park Trail

Ottawa

Length - 13 + 5 km (one way)

95% park path
5% road crossings, detours

Elevation - Flat, undulating path follows the river; a few short climbs to street level

Terrain - All paved, wide trail, bridges and dam crossings

Skill - Easy

Maps - Map boards, trail markers

Traffic - Typical city path users, busy on sunny weekends

Facilities - Parking lot, toilets, snack bar, benches, picnic tables, rain shelters, playgrounds, beach; food and lodging are readily available near the path

Highlights - Three waterfalls, dams, beach, quiet getaway

Phone - 613 239 5000

Website - NCC - Capital Pathways

Similar Trails - Rideau Canal, Upper Ottawa River, Cornwall Waterfront

Local Clubs - Ottawa Bicycle Club

Access - Many entry points on the route. Parking lots at these city parks along the way:

⊕**P1** Rideau Falls - Sussex Dr & John St
P2 New Edinburgh Park - Dufferin Rd
P3 Riverain Park - N River Rd & McArthur
P4 Donald St, west end
P5 Strathcona Park - Range Rd & Somerset St E
P6 Brantford Park - Clegg St, east end
P7 Vincent Massey Park - Heron Rd
P8 Hog's Back - Hog's Back R & Rideau River
P9 Mooney's Bay Beach - Ridgewood Ave & Riverside Dr
⊕Walkley Rd & Riverside Dr

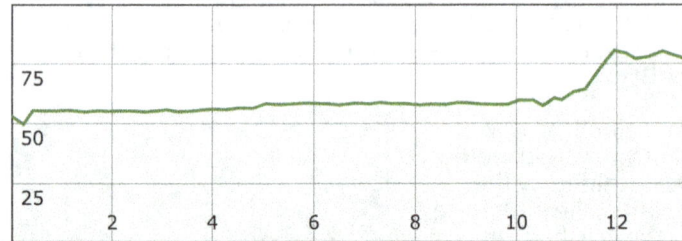

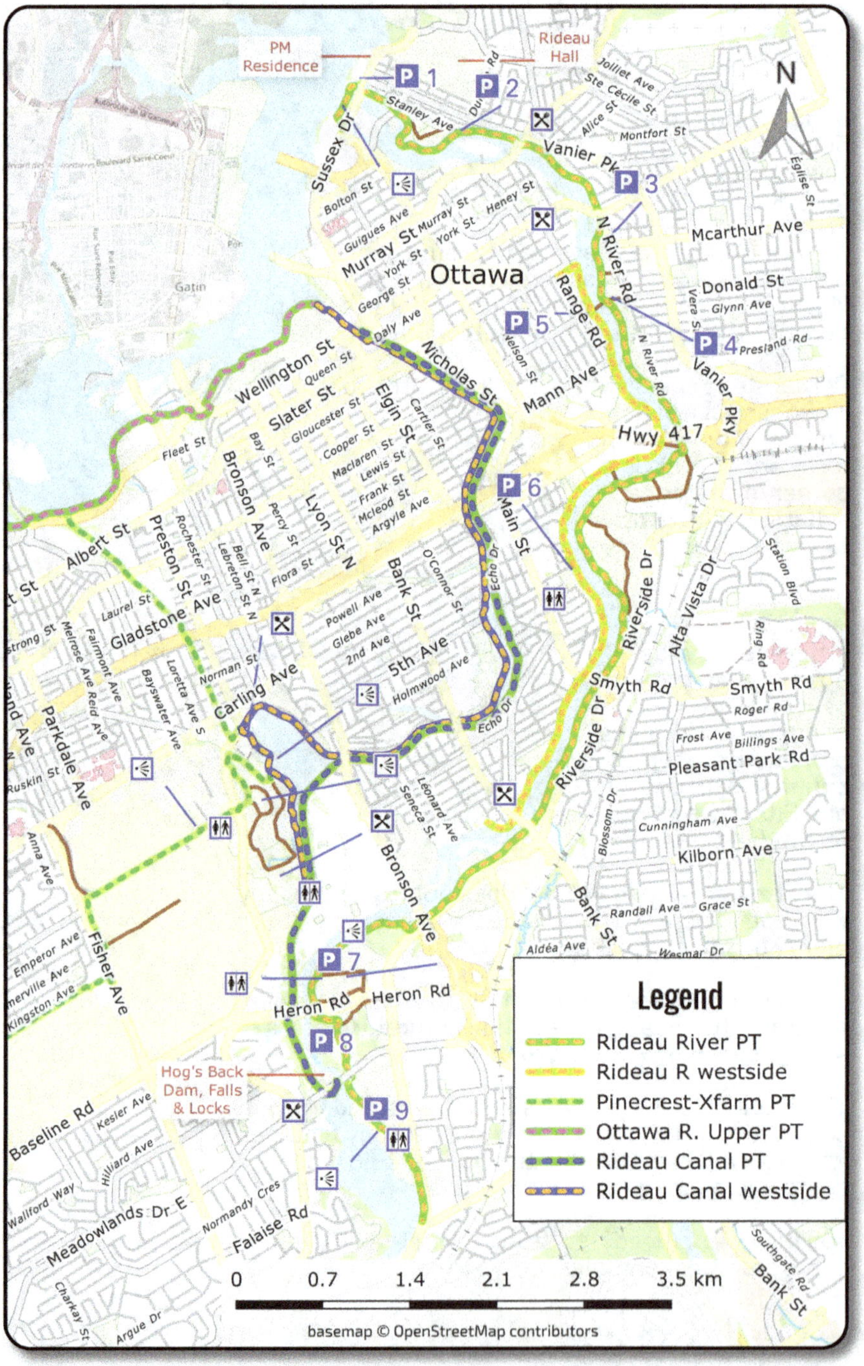

Review:

Ottawa's **Rideau River Park** trail is a **13 km** long winding path that follows this historic waterway through parklands, beside rapids, and past raging falls. It's one of the **best cycling pleasures** in the city.

photo Phil Meadows

Located in the heart of town, this **paved path** offers a **tranquil escape** that at times is removed from the sights and sounds of the busy city. It's a lovely mix of open, **sunny parkland** cycling interspersed with **shady, treed woodlots.**

photo Phil Meadows

The main route runs along the east banks of the **Rideau River**, with an optional west-bank ride in the middle section, a thin strip of greenway **5 km long**.

The **pedestrian Adàwe bridge** gets you across to the western section on the north end and the **Bank St road bridge** on the south end brings you back.

The highlights of this ride are **three waterfalls.** Just beyond where the pathway ends at **Sussex Drive**, the **Rideau River** spills over in two places into the **Ottawa River.** You are free to cycle across the dams spanning this impressive pair of falls - highly recommended.

On the south end of this trail are the spectacular **Hog's Back falls/rapids**. Take a moment to admire them, ponder, and realize why a canal was dug centuries ago to bypass this torrent.

A short ride across **Hog's Back dam** brings you to the Rideau Canal Pathway, an excellent return route to make this **almost a loop.**

When you get back to the north end, you need to sort out when and how you will connect back to the **Rideau River** trail via side streets (try **Somerset St E**).

If in need, you are **never far from amenities**, especially on the south end of this ride, where you will find washrooms, picnic areas, food, and even a beach (at **Mooney's Bay).**

For your kids, I saw numerous **playgrounds** on my trek that can break up the ride, the largest in **Mooney's Bay Park**. And a little further south the trail officially ends at the **Walkley Rd** street crossing.

It was nice to see my favourite path marker, a **painted yellow centre line** leading the way making it easy to follow. But if you wish to wander off on the **many other side trails,** map boards and signage will sort you out.

I do recall one or two road crossings at the lights; all other crossings use **road underpasses**. The path does come up to street level a few times on its own raised sidewalk. But for the most part, your ride will be quiet, safe, and away from traffic.

Whether you're **a tourist discovering the capital** or a local headed out on an after-work outing, this trail offers a natural, **relaxing cruise** through the centre of **Ottawa.**

It's an excellent ride in its own right and a great way to get to many interesting destinations beyond.

Riverside – Park Trail

Belleville

Length - 8 + 4 = 12 km (one way)

85% park path
15% road, crossings, detours

Elevation - Flat following the water's edge, short climbs over/under bridges

Terrain - Almost all paved, some gravel sections

Skill - Easy cruising

Maps - Map boards, a few trail markers; just follow the centre line

Traffic - Not busy, typical park path users: walkers, joggers, and cyclists

Facilities - Parking, toilets, benches, picnic tables, gazebos, and local pubs nearby

Highlights - Moira River, historic buildings, waterfront parks, gazebos, marina, Bay of Quinte

Phone - None

Website - Belleville on Bikes, Great Lake Waterfront Trail

Similar Trails - Grand River, Speed River, Rideau River

Local Clubs - Nothing local, Northumberland Hills Cycling Club

Access - From the north end here are a few parking lot suggestions:

⊕**P1** Riverside Park - north end of N Park St another lot is in park
P2 Two lots on Moira St E
P3 Lion Park - 57 Station St
P4 Riverfront lots behind Front St
P5 Forrester Park - Harbour Dr
P6 Herchimer Boat Launch - 22 Keegan Pkwy
⊕**P7** Zwicks Park - Hwy 62 & Mary St

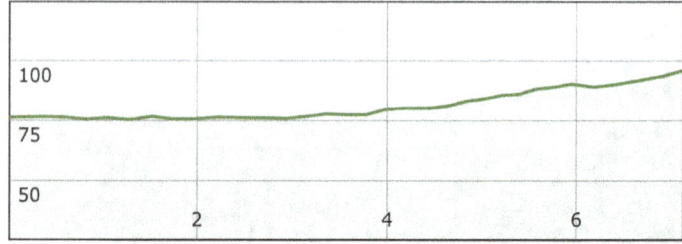

Review:

On the shores of the **Bay of Quinte**, I found **12 km** of leisurely bike paths in the city of **Belleville** while out visiting family. Just off **Hwy 401** in eastern Ontario, this bike route runs down the **Moira River** to the harbour and beyond.

These easy and well-maintained park paths consist of four sections. **Riverside Park** is on the north end, right off the highway; **Zwicks Park** is at the mouth of the river on the southwest side, and the **Bayshore** trail is on the east side. Connecting the three park areas is the **Parrott Riverfront** Trail, which runs along the river.

The city of **Belleville** is trying to promote cycling and has made connections with these snippets of trail to make this a safe and **idyllic journey with varying scenery.**

I did not see tons of signage, but a look at a map would remove any confusion if you felt lost. We easily found our way just by following the painted centre line.

A likely start to your ride would be at the north end coming off the highway at **Riverside Park**. Here you can leave your car and do a few loops in the park before heading down the path to the bay.

Take note of the **Quinte Mall** just west of the park; this may be a good spot to find lunch on your return.

On your way down there is a **"pirate ship"** playground to amuse your kids. The trail splits briefly, with fine gravel by the river's edge and an asphalt path closer to the street.

Numerous dams and concrete barriers in the river tell the story of how the **Moira River** has a long history of spring flooding that needs to be managed. Natural waterfalls cascade over a riverbed made of layers of sedimentary stone.

Eventually, this trail will take you over the top of a **large dam** to the other side. Now the path travels right on the edge of the river along a concrete walled route. Though this section isn't very natural, I can see it serves to protect the banks from flood damage.

The path backs onto **Front St** in the **old downtown** core. It's worth a look as this sleepy town is being revitalized with newly landscaped sidewalks and storefronts. We bought chocolate croissants at a French bakery and ate them as we admired the **modern metallic pedestrian bridge** that now spans the river, offering yet another neighbourhood to explore.

The last underpass at **Dundas St** requires a decision to head east or west. Both require about a **600 metre** road detour. I would suggest going east first by heading down to the marina and out onto the pier, then east along the water's edge to **Bayshore Park.**

This winding, quiet path along the **Bay of Quinte**—with pockets of parkland, gardens, and benches to stop at—offers good **photo opportunities** if you have a keen eye.

The path currently continues past **Herchimer Ave** as more of a short, overgrown gravel hiking trail to **Farley Ave,** if you feel the need. Eventually I can see this getting developed and going farther.

Note the monument to train history: yet another hidden railbed has become a park path.

As you ride back, you now have the option of crossing the road bridge at **Dundas St** over the **Moira River** to add **four more kilometres** to your ride by looping around **Zwicks Park**, or heading back the way you came. Traffic is light, so take the side streets perhaps, if no one is in a rush.

If driving **two hours from Toronto** for this outing seems intriguing, may I suggest staying overnight and also biking a **local Rail Trail** - either the **Millenium** or **Lower Trent** or the rougher **Two Lake** northerly ride.

Little else in the area offers off-road pleasure riding, so I am pleased to mention this location for you to explore on two wheels in this **belle ville.**

Tay Havelock – Rail Trail

Havelock - Perth

Length - 144 km (one way)

90% rail trail path
10% road crossings, detours

Elevation - Flat with higher grades to slopes than most RT routes

Terrain - Crushed stone, gravel, large rocks, double tracked, tall grasses, large "puddles," mud

Skill - Advanced

Maps - Map board at trailheads, route signage

Traffic - Bicycles, hikers, horses, ATVs, dirt bikes, snowmobiles, Nordic skiers

Facilities - Parking lots, info kiosks, not much else

Highlights - Farms, nature, rocky ridges, picturesque lakes, bridges, Tweed, Sharbot rail museum & beach

Phone - None

Website - Lanark County, Trans Canada Trail

Similar Trails - Northumberland RT, north half of the K&P RT, south end Hasting Heritage RT,

Local Clubs - None

Access - Parking lots are at:

P1 County Rd 50 south of Hwy 7, Havelock
P2 50 Louisa St, Tweed
P3 Hwy 41 south of Hwy 7, Kaladar
P3 Cannon Rd, Sharbot Lake
P5 460 Armstrong Line, Maberly area
P6 18471 Hwy 7, west of Perth

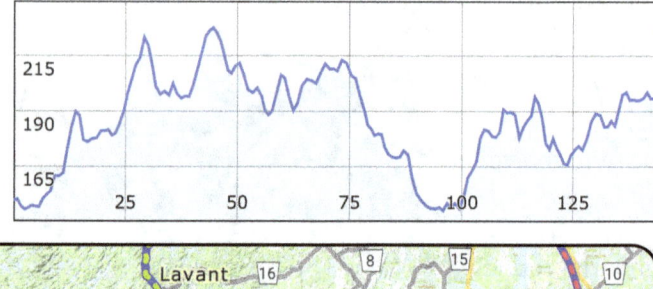

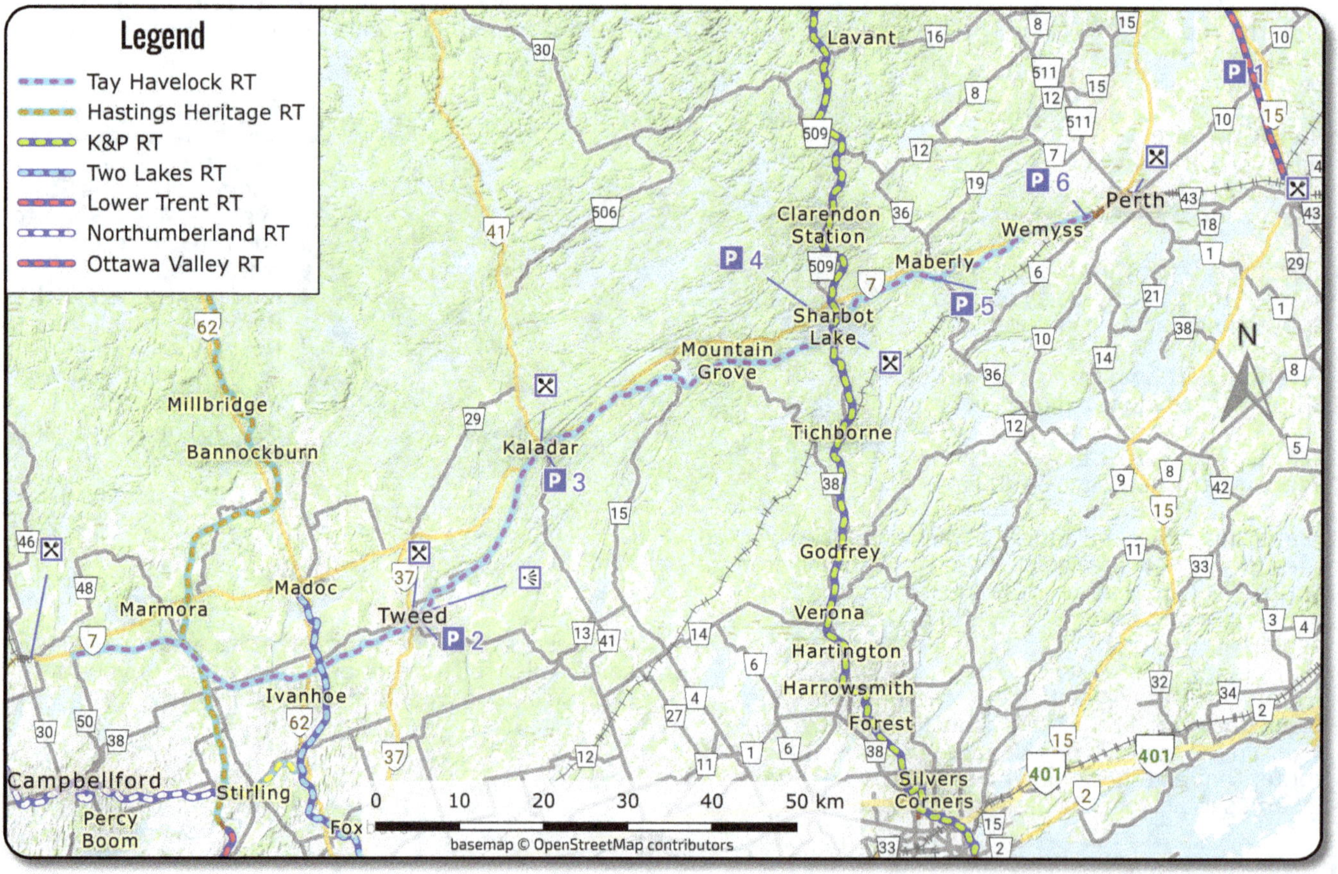

Review:

The **Tay Havelock Rail Trail** is a **144 km rugged wilderness route** that runs from east of the farming town of **Havelock** to the old rail hub of **Perth**. Well, almost—neither end of this RT goes into town on the railbeds, as these parts of the line are still in use.

For the **bikepacking enthusiast,** this makes an **excellent outing** on a loaded mountain bike or even better, a fatbike. I've ridden sections of it carefully (but not comfortably, LOL) on a hybrid bike with thinner tires.

It can be done with a **gravel bike**, but you have to pay attention to the occasional **rock outcrop** that could throw you. And when you get to **loose gravel and sand**, it may be more work than you bargained for.

I've rated this as an **Advanced Rail Trail** ride because of the **rougher terrain** and **wilderness aspect** (though it's not completely remote). There is certainly **evidence of ATV and snowmobile use,** yet I did not hear or see many travellers on this doubletrack trek.

This RT starts just east of **Havelock** and cuts straight through wetlands and farm fields as it swings down to meet the town of **Tweed** about a third of the way along, a welcome stop to rest and refuel.

Along the way, the **Tay RT** crosses the **Hasting Heritage RT** and, later, the **Trail of Two Lakes RT** for more riding options. Both routes offer similar terrain.

Once past **Tweed**, the **geography starts to change** as you enter the **rocky Canadian Shield.** From an aerial photo, you can see how the glaciers scraped the bedrock into **very long ridges.**

I remember driving near **Kaladar** down **Highway 7**, which parallels much of this section, and seeing rocky **barrens and picturesque waterways**. I thought this RT would offer the same views, but not so much. Fortunately, the scenery is **ever changing** and **not a wall of trees—a more open, savanna-like feel** than a dense forest of green.

I encountered a few long, **challenging water crossings** (mega-puddles/ponds) in the **lower marshy wetlands**. *Do I go through or around? Hmm, **is this my lucky day?*** This was in midsummer; in early spring it must be worse. Best to delay your trek for it to dry out. *(so I got lucky, stayed dry doing a bit of both... Ya gotta have some fun, it's only water.)*

I appreciated the old rail bed winding its way through the Shield; it gave the journey a little more interest. And I mostly won the **battle with the bugs** as long as I kept moving. *Oh look... here comes a good photo op, do I stop?...not for long!*

I did not see the other kind of wildlife on my treks **(deer, moose, or bear)** but they are out there, so be prepared for a possible encounter.

Next stop is **Sharbot Lake,** once an important **train hub** and still one for the bike touring kind. The well-established and smoother **K&P RT** crosses your path here, offering other directions to explore.

Sharbot is now a small vacation town with two or three places to eat and stay. Check out the **picnic area by the beach** and the fascinating little **outdoor railroad museum.**

After **Sharbot,** the trail takes you back into the wilderness with no amenities again 'til **Perth**. The **trail is better graded** and not so jarring on this section as it opens up to farmland again. (I think because it enters a new county that put money into it.)

This RT ends **4 km short of town** and if the traffic on **Hwy 7** is not to your liking, **swing down to Hwy 6,** which is the same distance into town.

This is one of the **longer cycling adventures** in this book and could take you up to **eight hours one way**. Consider staying over in **Tweed, Sharbot Lake,** or **Perth**—each community offers motels, B&Bs, and places to eat. And there are a few **campgrounds and B&B** establishments popping up along the way, too, if you look.

History - During the golden age of rail, passengers traversed Ontario from **Ottawa to Toronto** and elsewhere on a multitude of small lines, including the **Ontario and Quebec Railway** (O&Q), which started building track from **Perth** back in the **1870s**. The line was extended to Toronto in **1884.**

The O&Q main line was **199 miles long** and ran from **Perth** through **Sharbot Lake, Tweed, Havelock,** and **Peterborough** to the **West Toronto Junction & Parkdale**. Not until **1893** was there a route down the **Don Valley to Union Station**. Trains shipped hickory wood, pulp, and ore from local mines.

In **1884**, the CPR leased the line from O&Q—for **999 years!** But within a century, by the late **1980s**, most of the route had been abandoned. A rail line south of the **Tay-Havelock** was more efficient to use and still operates.

Built in the early **1930s**, **Highway 7** parallels much of the old O&Q Railway line from **Perth to Tweed.**

K Pace Way – Park Trail

North Bay

Length - 22 = 12+3+3+4 km (one way)

65% park path
35% road riding, detours

Elevation - Very flat path, 60 m climb to visit university

Terrain - All paved, raised curb paths, road riding on the paved shoulder, bridges, gravel side trail

Skill - Easy

Maps - Map boards, post markers

Traffic - Cyclists, Fatbikers, hikers, rollerbald, Nordic skiers (users vary depending on section); eBikes are allowed in pedal mode only (no assist) at 20 kph

Facilities - Parking lot, toilets, benches, picnic tables, bike repair stand

Highlights - Waterfront, lake views, wetlands, wildlife, downtown attractions, village of Callander, Nipissing University and Canadore College campuses

Phone - 1 888 249 8998

Website - Discovery Routes, Tourism North Bay

Similar Trails - Rainbow Route, The Hub

Local Clubs - N Bay Mountain Bike Assoc. - NBMBA

Access - These are suggested parking locations to start the ride:

P1 Lee Park - 800 Memorial Dr (has the iconic arch)
P2 N Bay Marina - Memorial Dr
P3 Omischl Sports Complex - 1175 Lakeshore Dr
⊕**P4** Cranberry Trailhead - west end of Cranberry Rd
⊕**P5** Nipissing Campus - College Dr & S Access Rd

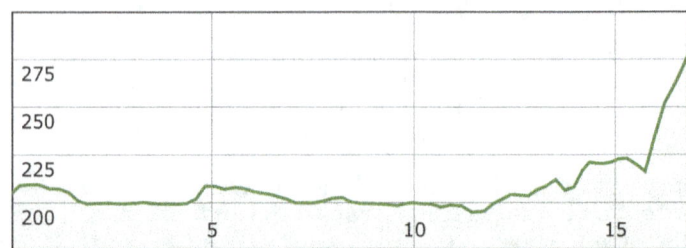

Legend
━ ━ K Pace Way PT
━ ━ Kinsmen PT

0 1 2 3 4 5 km

basemap © OpenStreetMap contributors

Review:

I'm pleased to finally add **North Bay** to my list of cycling destinations. The **Kate Pace Way**, part of the **Voyageur route**, is a collection of bike paths and road riding. This easy spin includes a mixture of wooded forest paths, wetlands, a RT segment and a cruise across the **downtown waterfront**. (I've added one big hill at the end, too.)

This route travels across town alongside **Lake Nipissing** on the city waterfront, offering **panoramic views of the lake**, which is so large you will strain to see the other side. It's certainly a place to see **dramatic sunsets**. The best part of the ride is at the south end, where you can ride **nature trails** and visit the **village of Callander.**

photo – Discovery Routes

For convenience, let's start from the waterfront marina in **North Bay,** where there is plenty of parking if you need it. Along **Memorial Drive**, the **K Pace Way** is a paved bike path, raised above the road. Heading south, much of it has been landscaped into parkland since the industrious railroad era.

photo – Caroline Jacqueline

Once you pass by the white sands of **Golden Mile Beach**, the trail curves inland at **Lee Park** for the rest of the ride. Soon enough you will see a baseball diamond and **Stanley Street**. This is where you can start the **Kinsmen Way**,.

If you ride under the overpass bridge and skirt by the playing field, you'll reach a wooded area that goes alongside the **railroad stockyard**, but unfortunately the forest path ends a few kilometres later at the **fire station on Marshall Ave.**

Looking at the map, I can see a way this trail could possibly continue, but for now, you'll have to take a **4 km road ride detou**r on the paved shoulder. Take **Booth Road** south to **Lakeshore Drive** (or my preferred choice, **Birchs Rd**, before that). Go east on either of these roads to meet what I believe is an old rail line, now paved. You will see it in about a kilometre. (On **Birch Rd**, take **Gibson St** to the end to find the entrance.)

The **Pace Way** signs point you south over a bridge over the **La Vase River** into the woods and wetlands. Keep an eye out for deer, heron, and turtles on this short section close to the wetlands that hosts multiple beaver lodges. I'm sad to say this part is soon over when you reach the golf course at **Cranberry Rd**. But hold on—I added more good times.

Consider a **3 km** ride into the village of **Callander** for a bite and a visit to the beach. Ride west, then south on **Fairway Dr** (which turns into **Osprey Cres**), then south on **Kilby Lane** and west on **Golf Course Rd** to avoid any traffic. **Main St** takes you south into town. It's easier to get there than it sounds, but you can look at a map or follow the **Voyageur Cycling Route signs** into the heart of Callander.

For some more nature in your ride, may I suggest continuing **3 km west** on **Cranberry Rd**. A gravel path goes to a cranberry marsh and **two lake lookouts** over **Callander Bay**.

If you wish for even more time on your pony, there's **4 km more** north of where we started. Once you get back to the marina, ride the other direction to **Main St W,** then head west on the newly raised bike lanes to **Gormanville Rd**. Turn north on that road and use those curbed bike lanes. It's a street with light industry, auto shops and family homes, nothing fancy here.

photo – Caroline Jacqueline

When you reach **Hwy 17**, your challenge (if you need one) is taking the roundabout to the left for a **60 m climb** on raised bike lanes up to **Nipissing University campus.** Are you game to ride around and explore the expansive grounds? If you've got gravel tires, another option is at the top of College Dr: turn right onto Monastery Rd to find an informal mountain bike/hiking trail starting at the old horse barn arch.

This route has a little more road riding than I personally would wish for—not something I expected in Northern Ontario, which I think of as so vast and empty.

The downtown North Bay waterfront has been revitalized, the **train station** is a city **museum**, and on **Main St** you can stroll by the old shops. This working town is no longer a **frontier outpost** of lumberjacks and prospectors: it is at the crossroads of road-, rail-, and waterways, and, as the arch in **Lee Park** proclaims, it's really the **"Gateway of the North."**

Killbear - Park Trail

Parry Sound area

Length - 6 km (one way)

97% park path
3% road crossings

Elevation - Mostly level, with a few quick climbs and turns

Terrain - Wide, crushed-gravel path with a few mud patches

Skill - Easy to Intermediate

Maps - No map board was seen, basic milestone markers

Traffic - Bicycles, hikers and deer

Facilities - Parking lot, comfort stations, park store, camping, beaches, swimming, hiking

Highlights - Rocky coastline, wildlife, peaceful

Trail Fee - Day pass or camping permit (and the only trail in this book that has a fee)

Phone - 705 342 5492

Website - Ontario Parks

Similar Trails - Awenda, Pinery, Bracebridge RMC

Local Clubs - None

Access - Drive 13 km north of Parry Sound on Hwy 400, then take Hwy 559 west for 19 km to get to the park gate. The bike trail is easily accessed from any of the campgrounds.

If you are visiting for the day, you can park at the:

⊕ Blind Bay & Killbear Park Rd
P1 Park Office
P2 Lookout Point Trailhead
P3 Visitor Centre
⊕ **P4** Lighthouse Point Trailhead

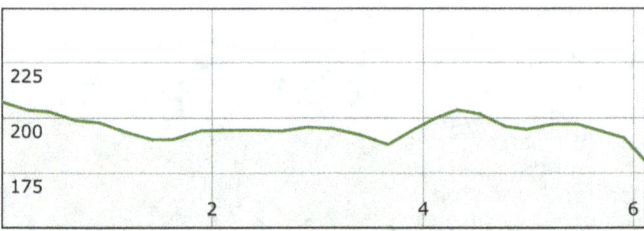

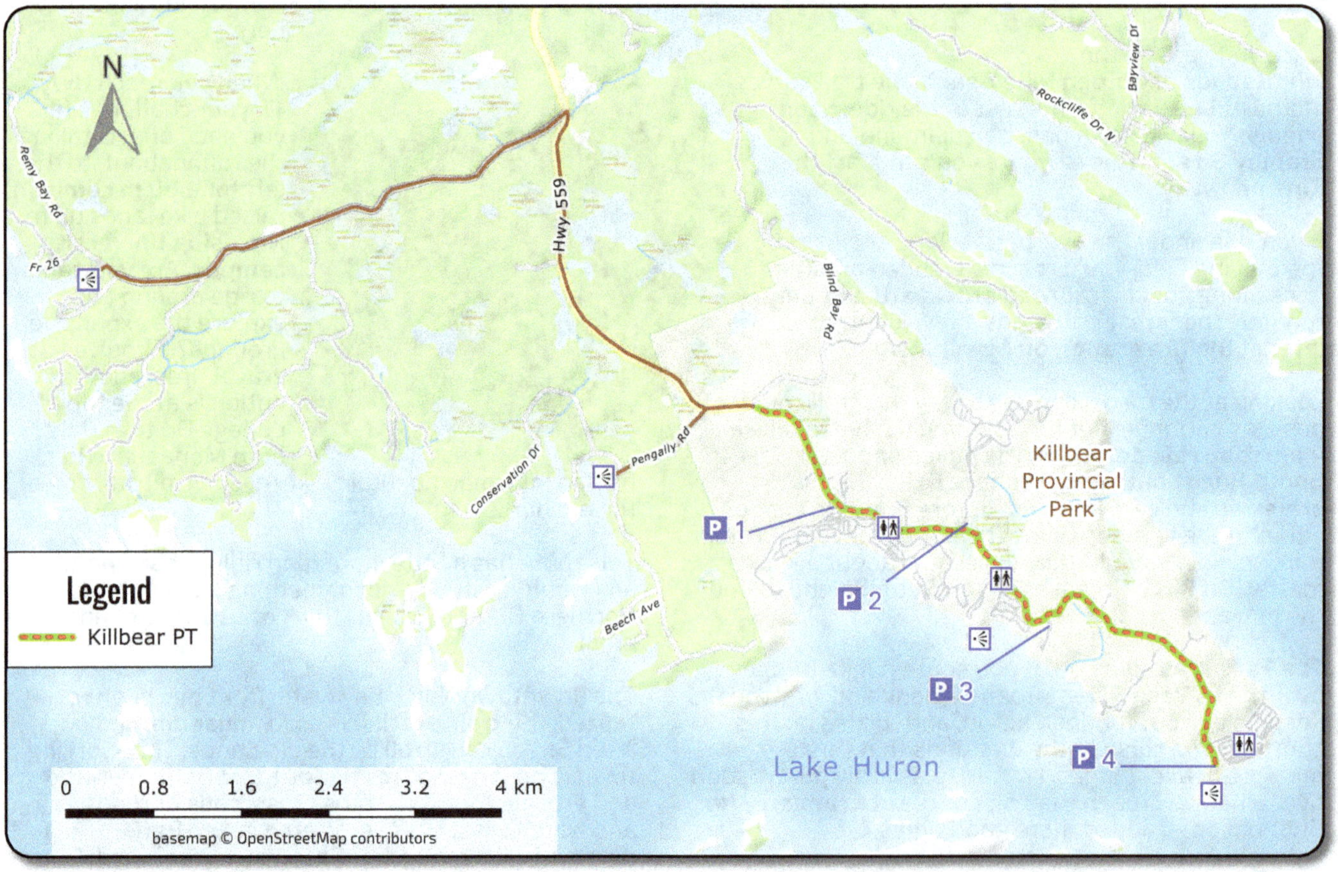

Review:

Up in cottage country, **Killbear Provincial Park** has **6 km** of forest trail to cycle through for the whole family. It offers a peaceful outing, well shaded and car free. Though not long at **12 km return**, it has a few hills and fast dips, so it's not all flat, easygoing.

Killbear is located on a peninsula west of the town of **Parry Sound**. As a three-hour drive from **Toronto**, this ride destination is best suited for campers at the park or those staying at a local cottage doing a day visit.

I was introduced to **Killbear** decades ago, when I was here with the **High Park Cycling Club**, now the Toronto Cycling Club. I returned a few years ago with the family to refresh my memory and **found it worthy** of this small review.

The **bike path runs parallel** to the park access road for the whole distance, but by no means is it straight and boring. It's separated from the road by a line of trees, which give the trail lots of **little twists and rock outcrops** to watch for.

We were delighted to **encounter deer** on the route that were so tame, they did not run off when we stopped to take pictures. I suspect they have seen many campers before us do the same.

This trail is wide and the **base is crushed gravel** for most of the way. There were a few muddy patches when we visited, but they may have been filled since then.

From the gatehouse, the path ends at the **lighthouse point**, a good spot for some hiking, pictures, and maybe a dip. (The lighthouse is not photogenic; better to call it a small light beacon.)

Killbear has a beautiful, **rocky coastline** with windswept pines, a favourite for picturesque views of **Georgian Bay** sunsets. You can go for a swim or lounge and read a book—what's the rush?

If you wish to **expand your ride**, beyond the park trails there are quiet secondary roads leading to secluded bays. Map out a route to **Pengallie Bay (2.5 km away)** or **Snug Harbour (8.8 km away)** for extra mileage and lunch at the marinas. When my group did it, skinny race tires were getting flats, so I recommend thicker treads when exploring the gravel side roads.

So now you know where to go when making plans to get out and relax on your two-wheeler. As for getting a campsite, book early! The season fills up fast.

Considering the number of parks and the amount of land we have in Ontario, this is one of only a few rides that I can recommend at a provincial park. Most parks have little to cycle beyond the dirt roads circling the campgrounds.

My hopes are that Ontario Parks will add more interesting and longer trails to bike on. With the surge in cycling during Covid and the extra money the Ontario government (Ministry of the Environment, Conservation and Parks) made at packed parks, in the last few years, this is warranted.

Kinsmen Way – Park Trail

North Bay

Length - 7 km (one way)

90% park paths
10% road riding, detours

Elevation - Level most of the way, sloping up at the end

Terrain - Paved, some gravel and sandy spots, bridges, tunnels

Skill - Easy

Maps - Map boards, trail signs, painted marks

Traffic - Cyclists, pedestrians, dogs, in-line skaters

Facilities - Parking lots, toilets, benches, rain shelter, local amenities & lodging nearby

Highlights - Quiet ride, treed urban path, ever-changing scenery

Phone - 705 474 5420

Website - Discovery Routes Tourism North Bay N Bay Conservation Area

Similar Trails - Rainbow Route, The Hub

Local Clubs - _North Bay Mountain Bike Association

Access - Lots of side streets to park on; I found only three lots you can try:

⊕ 673 Queen St
P1 Lee Park - 800 Memorial Dr (has the iconic arch)
P2 Memorial Gardens Arena - 100 Chippewa St W
P3 Laurier Woods Conservation Area - Brule St, south end
⊕ 309 Airport Rd

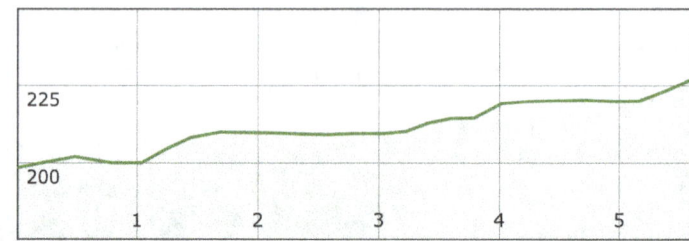

Review:

The **Kinsmen Trail** is a **7 km** winding path that follows the **Chippewa Creek** as best it can across town. It's a lovely bike ride that makes its way through neighbourhoods, playing fields, and woodlots, ending at the base of the escarpment.

By the waters of **Lake Nipissing**, the trail crosses the **Kate Pace Way** bike trail at **Lee Park**. The path immediately goes through a **tunnel** underneath train tracks, then over a bridge, and through **another tunnel** as it finds its way to safer, more quiet realms a few blocks away.

Though this route is a collection of on-again, off-again trail patchwork, you should be able to stay the course. As a **long-established path**, it has plenty of signs, painted pavement marks, and barriers to guide you.

There are road crossings and detours to complete this route. I still think you will be looking at a map the first time on it.

It's certainly not boring. All the **little twists and changes** as it threads its way along might make you think it is a longer ride than it is.

About halfway through it you will reach the only large open area on this narrow pathway at the **Thomson Park** sports fields, where the **largest ice arena in town** is.

photo - Caroline Jacqueline

It may get confusing here, so find your way through the trees across the creek to **Olive St W.** Continuing north of there, a few blocks of road riding is required, then a few more west on **High St.** to reconnect with the creek again.

At this point the route starts to slope up and the trees are more abundant. A brief crossing at the lights of busy **Hwy 17** gets you over into the **peaceful, shady woods** again.

Where the **Kinsmen Way** ends at **Airport Rd**, do a U-turn and head back the same way, **or try some side streets**. It won't be that busy.

May I suggest another bonus riding area I did a while back at **Laurier Woods Conservation Area**: this large, natural forest has ponds, wetlands, boardwalks, and rock outcrops. It's great for **birding.** And admission is free.

To get there, cycle back towards the beginning of the ride and find your way over to the end of **Laurier Ave** and across the tracks. There are maybe **six loops** you can try on dirt, gravel, and wood chip paths.

I did all **6 km**—even the hilly parts—**on a MTB** with not much of a sweat. On a city bike, it may not be all doable...but you can walk those parts. It is a beautiful hike (when the bugs are away).

photo - Caroline Jacqueline

So there you have it: three bike trails in this book from a city a third the size of **Sudbury.** Opportunities on your road trip to pull the two-wheelers off the car. Make a day of it! Explore this northern community and stay awhile.

Rainbow Route - Park Trail

Sudbury

Length - 13 = 6 + 7 km (one way)

75% park path
10% hiking trail
15% road detours & crossings

Elevation - Flat, gradual slopes with small hills

Terrain - A mix of paved and crushed gravel paths plus road detours

Skill - Easy - Intermediate, to say on track

Maps - Map boards, new trail markers

Traffic - Cyclists, joggers, hikers, dogs, kids and occasional road vehicles

Facilities - Parking lots, benches, picnic tables, downtown amenities

Highlights - Board array of sights from inner city to natural creek settings, downtown core, bird rock formations, industrial mining landscapes, Big Nickel & Dynamic Earth

Trail Fee - Free

Phone - 1 866 451 8525

Website - Discover Sudbury   Rainbow Routes

Similar Trails - Kinsmen in N Bay, The Hub in the Soo,   Guelph Royal

Local Clubs - Sudbury Cycling Club, Bike Sudbury

Access - Plenty of entry points but not so many convenient parking lots. Here are a few suggestions and good start points:

⊕ P1 Adanac Ski Hill - 744 Beatrice Crescent
P2 Rotary Park Trail - 360 Mountain St
P3 Downtown Paid Parking - 9 Elm St P4 Downtown Paid Parking - 250 Elgin St
P5 Lilac & Norman St
⊕ P6 1200 Kelly Lake Rd

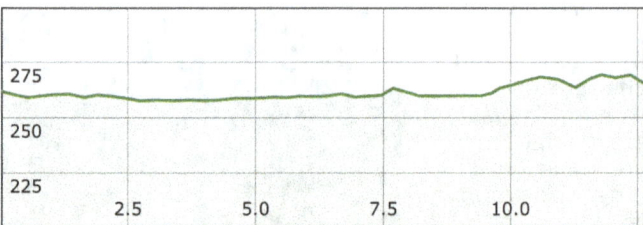

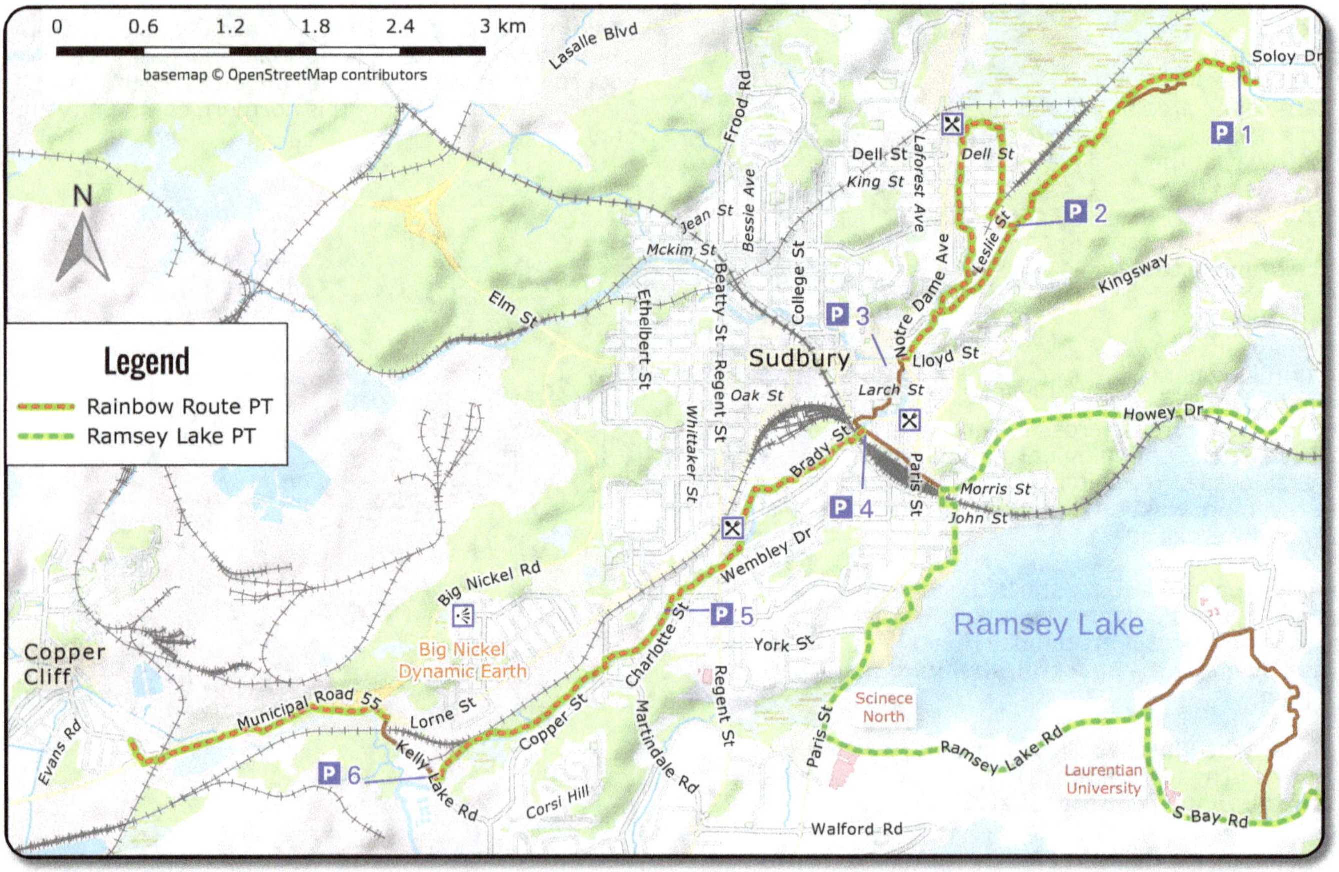

Review:

Recent improvements with the **Sudbury** bike scene has prompted me to give you **my version** of their **Rainbow Route**. I am using **13 kms** of this trail network to string a diagonal ride from the north end through **downtown Sudbury**, south out of town. I think you will like where it goes.

It is a **mix of urban creek riding, cruising by neighbour-hoods and industrial areas.** It is also a mix of riding terrain, changing a few times from a crushed fine stone base to paved asphalt. None of it is overly hilly, and **the route has lots of variety to it.**

photo – Kat Cameron

What makes it more of an I**ntermediate ride is not getting lost.** Unlike many of my other published rides that take little thought, **you need to pay attention.** There are a few more nuances to this route to stay the course. I did see a few gaps in signage and in some areas trail surfaces need "refreshing" but for most of it, it connects well.

Do the **6 km north section** or only the **7 km south section**, or both ends. **Three road detours** are required to make the connections. Sorry, there is no other way to make a long enough route, without a little street riding.

I found it tricky to find free parking downtown but let's start this ride description from there anyway. Going north, the trail starts at **Hnatyshyn Park**, a narrow band of trees that line **Junction Creek.** This is where **Paris & Lloyd Street meet.** In no time the path forks at **Mountain St.** Stay on the creek trail and ride up it into **Percy Park.** Then east to the other side to find **Percy St.**

I found an easy shortcut to the other forked trail. Pedal down **five blocks** to the **end of Percy** and cross the tracks (carefully) to **Myles St.** Jog down and over on **Leslie** then **Harvey St** to find the start of the **Rotary Park Trail**. This part is beautiful as it winds between the wetlands of the creek you saw earlier and against a **huge stone "mini mountain".**

In **2 km** it ends at the **Adanac ski hill** parking lot. The trail splits before that up to a platform lookout. I am not sure you can ride up it. The otherside has stairs going down. To get back, go back the way you came or you can shorten it by taking **Mountain St south** to meet the path later.

Reaching the south trail from **Hnatyshyn Park** requires less than a kilometre of road riding. This is done by zig-zagging through the busy **downtown backstreets** to get to the **pedestrian tunnel under the tracks at 158 Elgin St.** This is also the best area to find lunch after the ride.

The tunnel takes you out to **58 Riverside Dr** and the start of the **St. Catherines St Switchback** gravel trail, and welcomes you back to, you guessed it, **Junction Creek.**

It starts off going down to **St. Catherines St,** a paved back alley. Take this across **Douglas St W** and continue into the trees 'til you reach **Cross St.** Head south here (I saw no signs) 'til you see the opening by the right side of the armoury to get back onto the creek trail. You are **good for 3 km**, with three short road crossings. The creek trail has a few humps to it and gets pretty in some spots. It's a very **natural route** and I wish it went farther.

When you reach **Kelly Lake Rd,** head back or do the optional extra path: ride north for 3 minutes on the road to **Lorne St,** then take the **2 km trail** to the **Copper Cliff** community. The scenery has signs of what a stark, barren landscape can result from mining in **Sudbury.** Smokestacks in the distance, piles of waste mine tailings, settling ponds; a reality in parts of this mining town.

If you wish to see the **famous Big Nickel** and tour the demonstration mine at **Dynamic Earth**, a science museum, it is just up the road at **122 Big Nickel Rd.**

I have been keeping an eye on **Sudbury bike trail developments** over the years hoping to recommend a decent route. Since the last book much progress has been made. The city now has a **cycling web presence** and made an **interactive trail map**. Which means, they are committed to keeping their trails well managed, safe and properly signed. At least **that is the theory.**

Bike culture is slow to come around in the north, a land full of pickup trucks. I am pleased to offer this new trail and invite you to come explore the "great white north" one day, when there is no snow under your wheels.

*(Note - In an earlier review for the book, I mention the gravel/dirt trail along **Kelly Lake** as an added ride. A visit there this summer (2023) finds it only suitable for MTB riders.)*

Ramsey Lake - Park Trail

Sudbury

Length - 21 km = 12 + 9 (loop)

50% park paths
10% hiking trail
25% road bike lanes
15% road riding

Elevation - Hilly terrain, three big climbs, north end of loop is level

Terrain - Paved and gravel/dirt paths, boardwalks, road riding (on bike lanes most of the time)

Skill - Intermediate

Maps - Map boards, various trail markers (some missing)

Traffic - Cyclists, hikers, dogs, kids, cars

Facilities - Parking lots, toilets, benches, picnic tables, rain shelter, amenities on north road ride

Highlights - Lake views, rocky terrain, boardwalks, Science North, university grounds, beaches, fall colours

Phone - 1 866 451 8525

Website - Discover Sudbury

Similar Trails - The Hub, Kinsmen Way

Local Clubs - Sudbury Cycle Club

Access - Parking lots suggestions to start you loop from:

P1 Bell Park - 531 Elizabeth St
P2 Bell Park - York St & Paris St
P3 Science North - 100 Ramsey Lake Rd
P4 Laurentian University - S Bay Rd & Voyageur Dr
P5 BioSki Lot - west end of S Bay Rd
P6 Moonlight Beach - S end of Moonlight Beach Rd

Graph starts at P1 on the map

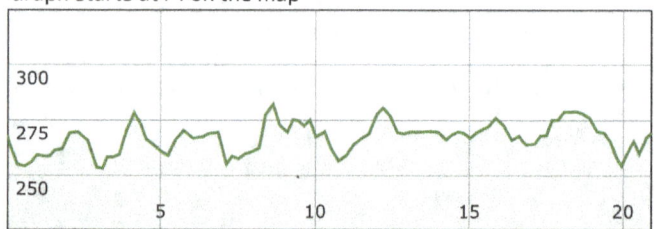

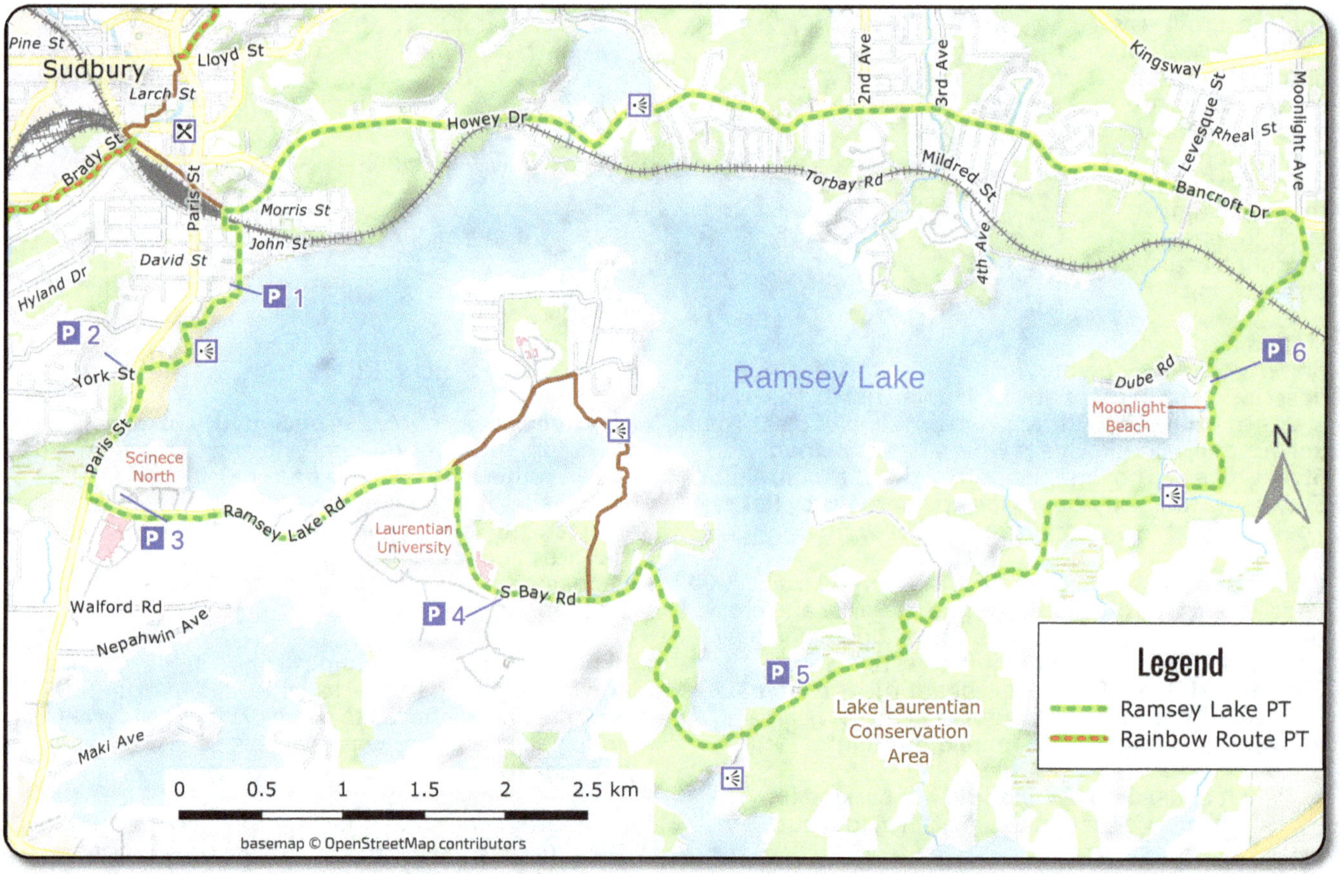

Review:

Built on rocky, hilly terrain, the city of **Sudbury** has a rugged look to its landscape. It became the **province's largest mining town,** due to the metal deposits left from a meteorite impact. (Though it's not obvious, you will be riding inside the crater zone.)

The **Ramsey Lake** route circles one of the largest of many local lakes and has **beautiful views of the water** dotted with sailboats and tiny islands. I am suggesting a **21 km bike loop** around the lake. If you prefer not to cycle on the road, even though there are bike lanes, this becomes a shorter **12 km path; one way.**

I am rating this ride as an **Intermediate effort** as there are some steep climbs the likes of which are not found else-where in the book. Hills totaling **142 m of vertical.** Are you up to it?

A good start point is the north end of **Bell Park** at the bottom of **Eliza-beth Street**. Let's head south through **Bell Park**, a lovely public space with a path by the water and a good spot for a picnic or to read a book.

When you get to the black rocks at **Science North**, ride around the corner. Or you could **walk your bike on the lakeside boardwalk** the other way around the science centre for a little tourist-type stroll.

As you find your way back to the street, on the other side, you'll see a paved path up **Ramsey Lake Rd.** Once you pass the rock walls **Laurentian University** will appear. You could cut through the expansive univer-sity grounds for a **look at the campus** and pick up the trail further along.

When you get to **South Bay Rd,** you can take that road up or continue around **Bethel Lake** on **Ramsey Lake Rd** for a little extra adventure (recommended). When you get to Bethel Lake Ct, go south across the marsh board-walk and up the rocky forest path for 1 km, then down

Arlington Blvd to meet S Bay Rd. Either way, you have done your first big climb. Woohoo!

But it's not time to celebrate yet. There is a second climb (that is easier to do in this direction), followed by a fast drop. As you pass the entrance to **Lake Laurentian Conservation Area,** you could pop in to do some excellent hikes or MTB trails, or just keep riding the road to the park gate near the **BioSki clubhouse.**

From here, a lovely, quiet **4 km gravel path** leads into the woods to reach **Moonlight Beach.** Half way along is a **photogenic open-water boardwalk crossing**. Don't fall in (lol). If it's a hot day, wait until you get to the beach before having a refreshing dip.

Beyond is the road ride back to complete the loop. One last hill climb up **Moonlight Beach Rd**, then go west on **Hwy 67.** It runs level from there. Or head back and do the two hills again.

Unless you're averse to car traffic, riding the bike lane back on **Bancroft Dr** will be less taxing, but not as pretty. There are convenience stores on the way. Did anyone say **ice cream?**

If you do keep moving down **Hwy 67,** it changes street names to **Bellevue Ave**, then **Howey Dr**, and ends at **Morris St.** Jog west a block to cross the pedestrian bridge over the train tracks. Now jog back a block east and you will be on **Elizabeth St.** Take this back to the starting point of the loop.

Are you ready to take on this tour for real? Find your way up to **Sudbury** one summer. My wife has family here and we go every year. There is plenty to see and do in Northern Ontario to make this part of your family road trip.

The Hub – Park Trail

Sault Ste. Marie

Length - 25 +3 km loop

85% park path
10% hiking trail
5% road crossings, detours

Elevation - Flat along water's edge; hill climbs to get to the north end of the loop; nice coasting down the other side

Terrain - Paved, some gravel mud and sand spots, long bridges

Skill - Intermediate (there are hills!)

Maps - Map boards, trail markers

Traffic - Cyclists, wandering tourists, kids, hikers, joggers

Facilities - Parking lots, toilets, benches, picnic tables, rain shelter, food mall, lodging

Highlights - Waterfront, Whitefish Island, locks, dams, bridges of all shapes, evergreen forests

Phone - None

Website - Tourism Sault Ste. Marie

Similar Trails - Ramsey Lake, Pace Way, Granger Greenway

Local Clubs - Sault Cycling Club

Access - You could try street parking in neighbourhood areas. Here are a few parking lot suggestions:

P1 Bellevue Park - 1310 Queen St E
P2 Waterfront - St. Mary's to River Dr to Foster Drive - many lots, most paid
P3 Locks/Canal Historic Site - 9 Canal Dr
P4 False Creek Conservation Area - 135 Second Line
P5 Finn Hill Park - 184 Black Rd

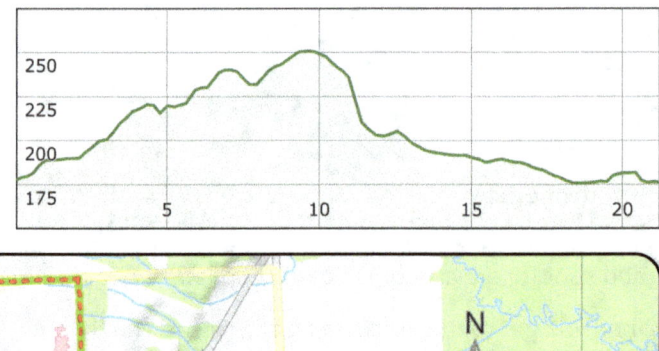

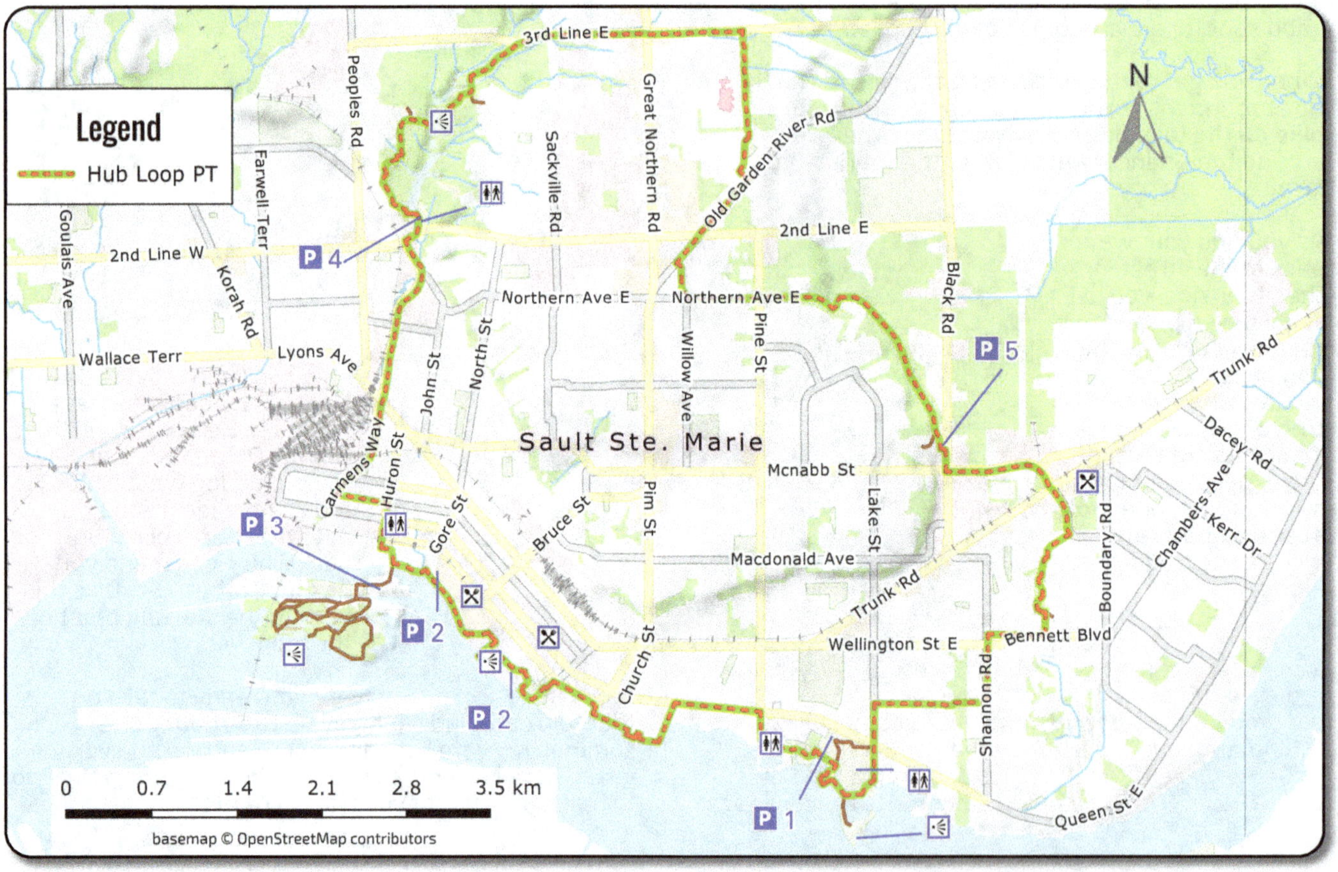

Review:

Here is a trail loop that's worth a day ride if you're in **Northern Ontario**. The **25 km John Rowswell Hub Trail** or simply **The Hub**, as it is called, **circles the city of Sault Ste Marie** (the Soo). It comprises a variety of visual settings that will give a rider a sense of this city that's far from one-dimensional.

There is the developed **tourist waterfront**; the **forest section; a business area, a hospital, Algoma University, Sault College;** and another stretch of cycling through quiet **residential neighbourhoods.**

This **paved trail** is flat by the water's edge with some sizable hills on the back side leading up into the best part, the wooded areas of the loop.

During a hot summer day (yes, they do have those here), we spent a sunny afternoon cycling the waterfront, looking at the locks and enjoying this trail.

the waterfront to visit the **art gallery** or the **bush pilot museum**, pick something up at the mall, or relax at a brew pub.

But since most of you bought this book to be on a bike to get some mileage in, **let's keep going.** Take on those hills, get some exercise, and **earn that ice cream!**

photo – Colin Field/Sault Tourism

By now you will have noticed signposts for the Hub trail. Follow them away from the river north to **Albert St W**, then left to take the cycling path along **Carmen's Way.** Not much here except the **railyards and Algoma Steel** beyond.

Your goal is **Fort Creek Conservation Area**, a beautiful, winding ride through the lush forest and across **four bridges**, one with a **135 m span**. Wooded areas will be a buggy zone at certain times of the day, likely 'til midsummer.

At **Third Line**, find your way east across and around the hospital grounds. (Handy if you need oxygen for the climbs, lol.)

photo – Konrad Wojcik/Sault Tourism

Park and start anywhere along the modern and touristy waterfront. The paved path winds along flower beds and benches by the flowing waters of the **St. Marys River**, where freighters pass and cruise ships dock.

Further west, take the trail to the **old historic locks** by the water **power station**, a side trip I recommend doing. **Cross over the locks** and circle around the **Whitefish Island gravel trails.** These **3 km** of narrow paths lead to **boardwalks, scenic views of the rocky rapids**, and in the distance a dam and locks that permit large ships to enter **Lake Michigan and Superior.** The trail passes underneath the expansive international bridge to the American side.

This might be the extent of the ride you can fit in or do on your travels. You might want to meander up the street to check out the **train station** (home of the famous **Agawa Canyon Tour Train**), or head back to

The next enjoyable part is another **2 km** stretch of northern evergreen forest at **Finn Hill,** going down hill…wheeeee! Once at **McNab St,** you are into the urban street/park part of the tour to get back to **Bellevue Park.** There you could go to the point for photo ops, then ride to the downtown waterfront again for an après snack, be it a cone or a pint.

I'm thankful to a reader who emailed me to enlighten me about this dynamic trail. If you're passing through town or staying awhile, pull your bike out for this spin or others mentioned on the city tourism site (MTB at Hiawatha). The hotels and dining options along the waterfront make this a **great holiday destination.** And **fall colours are famous up here.**

10 Extra Rail Trails

This collection of **ten extra Rail Trails sums up what is left** in the province. Between my two Park & Rail books, that's it as of 2023. I wanted to give them a mention. Not a lot can be said and not all have been ridden by me, so I kept it short.

Some listed are repurposed as more of a **Park ride experience** on an old rail bed. Others are straight, short snippets of off-road riding in the country, good to **incorporate into a longer ride.** They all get you out in different corners of Ontario to play the tourist and **stretch your legs for a spin.**

There were originally so many train tracks laid way back, going every which way; it is hard to say what's left in the future to repurpose as a recreational trail. In the last decade, there has been an **upsurge in Rail Trail development,** which will probably result in more routes being developed and existing ones being resurfaced in the next decade. It's a slow, expensive process with a lot of potential.

Carleton – Rail Trail   *Ottawa – Carleton Place*   Eastern Ontario

Length - 31 km (one way)
95% rail trail path
5% road crossings, detours

Terrain - crushed stone, gravel, paved sections
Traffic - Cyclists, hikers, snowshoe, Nordic skiers
Highlights - Historic town and river of Carleton Place, urban trek through Stittsville and Kanata, woodlots
Website - Trans Canada Trail
Access - Start of Fitzgerald Rd in Bells Corners ending Coleman St. and Queen St S in Carleton Place

⊕ **P1** Impark - 25 Fitzgerald Rd, Nepean, fee
P2 CARDELREC Recreation Complex - 1500 Shea Rd, Stittsville
⊕ **P3** 29 Coleman Street, Carleton Place

As the name implies, this rail trail helps connect cyclists from **Ottawa to Carleton Place,** either to visit this **historic town** or continue on the new **Ottawa Valley Rail Trail.** It's got a few bends in it, but it's pretty straight going, with a gradual **60 m slope up from the Ottawa River.**

Starting in **Bells Corners,** you can reach it on a number of **Greenbelt trails.** This **Trans Canada Trail** segment is well established and well used. It cuts through **Kanata** and **Stittsville,** and then you are in the countryside, traversing wetlands and woodlots. Eventually, it takes you underneath **Hwy 7** into **Carleton Place.** A short road ride on **Coleman Street** further SW will connect you to the **Ottawa Valley RT.** In **1870,** this track went all the way to **Brockville,** and it's yours to ride today.

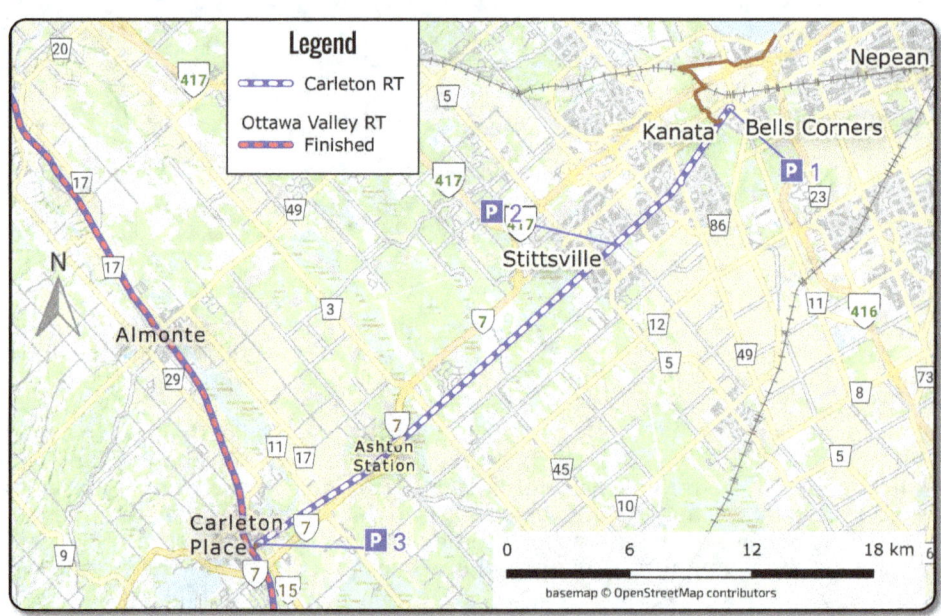

Osgoode Link Pathway – Rail Trail   *Ottawa - Osgoode*   Eastern Ontario

Length - 18+ km (one way)
95% rail trail path
5% road crossings, detours

Terrain - Stone dust, gravel
Traffic - Cyclists, hikers, horseback riders, Nordic skiers
Facilities - Parking on street, no washrooms, bike repair stations
Website - Surprisingly none
Access - The new LRT can take you to Bowesville Station to start the ride or park here:

P1 6187 Mitch Owens Rd
P2 5484 Osgoode Main St, Osgoode
⊕**P3** Osgoode on Buckles west of Nixon Dr

Here is another snippet of long-established Rail trail south of **Ottawa**. It's straight and doesn't connect very well with any other bike trails (currently, but...). Part of the north end of the railbed has been reclaimed to build a new LRT line.

I've read that when the dust settles, there will be a **new multi-use path running the full length of the LRT.** That would be ideal and give riders **an escape route out of the city.**

For now, it starts below **Earl Armstrong Road** and goes on past a golf course, a patchwork of woodlots and farm fields, and rural subdivisions, ending on the south side of the **town of Osgoode**. With **only a 12 m decline in 18 km**, it's a flat one, all right.

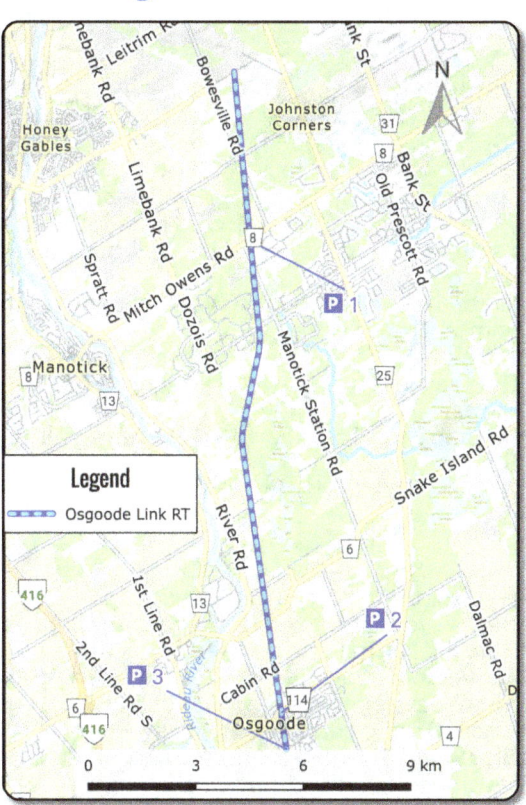

Sutton - Zephyr – Rail Trail   *Sutton*   Central Ontario

Length - 11 km (one way)
97% rail trail path
3% road crossings

Terrain - Fine crushed stone, gravel, puddles
Traffic - Cyclists, hikers, horseback riders, ATV enthusiasts, dirt bikers, snowmobilers, Nordic skiers
Facilities - Parking lot
Website - None found
Access - Parking lot P1, otherwise by the side of the road at:
⊕**P1** 33 Catering Rd, Sutton
P2 258 Crydermans Sideroad
P3 5541 Ravenshoe Rd, Brown Hill

I've included the short **Sutton-Zephyr RT** for those looking to do a **quick spin north of Toronto** just south of **Lake Simcoe.** It does not connect well with other trails and sits alone, unloved. My visit was enjoyable. It's a quiet excursion, nothing fancy, but it **crosses the Black River a number of times,** which makes it a little interesting. I think it's called the **Black River** because you cannot see the bottom. The terrain needs repair, as rogue ATVs have put in a few ruts and puddles.

The crushed stone base turns into a sandy dirt track by the time you get to the river **beyond the Hwy 48** crossing. You might turn around at that point, from the look of it. I managed on my MTB to go on to the river; it's missing a bridge and there is no way to cross. I hope that one day a span will be built across to ride into the **Zephyr Forest Tract**; I just saw that **York Region** bought the trailway and will be fixing it up, so it's possible. We will see what develops in the next few years.

Afterwards, check out the **Simcoe waterfront** around **Jackson Point.**

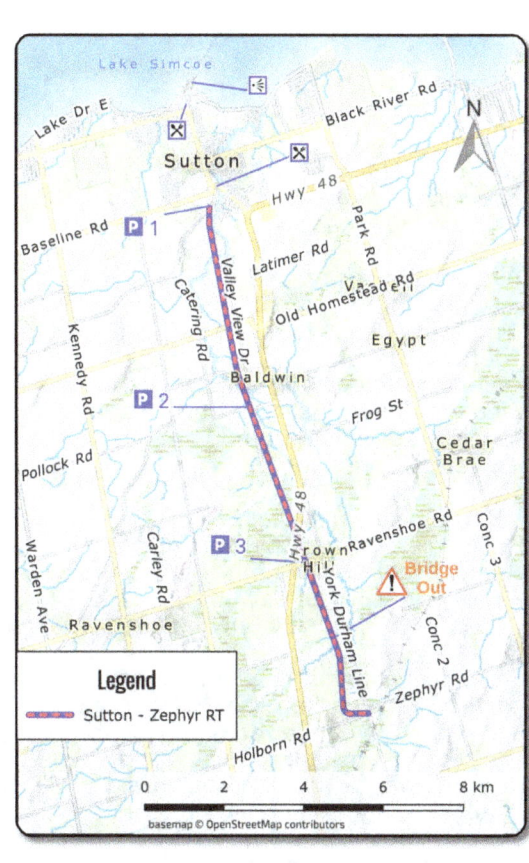

Watson – Rail Trail   *Sarnia*   Western Ontario

Length - 16 km (one way)
90% rail trail path
10% road crossings

Terrain - Crushed stone, gravel, asphalt
Traffic - Cyclists, hikers, Nordic skiers
Facilities - Parking on street, outhouse, benches
Website - Ontario's Blue Water coast - Lambton County
Access -
P1 Clearwater Area - 1400 Wellington St, Sarnia
P2 Blackwell Trails Park - 1430 Blackwell Rd
P3 Mike Weir Park - Hwy 7

If you ever make it to **Sarnia** with your bike, they have repurposed a rail line into the **Howard Watson Nature Trail**. Starting above **Confederation St**, it travels **straight north** between neighbourhoods **under Hwy 402** and curves gently east past **Blackwell Trails Park**. Here you could do a few loops around before continuing. A crushed packed gravel path that was resurfaced many years ago from a **CN Rail abandoned line.**

Trees that line it have grown in, signs mark the way, and recent upkeep makes it **an inviting nature trail**. Onward this path curves, heading out of town near the southern end of **Lake Huron** and going straight alongside **Hwy 7** to just before the **village of Camlachie.** There are opportunities to see the waterfront by looping back on **Egremont Rd** when you get to the end of the RT. Follow it west and continue on **Old Lakeshore Rd** to the bike path till it comes out to **Mike Weir Park** and meets the RT again. A sure-to-please excursion.

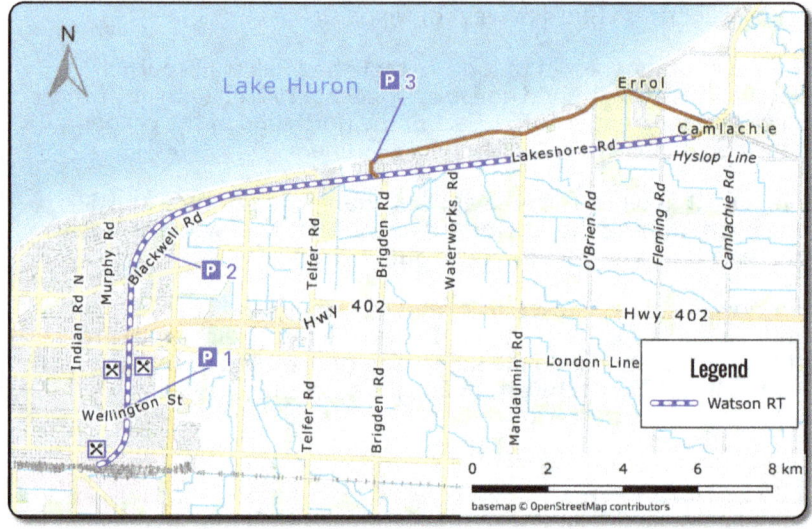

North Perth – Rail Trail   *Listowel*   Western Ontario

Length - 21 km (one way)
95% rail trail path
5% road crossings, detours

Terrain - Crushed stone, gravel, paved asphalt
Traffic - Cyclists, hikers, horseback riders
Facilities - Parking on street, benches
Website - Municipality of North Perth
Access - Street parking and try these suggested lots:

⬦ Henfryn Line & Davies St
P1 Kinsmen Club - 555 Binning St W, Listowel (old train station)
P2 Main & Arthur St, Atwood
⬦ Line 88 & Lincoln Ct, Gownantown

This old abandoned segment awaits north of the **well-known G2G Rail trail.** It starts in the **hamlet of Henfryn** and goes **6.5 km straight to the town of Atwood,** where it does a **90-degree bend** and continues on 8.8 km to the larger town of **Listowel,** then a little further on, to **Gowanstown.** In the future it may go to **Palmerston,** but

currently this segment is incomplete. And going the other way, who knows how far it might extend.

This is a **flat farm-country ride** with some shade, but mainly out in the sun. You can find a coffee shop in **Atwood,** a bakery in **Gowanstown,** and all your needs met in **Listowel.**

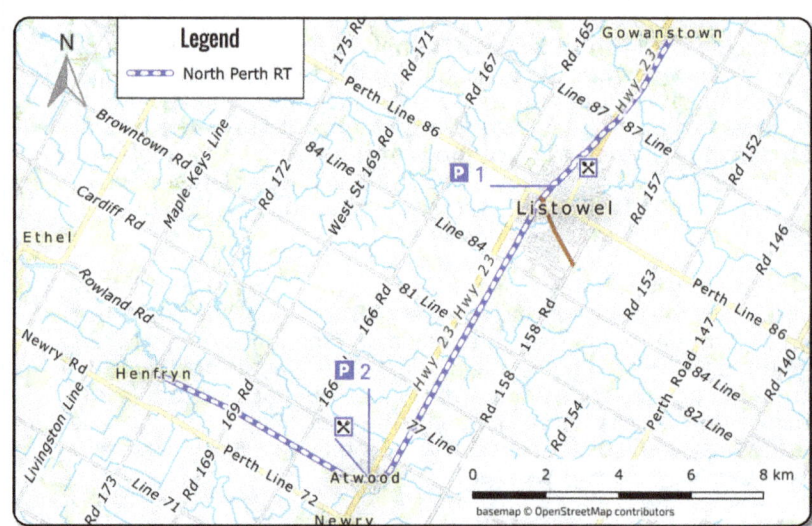

Hickson – Rail Trail *Woodstock* Western Ontario

Length - 10 km (one way)
95% trail path
5% road crossings, detours

Terrain - crushed stone, soil
Traffic - Cyclists, hikers, Nordic skiers
Website - City of Woodstock
Access - Start at P2 to do the RT or P1 to do the extra brown tracks: for bonus trails
P1 river bridge - 391 Tecumseh St
P2 Pittock Park Rd. & Frederick St
P3 745137 Oxford Rd hwy 17
⊕ **P4** Hickson Park - 100 Loveys St E, Hickson

This established short **10 km** old railbed **runs north from Woodstock** to the **village of Hickson**. It offers a tree-shaded, natural setting, away from the road, that travels through farm fields and small woodlots. Only **three road crossings** and you are there. P2 would be a good start point.

If you take the trail **the other way for 800 m**, you can connect with the **Thames riverside path** going east in **Woodstock.** From the **Tecumseh St** bridge, the **Pittock Trail** goes for about **6 km** on a wooded path through **Roth Park** past the dam to **Oxford Rd 4.** Going the other way, you can **explore the loops in Burgess Park** for another **4 km.** Looks like fun! Then, only minutes away, downtown **Woodstock** can feed you well.

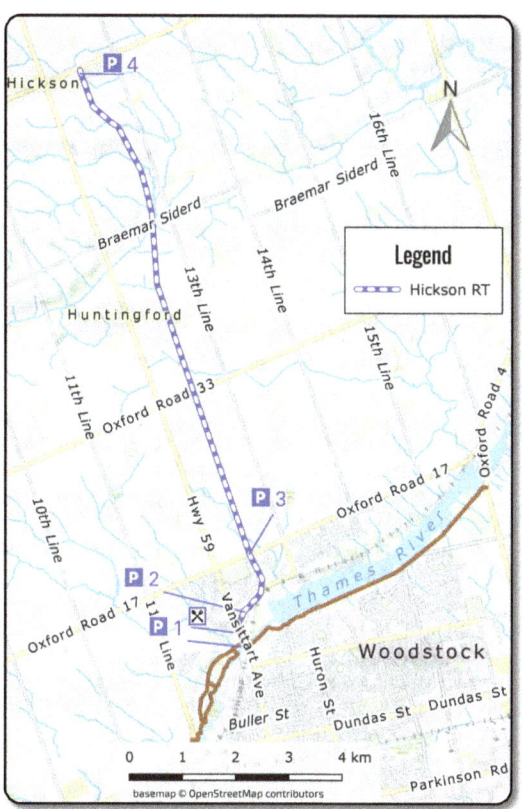

Bauer – Rail Trail *Welland* Central Ontario

Length - 6 km (one way)
95% trail path
5% road crossings

Terrain - Flat paved asphalt
Traffic - Cyclists, hikers, Nordic skiers
Facilities - Parking on street, benches
Website - Surprisingly none
Access - Find street parking by the trail in Welland or at the parking lot here:
⊕ **P1** 48 Port Robertson, Font Hill
⊕ 12 Colbeck Dr, Welland

I just noticed the **Steve Bauer Trail** in **Welland** on a map last week. He was a **pro cyclist** who made us proud at the **Olympics** and on the **Tour de France circuit.** And this is **the only Ontario bike trail** I know of that is named after a famous cyclist. Oddly, there aren't any more.

The route curves north from the bridge, crossing the **Welland River** near the centre of town. It follows the busy **Prince Charles Dr N** up for a few blocks through open, grassy parkland. After you cross **Thorold Rd** (carefully) it carries on as a quiet, tree-lined path, by neighbourhood backyards where the residents are surely glad the noise of trains has been replaced with silent bicycles.

After the bend, it parallels **Clare and Line avenues,** ending just outside of town in **Font Hill.** There are some mean hill climbs on the other side I remember, but you won't see them. **In 2020 it was completely paved** so that the whole railway line is accessible to all.

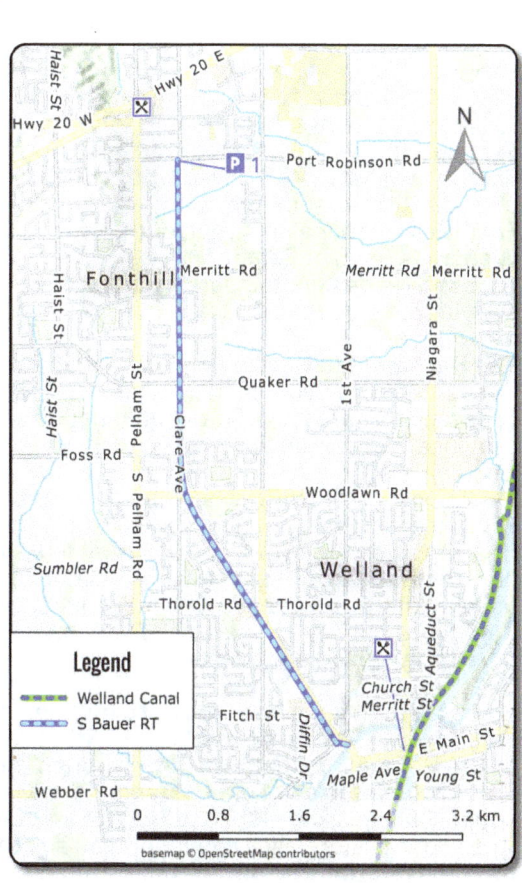

Centennial Bikeway – Rail Trail

Burlington Central Ontario

Length - 8 km (one way)
95% park path
5% road crossings, detours

Terrain - Crushed stone, gravel, asphalt
Traffic - Cyclists, hikers, horses, ATV, dirt bikes, snowmobiles, Nordic skiers
Facilities - Parking on street, outhouse, benches
Website - City of Burlington
Access - Three large parking lots, or pick a side street and take your chances:
⊕**P1** Sherwood Forest Park - 800 Fothergill Blvd
P2 Nelson Park - 621 Belvenia Rd
⊕**P3** 410 Martha St, downtown Burlington, fee

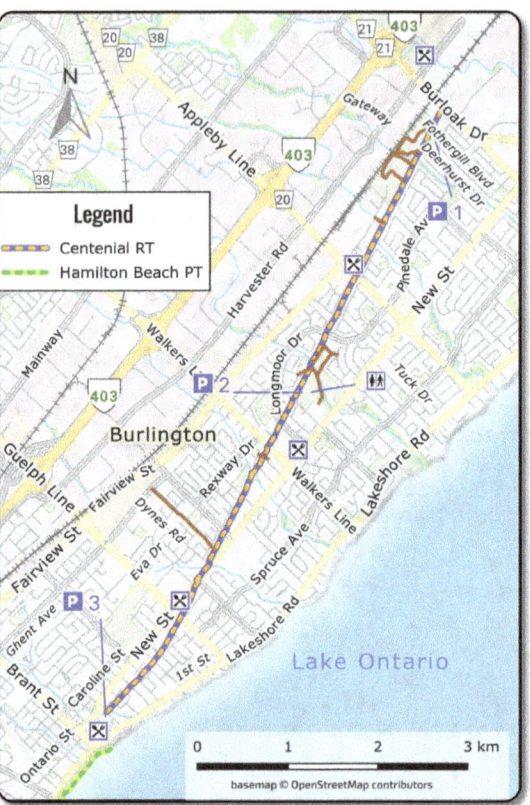

This linear corridor was a rail line at one time, but **no signs of it remain now.** Cutting diagonally across the city of **Burlington**, it is a wide paved Park path along a green space that's a tad boring and could use some extra landscaping. This peaceful, tree-lined ride passes backyards and sports fields on its way from the city centre to **Burloak Dr.**

It is an easy, level paved path to cruise on, away from road traffic except at crossings (most have lights). The city recently jazzed up the **Elgin Promenade section** in the downtown area where the trail ends and where you can find a cafe. I first used this path to get from the **Appleby GO station** down to the **Hamilton Beach trail**. Worth adding to your itinerary for a good day ride; you find the start of it **west of the waterfront pier.**

Hastings Heritage – Rail Trail

Trent R. - Bancroft Eastern Ontario

Length - 158 km (one way)
90% rail trail path
10% road crossings, detours
Terrain - Gravel, rocks, sand, mud and large puddles
Traffic - Cyclists (MTB), hikers, horseback riders, ATV enthusiasts, dirt bikers, snowmobilers
Facilities - Parking on street, outhouses
Website - Town of Bancroft
Access - No designated parking lots found. Park on the shoulder of side roads.

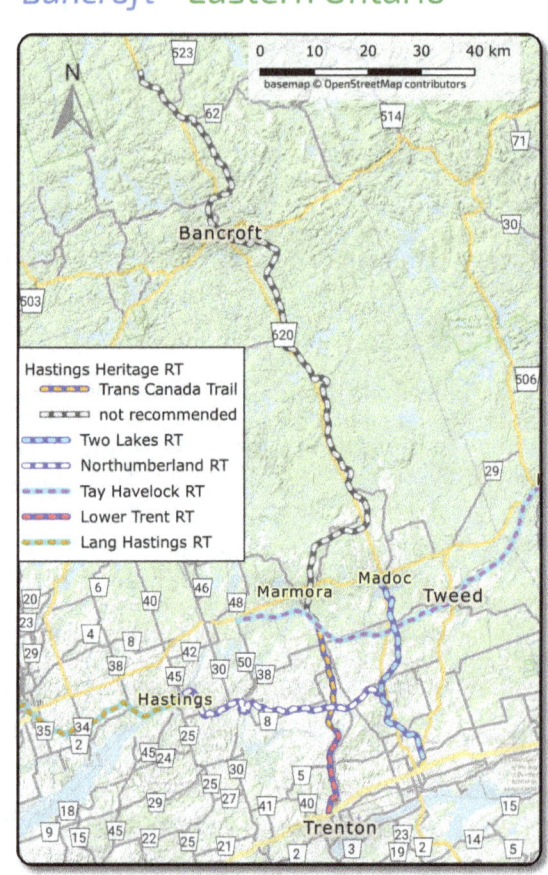

The **Heritage Trail** is showing up on maps and riders are taking notice. I have added this RT as **a warning to any adventurous types.** (There are lots of other abandoned, lost RT lines in the province that are similar.)

This long old rail line starts off as the **pleasant Lower Trenton RT.** Once it crosses the **Trent River,** the name changes to the **Hastings Heritage Trail,** and it's **open to ATVs.** This is your clue the **riding could get rough.** A section of it in the middle is used by the **Trans Canada Trail** to connect the **Northumberland RT** to the **Tay - Havelock RT.** Not resurfaced and bumpy, it's **a tough go on a gravel bike.**

Beyond this, it goes from **rough to hellish** north to **Bancroft** and further. **ATV traffic has trashed it!** I have read mountain bikers' complaints that travelling through the bush there is nothing to see, it's full of bugs, and there are few towns to support bikepackers. Plus they want $5 a day to MTB this rutted minefield! Only a commando on a Fatbike might make it. **Best to wait this one out.**

Friendship - Harry – Rail Trail *Fort Erie - Port Colborne* Central Ontario

Length - 24 +15 km (one way)
85% rail trail path
15% road crossings, detours

Terrain - Paved and crushed stone base
Traffic - Cyclists, hikers, Nordic skiers
Facilities - Parking lots, benches
Website - Fort Erie, Niagara Peninsula Conservation
Access - Parking lots at:

⊕ 1111 Edgemere Rd
P1 351 Crescent Rd, Fort Erie
P2 273 Ridge Road, Ridgeway
⊕ **P3** Welland & Durham St - Port Colborne

⊕ 10177 Cement Rd, Port Colborne
P4 Wainfleet Wetlands - 10628 Quarry Rd
P5 12026 Station Rd
⊕ Hutchinson & Minor Rd

I am combining the **Friendship Trail** out of **Fort Erie** with the **Gord Harry Conservation Trail** that continues beyond **Port Colborne.** They both were once part of the same **Grand Trunk rail line** running across the north shore of **Lake Erie.** The Friendship path is paved, straight, and rather flat. The Harry Trail is a fine crushed stone and it too is very linear = potentially boring.

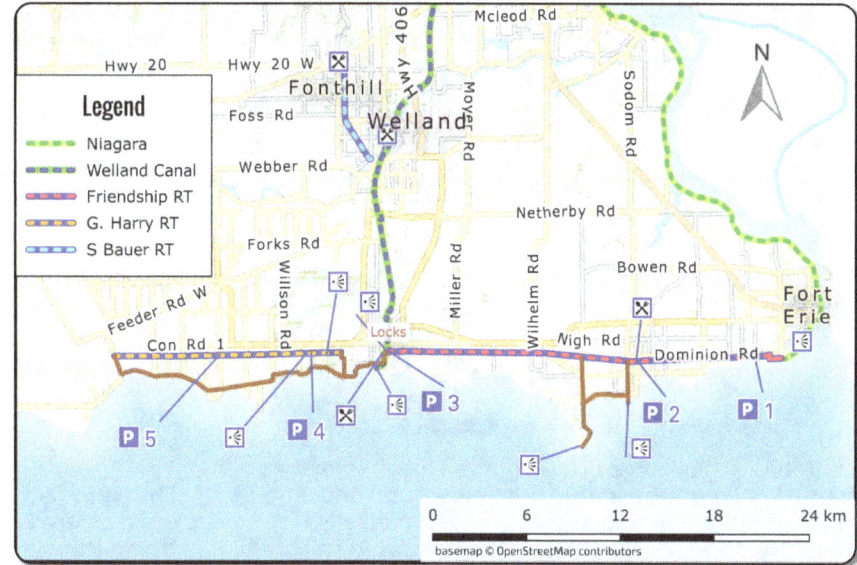

So let me add some interest to them. On the **Friendship RT,** consider side trips down to the lake to **tour Crystal Beach,** once, in a bygone era, **a resort town with an amusement park and dancehall.** Venture down to **Point Albino** to view the rocky shores and an **unusual historic lighthouse.** This path also connects the **Niagara River trail** with the **Welland Canal bike trail** for more mileage, great sights, and a full weekend of riding.

Unfortunately, **this rail trail does not go through Port Colborne.** You need to do a street detour and pick up the Gord Harry path on the west side of town, off **Cement Rd.** The highlight of this section is **Wainfleet Wetlands Conservation Area,** where there's an **old quarry, clay pits,** and open rock. It's a good place for **birdwatching.** Once you get to **Hutchinson Rd,** head back or **take the coastal roads** for views of the lake and cottages. (Take care, the road does not have shoulders.)

Rail History

★ A Brief History of Ontario Train Transport ★

(Not the boring version)

I wanted to pass on a little bit of railroad history, as **half the bike paths in this book use them** and, unbeknownst to many riders, sections of Park trails **secretly do**. I am not a **ferroequinologist** (a rail buff), but after researching the history of **50 Rail Trails** (RT), **I've learned some things**.

For almost a **hundred years, before our time,** train travel was a big thing, **HUGE!** After having nothing but **horses and wind power** for so long, the **steam engine was the new tech** poster boy of that era. Hard to believe, but just like in modern times when a **great leap forward in convenience and technology** appears, this world was abuzz with **TRAINS!**

Let me take you through an **abridged version of the rise and fall** of Ontario train transport. You will see how **many things never change**; only technology does.

1850S · TRANSITION

Before trains, Ontario was **wilderness covered in trees**; travel was done by **horse and stagecoach** on muddy, dusty paths. **Ships were the main means of transporting goods** to market and people (immigrants) to new frontiers. **Canals** were built at great cost to help open up the land and shorten routes. Ships could **carry great loads** efficiently, but **only as far as a port** or shore—beyond that was a problem. And in the winter, when the waters froze over, ships could **not move at all**.

The first steam locomotive was invented in **1804** and trains rapidly began to be widely used in England and elsewhere in Europe. Of course, the new colonies in Canada were interested in this modern, efficient, faster way of transportation. The **first locomotive in Ontario left Toronto** on tracks to **Aurora** in **May 1853**; a few years later, the tracks were extended to **Barrie. They're still in use for Metrolinks GO service.**

1860S · THE BOOM YEARS

Trains had the advantage of crossing over land to connect isolated communities, mining, and lumber enterprises; ship grain; and open up the province to settlement. There were several train **booms and busts.**

Like current-day venture capitalists and big business, investors and opportunists of the day were **keen to get involved and make money**. In addition to businessmen (sorry, it was a man's world in the rail business), there was also interest at all levels of **government to aid**—and basically fund—track-building projects. Growth-focused governments needed to expand into, settle, and transport goods over large areas of the province. There were strategic reasons (economic and military) to connect communities and make Canada more cohesive. **Every community wanted a track to come to town;** politicians could buy votes by supporting more trains.

The train tech race had begun. **Government grants were offered to any railway that built over 120 km of track.** Bonds guaranteed a return, which led to a rapid expansion of lines even when they were likely not going to turn a profit. Tracks crisscrossed the province, **the race was on.**

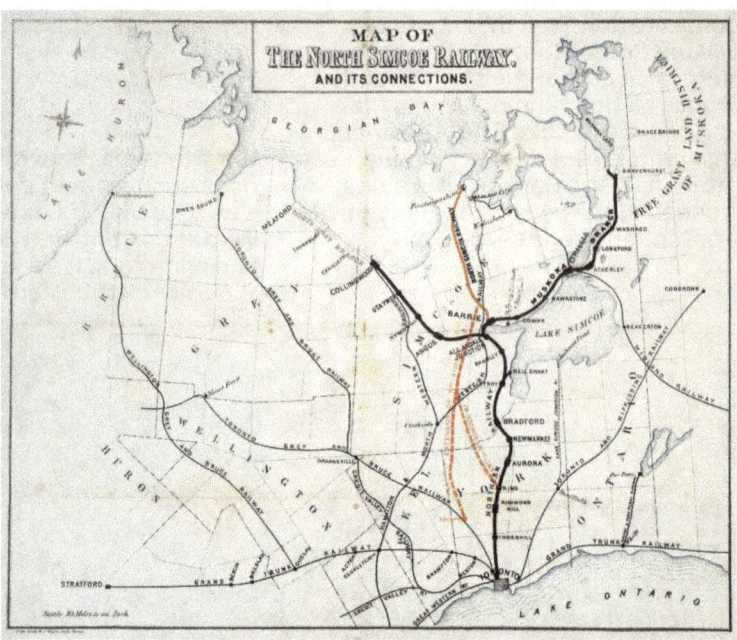

Rail lines are an **expensive endeavour**, especially in the Canadian wilderness. Money was required to survey the routes, build bridges, establish causeways over wetlands, and blast rock cuts to run track. Crews of hundreds were employed for years at a time to lay the stone ballast, set the ties, and hammer in the rails with spikes.

Small railroads competed with each other to run track to untapped areas, taking away business from the shipping industry—and **hoping to survive the startup costs.**

Entrepreneurs would often **build competing lines going in the same direction.** Their goal was not only to **take a piece of the pie** but also attract new business by building a **more direct, faster railway**. This could be achieved by surveying better, **more efficient routes** with fewer inclines for heavy trains to climb. Trains can travel faster on a straight track, so the least amount of sharp turns would be incorporated.

Not everything was rosy for these competing lines. Many of the best routes were quickly snapped up, and farm and crown lands **became unavailable.** The **rights to cross over private land and other train tracks** were not always granted, so would-be builders had to reroute through marshes, build extra bridges, or launch **expensive court challenges.** Existing railroads were **not going to make it easy for newcomers.**

Once competing railways were up and running, passengers, farmers and industry no longer had to **pay high transport fees set by a monopoly** train line. This competition created tighter margins, cheaper fares, and large debts for small railways trying to maintain track and buy rolling stock.

1900 - 1930 · THE GOLDEN AGE OF RAIL

By the turn of the century, you could **travel to all corners of Ontario** on an established network of train lines to visit family, go on vacation in style, or ship goods with ease. The **war effort of World War I** boosted train traffic, and **passenger volumes peaked in the 1920s.**

With the arrival of the **Great Depression in the 1930s**, there was a dip in ridership, but **World War II led to another surge in train traffic.**

For industry, the **widening of the Welland Canal in 1932** and the **opening of the St. Lawrence Seaway in 1959** gave Great Lakes access to **larger freighters,** changing the importance and **cost of train vs ship transport.** And the car was about to change everything for passenger train travel.

1880S · STANDARD GAUGE & THE RECESSION

Eventually, this **overexpansion put railroads into debt,** and government funding was **bankrupting the provinces.**

But it got worse. In the beginning of the train era, **tracks were built at different widths around the world.** Train cargo could be shipped only so far before it had to be **transferred by hand to another train** on a different gauge. In **1851**, a **standard width was established** in Canada: 1.435 metres (4 ft + 8 1/2 in). The US followed suit in 1863. Many Ontario railroads had to **spend more money to resize their tracks**, which was a **massive undertaking.**

Then came the economic **Long Recession of 1873 to about 1896** which forced many small railways to **consolidate, merge, or go bankrupt and be bought out by others.**

The **Canadian Pacific Railway (CPR)** was born in **1881** and the federal government offered it a sweet deal and a bit of a monopoly out west. The **CPR** is one of the two major remaining train services we have today. The other, the **Canadian National (CNR)**, was established in **1923** as a product of the Canadian government to bail out, merge, and nationalize four railways (the **Grand Trunk, Grand Trunk Pacific, Canadian Northern, and National Transcontinental**), saving them from poor management and overexpansion.

1950S · THE DAWN OF THE AUTOMOBILE AND AIRPLANE

The construction of new roads freed citizens to buy cars and **travel on their own time.** Gas was cheap and new highways emerged; **truck transport was more flexible and could reach further than train tracks.** The **age of the auto was here.**

After the war, **airlines took over as the fastest way of mass transit.** You could fly farther than any train could take you. When engines went from prop to jet, and fares dropped, the public was on board (literally).

Railroads had to **cut back and begin abandoning tracks.** At first, when service declined, Ontario cities and towns complained, and **government forced railroads to continue** operating for the "good of the public." In response, many companies ran trains purposely late or at odd hours, and they didn't publish their schedules. **They sabotaged their own passenger services** so the public would not use the train and hence they could **claim it was not needed.** They were more **interested in freight,** where profits are more easily made. But even this would eventually begin to scale back.

After private railways showed such disinterest in serving the public, **GO Transit in 1967** and **Via Rail in 1977** were launched by governments to redevelop rail passenger service again.

1980S · THE END OF THE LINE

A lot of decommissioned tracks were abandoned, with **rails torn up** and **bridges sold for scrap,** in the last hundred years. Those early routes are long gone, with portions **sold off to farmers or made into county roads** or right-of-ways for gas pipelines and hydro towers.

In memory of Chis Lohan, a CP man.

In the **1980s**, a few activists and politicians began thinking it would be a great idea to **repurpose these unloved rail** lines into **recreational trails;** this was the basis of the Rail trails we have today. Railways were sometimes kind enough to **donate the land "as is" to divest themselves from any responsibilities,** such as environmental cleanups.

There has been a **surge in the last two decades to restore long-lost rail lines,** which has resulted in a network of trails only an ATV enthusiast could love. Communities and regional governments have started to come around to the notion that actual bike trails would not only **help local users stay fit, but would also be a boon to the economy by attracting tourists and visitors.**

The development of rail trails has really started to pick up, and I think these are exciting times. Could all these trails grow enough to **support local B&B and camping spots, and other tourist amenities?**

If there is **enough infrastructure** to support overnight bikepackers in terms of food and lodging along the way, maybe it will put Ontario on the map for this activity. **Quebec, BC, PEI, and the USA are all ahead of us.**

The potential is there for the **K&P, LE&N, G2G** and the new **Ottawa Valley, the Bruce** and the **Grey rail trails** to **become bike touring destinations in time.** These trails just happen to come to mind now, but almost any RT could become attractive if it offers good cycling, quaint surroundings, and relaxing vibes—and maybe a little piece of Ontario history. If we come, will they build cafes, craft beer pubs, B&Bs, and motels?

And may I add that in the future there is always the possibility that some of these routes **may again serve as mass transportation**. Might we see electric bullet trains or hyperloop tubes in fifty years?

★ RAIL HISTORY ★
CONTINUED FROM REVIEWS

Escarpment History - During the 19th century, many railway companies made efforts to build a track bed up the formidable Niagara Escarpment to reach **Lake Erie**. It took until 1881 for the **Hamilton and North-Western Railway (H&NW)** to lay track all the way to **Port Dover,** a project which was originally begun in **1834** by a company called the **Hamilton and Port Dover Railway.**

Hamilton and **Toronto** were competing to be the **main rail shipping centres** in the region, and this route now ran from **Lake Erie** to the **Hamilton** docks on **Lake Ontario.** Due to railway consolidations, the line changed hands many times. The **Grand Trunk Railway** ran it for a few decades, but in their haste to expand, they ran out of money, and by **1928** the entire track became part of **CN Rail.**

By **1997** most of the track was decommissioned and either repurposed for recreational trail use or turned into farm fields.

Uhthoff History - The **Georgian Bay and Seaboard Railway** (GB&SR) was operated by **CP Railway** starting in **1908** to compete with **the Grand Trunk Railway** (GTR) network. Grain from the prairies came from freighters **(lakers) to Ontario ports,** and was then shipped by train—the fastest way east to **Montreal or Halifax docks**. (The Welland Canal and St. Lawrence Seaway had not yet been built.)

By **1912,** the short-line route was complete: **140 km** from **Port McNicoll,** the terminal town built by CP; through **Orillia; a**nd down around **Lake Simcoe to south of Lindsay.** (The **South Victoria RT** in my first book.) Passenger service ran daily beyond **Lindsay to Havelock** until the early **1930s.** By **1937,** the line stopped in **Orillia.** There wasn't enough traffic after the **Welland Canal was opened;** a sea port was built in **Churchill, Manitoba**; and the Great Depression hit.

Over the years, less track was used; **Port McNicoll** was closed in **1992** and the spur line to the **Uhthoff quarry** shut down a year later. This spur is the recreational trail—and it's still under development.

CASO History - The **Canada Southern Railway** (CASO or CSR) built this line and started operating steam locomotives in **1869.** The route went **350 km** from **Windsor to Essex, St. Thomas,** and **Waterford** on to Fort Erie.

Later, due to financial troubles, it was leased to the **Michigan Central Railroad (MCR)** in **1883** and the **New York Central Railroad** (NYC) in **1929,** both owned by the American **Vanderbilt railroad empire.**

The town of **St. Thomas,** being in the middle of the line, was established as the headquarters and became an important rail hub. In **1985 CN & CP** purchased the former **CASO** line together to acquire the **Detroit rail tunnel and bridge over the Niagara River**. By 2001, the tracks had been lifted and the rail line was donated to the counties. Sections are being slowly transformed into a recreational trail.

Grey History - This track from **Toronto to Owen Sound**, with **Orangeville as a hub**, was completed in **1873** by the **Toronto, Grey and Bruce Railway (TGBR)**. Cordwood used for fuel, and quarry stone and gravel for cement were delivered to Toronto along its narrow-gauge track.

Ten years later, the original track was **changed to the wider standard gauge** common with other rail lines and the line became part of the **CPR** soon afterward. **Owen Sound became a busy port** for freight and passengers. **Grain elevators** were built and a shipyard opened. In **1884, CP** started passenger steamship service to **Sault Ste. Marie** and **Fort Williams (Thunder Bay).**

By **1905 CP** decided it would be **more efficient** to have a rail terminus closer to markets, and began work on building one in **Port McNicoll**. This was the start of the **decline of Owen Sound**, which had room for **only five vessels to dock** and a **steep grade heading out of town**. When the **CP grain silos burnt down in 1911**, they were not rebuilt, and headquarters moved to the new terminal further south in **Port McNicoll.**

Passenger service stopped in the early **1960s**. Grain continued to be shipped until the federal grain rate subsidy ended in **1989**, which caused this elevator and larger ones at **McNicoll, Midland,** and **Goderich** to close. **1995** was the end of the line.

K &P History - The **Kingston** and **Pembroke Railway** (K&P) was built to transport raw materials from the lumber and mining industries and aid farmers in delivering agricultural goods to eastern markets. It was completed in **1884** to **Renfrew** and not **Pembroke**, as another railway had beaten them to it.

Prosperity was short lived and by the turn of the century, it became **a CPR** asset. Beginning in the **1950s,** portions of the north line closed; the last section, from **Tichborne to Kingston**, shut down in **1986.**

The **K&P** is affectionately remembered as the **"Kick and Push" railroad.** Why? They say passengers had to get off to "kick and push" it as it was under-

powered and slow on the steep grades and tight curves, of which there were many.

Others say it came from the way the train would "kick" the uncoupled cars into a yard siding track and come around and "push" the coaches into the station. Or was it the sound of the steam locomotive?

Lang Hastings History - Briefly the **Grand Junction Railway (GJR)**, then part of the **Midland**, then the **Grand Trunk Railway,** this line was eventually sold to the **Canadian National Railway (CNR)**. As with most commuter lines, users were switching to cars by the late 1950s, but freight kept the line functioning for another decade. The old railbed was developed as a recreational trail after 2012.

A notable accident happened in the middle of the summer of **1884**, when a **locomotive left the tracks** and buried its nose in the mud of a swamp west of **Keene** Station, followed by seven train cars. Amazingly, no one was seriously injured. The papers reported it was an inconvenience that this made passengers late that day. A larger train from **Belleville** came later to pull it out of the mud.

Ottawa Valley History - In **1859**, the **Brockville and Ottawa Railway (B&O)** was opened from **Smiths Falls to Almonte/Mississippi Mills.** After **1864**, it was connected to Arnprior, then Renfrew in **1872**, and in **1876** it was extended up to **Pembroke**, on the **Ottawa River**. The B&O merged with **Canada Central Railway** (CCR) in **1878.**

To be compatible with other rail lines in the area, the **B&O's rail gauge** (width of the tracks) was changed in **1880**: tracks were narrowed from broad gauge to standard gauge for the **200 km** between **Brockville** and **Pembroke**. Certainly this was a major undertaking happening in the province to avoid having to transfer items between train tracks of **different widths**. Shops were kept busy changing the rolling stock for the **gauge conversion.**

Another **150-odd-km** section between **Mackey** and **Mattawa** was converted in **1881,** shortly before the **CCR** leased the line to **CP Rail**, which ran freight along the line for decades. The tracks were pulled up by **2012.**

The south half of this railbed, from **Smiths Falls** to **Petawawa** was resurfaced for recreational use in 2022. Work on the section to **Mattawa is** likely to continue for a few more years.

Bike Security - Lock it Up

You love riding your bicycle and you want to keep your dear friend as long as you can. Unfortunately, I have to bring up a fairly serious problem in this world, and that's **bike theft.** (The other main reason people hesitate to cycle is **street traffic**.)

Last year in **2022 Toronto** had over **3,000 bikes** stolen, **Hamilton 500**, (**Vancouver has the highest**, 4x as many per capita). And **25%** of cyclists never replace them. Most were not recovered. As you might suspect, locking up your bike downtown in any city is a risk.

Hot spots for thefts are health clubs, schools, retail outlets, restaurants, and in front of homes. In a smaller town or in the country, the **odds are a lot lower,** but bike theft can happen anywhere.

Because a bicycle is so light, portable, and expensive, it's a favourite item for thieves to steal, with a good chance they won't get caught. And it is such a great getaway vehicle, too!

There are **two main kinds of bike thieves:** the **opportunists** who may not have any tools, but spot an easy take and act on impulse. And the **experienced pro** who knows a good bike when they see one, plans the crime, and has a bag of tools for the dastardly deed.

I bet you **half the cyclists you know** (maybe even you!) have had a bike taken in their lifetime. In front of our house, two bikes were taken from our SUV overnight. Did I leave it unlocked, or did they have tools? No trace...

A friend of mine had her bike stolen from her third-storey apartment balcony, another riding buddy leaned his touring bike against a bakery shop window, went in for one minute to get a muffin, gone! All heartbreak stories...

Let's not make the next one yours.

The Strategy

Here are some **prudent measures** to keep your steed within your grasp and not someone else's. I'm going to focus on **tactics we trail riders need to employ. (** I'd have to write more pages for commuters in the city and those who want to park a bike safely at work or while shopping.)

Basically, **your bike has to be not appealing to take, and a hassle for anyone who tries.** Thieves want a **quick, easy job. They do not want to get caught** working on disabling your security measures. So by **increasing their risk** to do so, you may get them to **move on to softer targets.**

Let's start with the bike(s) you own. In general, the more expensive a bike is (or looks), the more appealing it would be for a thief to acquire. When you're buying a new bike, ask yourself: "Do I really need to spend that much money to have fun on two wheels?"

I certainly wouldn't suggest you drop $10K (even $5K) on a bicycle unless that's loose change for you, or you're training for the Tour de France. **Looks are everything: if your bike is shiny, new, and expensive it is more likely to disappear.**

Some cyclists have been known to paint and scratch up their expensive bikes to look ugly and less desirable. That seems a bit extreme.

Don't Advertise

If a thief doesn't know about your pride and joy, they won't come looking for it. Store your bike in a locked, safe area and **don't tell the world where that is.** Posting bike glamour pictures on social media can invite trouble. Same with a condo storage room with a door sign that says "Bike Locker."

Even sharing your ride routes that **start from your front door** on cycling apps can **tell thieves where you live and what you own.** I have even heard of cyclists being followed home, so thieves can return later, and make off with the goods from your garage or shed.

When you transport your bike, try to **keep it hidden.** Take the front wheel off and **lay it in the car or van**, covering it with a dark blanket, away from prying eyes.

That's not always possible: many of us have bike racks on the car roof or hanging off the trailer hitch. Those are risky places to leave your bike unsupervised. If you go to a restaurant after a ride, park close to the eatery, **ask for a patio table,** or at least sit by a window to be able to **keep one eye on your bike rack.**

Use the Best Locks

You spent a fair amount on your bicycle, now it's time to spend a small percentage of that to keep it.

Don't go cheap now and buy a lock that's only cosmetic. Pick up a **U-lock rated for some serious security attacks** and a **thick cable or chain.**

Read over the specifications of the locking devices. Understand what level of security they are rated at and what protection they give. Also learn how to use them properly.

Can the lock be cut, pried open with a bar, or broken with a hammer against something hard like the ground or a wall? Is the hardened steel cable/chain link thick enough to be a hassle to cut through, slow them down?

The **U-lock goes around your frame, a stationary object, and your rear wheel** if possible. The **cable goes through the other wheel** and anything else you want to hold on to, then connects with the U-lock. The object (pole, fence, bike stand) you attach your lock to has to be **firmly grounded.** Check that it is **not easily cut or broken,** and that it **can't be disconnected or slipped over.**

Consider taking the front wheel with you. (Though a thief may just steal another bike's wheel to ride off with yours.) **Remove any loose accessories** - lights,

seat post, bags, odometer...these items are often **stolen by opportunistic riff-raff.**

What if you're out with NO LOCK, but you have to leave your bike for a minute? Pray. And take the front wheel with you, take the air out of a tire, change the gears into the wrong ones, drop the chain—anything that slows down a getaway while **you make haste.**

You Are Never 100% Secure

Unfortunately, **locks will slow down a thief** but if they really want to take your prized bike, **they will.** Even the best locks will only give you **four minutes of protection** against the efficiency of an **angle grinder attack** before they fail.

Sad but true. Locking up your bike out in a **busy area may help,** but some are brazen enough to pull out from their gym bag a pry bar, hammer, hacksaw, cable cutters, or noisy portable angle grinder and do their dirty work.

A bike in a garage pretty safe, thieves extra **seclusion** on preventive have. Stored in your basement is even better, but going out for an errand gives them enough time. You just can't win. hidden, locked away or shed should be but this also gives time to **work in** whatever diabolical locks and alarms you

Hey, I don't want to get you paranoid, there isn't a thief under every rock, just **be security conscious** for **criminal opportunities**.

And I could go on but you get the message: **be vigilant.** There are **crime data maps and stats** on websites that could **put your mind at ease** if you live in a **low-crime-rated ward** of the city.

Travelling

When on a road trip, you need to keep your bikes safe. Leaving them out on a rack locked up overnight is very risky.

At a motel/hotel with no secure parking, ask to get a **room on the first floor** and park your car **by the room door** or under a **bright street lamp**, perhaps within sight of a **security cam**. Some hotels have a **secure bike/gear lockup** where your only risk is hotel employees and other guests.

It's a question of: **"How safe is it in this area/town?"** All vehicles have alarms, which help, but if you're worried about a **"smash and grab,"** you could **also lock your rig up inside the car**.

When in doubt, notch it up a level: take the front wheel, the seat, or **the whole bike with you into your room** if you're concerned.

Recovery

Before your bicycle goes missing, register your ownership into a local police database.

If a tragedy does occur, this may help your bike to be returned one day.

Over 90% of us do not register our bicycles, so return rates are **low: only 5%** of bicycles recovered are reunited with their owners. Most bikes go to auction because police have **no idea who the owner is.**

It's worth adding your bike's **make, model, colour, and serial #** to **bikeindex.org.** There's also an excellent free global app to register bikes called **529 Garage** at **project529.com**; Ottawa, London, Kingston, Halton, Niagara, and other regions partner with this app.

Get on it! At the very least, **keep your receipt and serial number with some photos handy** in case the worst happens. You can also invest in a **bike GPS**

tracker and maybe buy **bike insurance** for added comfort.

I ask my local bike shop if they **check serial numbers** with the police when repairs come in; **they do not.** I was told the system is not set up to make this easy enough to do; it should be. And why are bike shops not **registering new bikes** sold for us?

If your old friend gets stolen, you can try **Facebook, Kijiji, Craigslist, and eBay marketplaces** to see if it pops up for sale. Talk about the theft on **forums and social pages** and get the word around the neighbourhood. You never know, sometimes a bike could already be in another town or just sold privately to someone local.

And **if you buy a used bike, please check the serial number before you buy**, so you are not supporting the black market.

I hope this little talk spares you any grief. I know it's more to think about and those **locks are more weight to carry.** Once you set up a **security plan** and implement it, go have some fun, and chill.

The rest is fate and a bit of good luck. You have done your due diligence...

I am not going to suggest you
sleep with your bike
...unless it's worth $10k.

Cycling Safely

Be Aware, Be Seen!

I bet you enjoy cycling a lot. How can I tell?...you bought a book about it. And I'm sure you want to **continue riding forever** and have your future eBike buried with you when you go at age 110.

Life is full of risks and the consequences associated with them. We constantly **work out the odds** and **make decisions,** hoping they are good ones. Cycling for the most part **is a safe sport** but it can **lead to mishaps** and death. The likelihood is very low, **but it does exist.** Yet I see too many cyclists not considering the potential hazards on the trail and, even worse, on city streets.

Let me run through my observations and suggestions and then **you can make your own decisions. My goal is to ride another day.** I thoroughly enjoy cycling and want to continue doing it **as long as I can. It is as simple as that.**

So on the whole, I analyze what cycling is and the environment I do it in. What are the **potential hazards** that could cut short my fun in the saddle? Some I have no control over, but for the ones I do, **I want the odds to be on my side.** I stand a better chance to evade a mishap or at least **suffer less if one does occur.** Many of my actions are automatic, **second nature, conditioning,** like looking both ways when you cross.

BTW, I do not constantly **think about these issues, nor worry about them.** I simply am proactive and mindful of my ongoing situation as I pedal, enjoying the ride for what it is.

Be Aware

My first objective is to **be aware of my surroundings** as I ride. **Who/what** is coming at me, or may turn into my path? Could that blind corner or hillcrest ahead hold any surprises? **Is there a potential hazard** approaching from the rear?

To answer those questions, **my senses need to be on standby.** I do not wear earbuds playing loud music. I do not make phone calls or text while riding. These are **distractions when I need to be able to hear** what is quietly approaching from behind, the honk of a horn, or an ATV. (I have played music occasionally on a lonely singletrack trail, but

never when it's busy. And even then the volume is low, and I use just one earbud or the loose-fitting kind.)

Even **chatting over to your riding mates** for too long, or daydreaming and not focusing on what is ahead can lead to mishaps. I have had it happen.

You have to look out for others not readily seen or who are unaware of your approach. Where are they and what sudden moves could they make that could jeopardize your pleasant day in the woods? **What evasive action** would you take if they dashed in front of you, and suddenly stopped?

For us trail riders, our surroundings can also involve **wildlife encounters.** I have seen a **few snakes, deer, partridges, and turkeys** cross my path. We both get startled, and they run off. No **moose or bears** yet, but up north it's a possibility. A little chatter between cyclists or a bear bell will help to keep them away.

Being aware of **traffic in cities is on another, even more heightened level.** So much can happen on a busy road: **cars pulling out in front of you, people walking out from between parked cars, doors opening, trucks turning, no shoulders, potholes**...ya, it can get to be a bit of a gauntlet riding the road. Thankfully this book has very little of that "excitement."

Be Seen

When I am on the road I want cars and trucks **(everyone!) to see me.** Drivers are programmed to look out for **large vehicles;** a bike is a thin, small object that can be tough to see, and **bicycle awareness is still not that common**.

I recommend **wearing something that is a bright shade** (I like red, yellow, or orange), be it **a jacket, a colourful jersey** or **helmet,** maybe even your saddle bags or backpack. You don't have to look like an orange traffic cone, lol. I might not be fashionable but there is **a good chance I'll get noticed**. My cycling fashion can suffer as long as it helps keep me safe.

Here is a chart of **how effectively different colours are seen and at what distance. You can see **black**

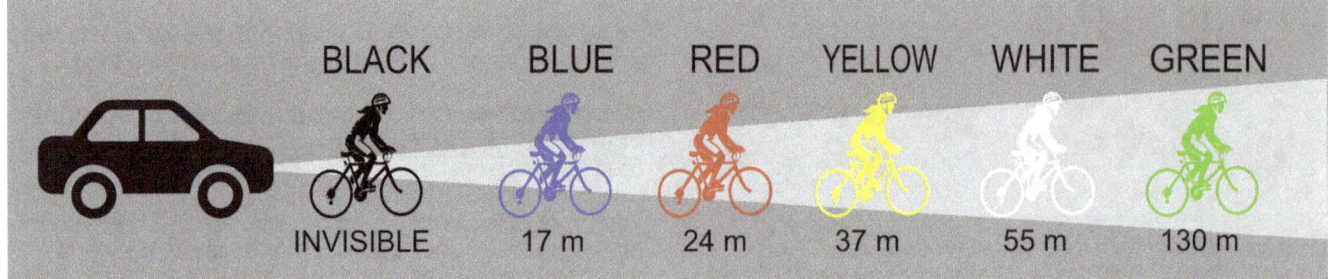

BLACK	BLUE	RED	YELLOW	WHITE	GREEN
INVISIBLE	17 m	24 m	37 m	55 m	130 m

gives you no edge: you are virtually invisible. This is why stop signs are red and warning markers are yellow while ninjas and cat burglars dress all in black.

I am **disappointed in the cycling industry that pushes fashion over function.** Even **reflective safety marks** on clothing have been reduced. The current trends of black and grey activewear and **dull bike colours** and accessories are not going to help you be seen.

They actually do the opposite; they endanger your life! When I see **black cycling club jerseys,** I just can't believe **they are not thinking this through.** Black is also **hot to wear in the sun** and **attracts bugs.**

I also wish cities would bring this to cyclists' attention through **public awareness campaigns,** as most road riders seem to be **oblivious to their lack of visibility.**

So find some bright, fun colours that stand out and say, **"HEY There, I'm on this trail/road! Just so you know!"**

At night, or even during the day, using these new **LED bike lights** is a wonderful idea. They're cheap, small,

and bright, with long-lasting charges or batteries, so there is no reason why you would not use them. And many of them can blink, too, as another way to say "Here I am—take notice!" Adding **reflectors** is another smart idea, if you wish.

One last item: pedestrians and others on the trail appreciate **a bell.** Bikes are pretty quiet and can sneak up on someone. If startled, someone may jump in front of you, or if they don't hear you, the moment you try to pass they may cluelessly **step into your path.** A polite **"ding ding"** or a call of **"on your left"** before you pass on their left is the norm. A bell also helps the traffic (walkers with earbuds, kids, dogs) register that you are coming.

Why Wear a Helmet?

Silly question, **we all know why**. And most of you do, but for those who still don't... Here are **my reasons why it's a good idea** and not a hassle to wear.

I have heard the arguments about why a helmet is not needed. It goes something like this: **stats show how few get hurt, so the risk is low**. People will state how many years they have ridden a bike and nothing has happened, **so why worry?**

Applying the same logic suggests that **they do not wear seat belts in cars or planes.** Again the odds of a crash are slim. But if there is a crash...

The thing is, stats and working the odds are not what you should use for reasoning. **It is the severity of the possible outcome,** if and when a crash does happen, that should be your gauge. You only have to fly off your bike **one time** for a disaster to happen. If you're not wearing a helmet, what will help save you?

I also hear **"Wearing a helmet makes you more confident, so you take more risks** and your chance of injury will go up." **I don't agree.** Not once while mountain biking did I think "I've got my trusty helmet on today, so let's go flying off that jump."

Actually, in the world of mountain biking, **everyone wears a helmet, everyone!** Yet on the streets of any city in Ontario, **so many road riders do not.** And I consider that **a way more dangerous cycling environment** than a trail lined with trees.

I rode a bike for decades without a brain bucket. There was little public awareness back then and it just was not something you could buy. Times changed and I eventually joined a cycling club **where you had to wear a helmet** to ride. So I tried it and now if I were to ride without one, **I would feel out of place, vulnerable.** You get used to it.

Not convinced? Well, I won't suggest you **hit yourself on the head with a 2x4,** but do you remember how it feels when you **smack your noggin on an upper shelf?** Not so pleasant an owie, eh? Now think about hitting it at **30 kilometres an hour.**

Helmet doing its job

Helmets also **reduce the amount of sun and bug bites you get.** (I use a visor on my helmet regardless of what roadies think is not aerodynamic or fashionable currently. I'm practical.) And **too much sun can later lead to skin cancer;** my dad got it playing tennis. Use a sunblock lotion with a rating of **SPF 30 or higher.**

Parents, the **Ontario law states your kids have to wear a helmet 'til they are eighteen,** then it's optional. You should **show by example.**

Another prudent good measure for your cycling well-being is wearing **padded cycling gloves.** Not only do

they help with **friction and vibrations from the handlebars,** they will spare your palms from **getting road rash** when you crash and your **hands instinctively reach** out to break your fall. I do not want to put fear into you. These measures **should do the opposite**—give you some **sense of**

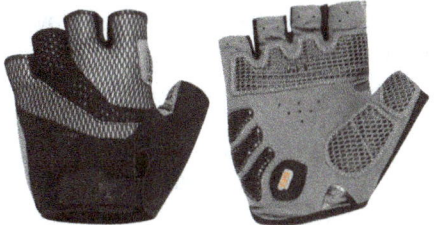

comfort and confidence. By following these **proactive safety tips, you lower the odds** of injury significantly (not entirely).

What is left in your safety cycling equation is **your cycling behaviour: how you manage and ride the terrain,** deal with obstacles, descend hills, and so on …and how you share the path with others. Do you know the rules of the road and what the signs mean? Do you follow them?

Finally, **ride within your ability, stay in control, and don't overdo it!** Improving your skills will pay off when you need to take evasive action. **Wear your helmet properly** so it works. Charge your light batteries so they are ready. **All the little safety things add up.**

Now you can relax, knowing you are making a conscious **effort to avoid injury,** so **you can continue to enjoy the sport you love** 'til you hit your 110th birthday.

eBikes- In Your Future?

Let me touch upon a few points regarding the **ever-evolving eBike universe** and why one could be good for you. I'll mention the **two types of electric motors** that are used and their pros and cons. And finally **where you can ride them,** and the basic laws in Ontario about using them.

Why you might want one...Eventually

I know some of us are wondering "Is now the time to get an eBike?" (or "Will I ever get one?") Shiny and new in bike stores, they certainly have added **more tech into cycling** than our trusty mechanical bikes at home.

Believing in the old adage **"If you don't use it, you'll lose it,"** I don't plan on getting one 'til I have to, and I'm in my sixties. But there might come a day when I still want to cycle, but may have more limited capacity due to aches and pains.

This is why I think eBikes are a great invention. They enable many people to ride who might not otherwise be able to, either **because of disabilities** or because they're getting on in years and **don't have the endurance** like they used to. It's wonderful to see how eBiking can extend a senior's cycling days to **continue to enjoy their pastime** and benefit their health.

Even if you don't have physical issues, you may still want to get an eBike because you can go **farther and faster** in a day than you can just with leg power. Hills become less of a consideration; you can take on more of them without bonking out. Bikepackers can take more with them on a trek and not be so weight conscious.

It also **helps you to keep up** with your cycling group (or a faster spouse who just can't wait). My wife bought one and she loves it. She even rides it to work some days without getting all sweaty. And if it starts to rain, it gets dark, or you have travelled too far, **give yourself an e-boost** and you're home in no time.

Definitely test ride a number of different models to see what you like and how it feels and handles. I've seen some very sleek road bikes that **you can hardly tell** are eBikes. Others are **built like tanks** for the outback and look it, too. Just remember: when the battery dies or you have to lift your bike into the house or onto a rack, **weight is always a consideration.**

Two Types of Motors

Though there are variations to this, the **two prominent styles** of electric bicycles are the **hub drive** and **mid drive** configurations. Here is what the differences are in motors and their riding characteristics.

Hub Drive

This is the **cheaper** method of motorizing a bicycle. The **motor is encased in the hub** of the rear wheel; some front wheel drive hubs exist, too. Even though there are gears on the rear wheel, the **motor runs independent** of what gear you pick when you are pedaling. Not so good on hills.

The effect is more like the bike pushes you and you **control the speed throttle** with a lever on your handlebar. **You don't need to pedal to activate the motor** but on battery power alone the ride will be short.

These are also **heavier bikes** and in turn come with **wider tires** and a heftier frame. They're **not as nimble** as you may wish when riding. The **quick acceleration** might be a little startling at first and the motor could be noisy.

Mid Drive

This type of electric bicycle has the motor down in the **centre crank assembly area** where you pedal. It's much more sophisticated and **smaller**. These are **pedal enabled/assited eBikes that only turn on while you are pedaling.**

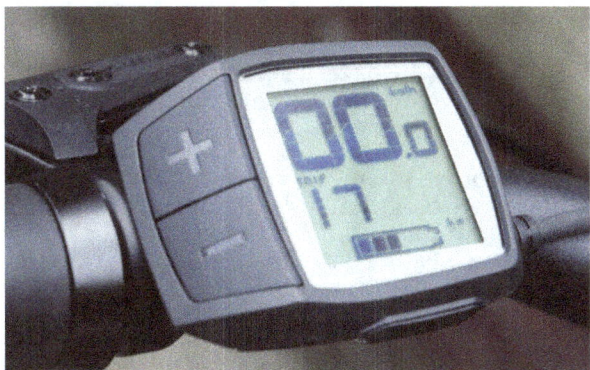

On the handlebar you **pick a power level** from Off up to Turbo, depending on how much extra **help you want with your pedal strokes.** A mid drive motor drives the crank and chain instead of turning the wheel itself. This **increases the torque and range** you can get if you select the best gearing to go faster or climb hills. It also extends the **battery efficiency.**

This design produces a more traditional cycling experience, with the motor assisting the rider pedaling. They are **lighter, well balanced,** and look and feel more like a regular bicycle. But with all that wonderful innovation comes a **higher ticket price.**

Battery Power

When you're shopping for your eBike, check how long the bike can go on a single charge. For many eBikes, you can expect a **70+ km** ride with moderate battery use (less if you're on Turbo all the time).

Although the heavy battery pack that powers the bike can be part of the rear carrier, it is **best mounted on the centre frame for balance.** These rechargeable batteries are expensive; you should be able to remove them for security and for charging elsewhere.

Battery range, weight, and costs are getting better every year. Right now, lithium battery packs are very expensive, at around **$1k to replace.**

Acceptance

eBikes have evolved in the last few years as **a more accepted means of transportation.** At first, politicians and the general public were curious about them, but **unsure what to make of them.** Many communities put the brakes on where you could use them. This uncertainty has now passed and in time I believe this will be a non-issue.

Most trails have taken down their signs and welcomed these new-fangled contraptions. (Of course, you should check to be sure.) There is still some **public resentment** among regular cyclists that you are **lazy riding an eBike.** Umm, maybe, but at least you're on a bike and not your couch. I say to those who may be a little judgy (or maybe envious?), don't jump to conclusions. Some eBike riders may have **hidden disabilities.**

I know many of you are considering buying an eBike and have asked me where you can and can't go. (I can't tell you; it's hard to track.) In general, **any public path or trail in Ontario allows eBikes** that meet **these provisions:**

- Looks similar to a standard bicycle with handlebars
- Motor engages only when a rider is pedalling
- Maximum power output of 500 watts
- Max speed is set at 32 kph (20 mph)

These are called "Pedelecs" or "Pedal Assisted Bicycles" or "Class 1 eBikes."

Naturally, if in doubt, go to the Ontario provincial or local government websites for clarification and current requirements. Some **local governments may add by-laws** of their own to limit use. The times are changing…and at times, **old signs are slow to come down.**

Europe has **electric kick scooters everywhere;** here, they are not allowed currently (2023) on any Toronto byways, yet they exist. Nor, technically, are **hub motorized eBikes** allowed on park trails.

With public acceptance, I hope these alternate means of transport get sorted out to **see more cars off the road.**

Signage Standards - Show Me the Way

The goal/purpose of good trail signs is to **guide you along a path in the right direction with the least amount of thought.**

If they're done well, your cycling experience will be **easy to navigate, making for a pleasant trip.** Likely **you won't even notice how smoothly you progressed** along the route.

If you feel like your ride is effortless—in terms of route finding, anyway—**you'll want to do it again.**

My hope in writing this book is to send cyclists to great trail destinations that provide directions they can follow without getting frustrated or worse, lost!

I've been cycling for decades and have ridden hundreds of Park, Rail and MTB trails/paths everywhere in the province. So **how successful are trail builders** at guiding us on these public recreational trailways? Here are my observations.

Let's look at the basic art and science of signage. As a **visual form of communication** for **fast-moving cyclists**, it **needs to be short and to the point**, using **symbols or words (or a combination of the two)** to get a message across.

Road riders benefit from a well-established, province-wide standardization of road signs that are universally known (more or less). **Riders can count on these road signs to guide them;** only the loneliest of dirt back roads might have signs missing.

On the other hand, **mountain bikers are used to having only a few signs** to guide them, maybe none, and **that's all part of the sport:** a sense of exploring the unknown, perhaps getting lost (hopefully briefly,

maybe a number of times), but we always find our way back eventually.

Park & Rail trail rides are somewhere in the middle, depending on where you go. **Because there are no provincial standards for trail signs, you never know what to expect** when you arrive at an unfamiliar trailhead.

Each city, borough, town, and county does its own thing. Then there are the standards set by **Ontario Parks, conservation authorities, and regional park systems.** All are slightly different in design and implementation.

What this means is that with nearly every new trail you ride, you'll have to learn the nuances of that site's particular signage language.

In the first few kilometres of riding, hopefully, you'll understand **how the signs are giving you guidance** as to where you are going, how far away things are, when to turn, and where there are other route options, sights to see, and exits and toilets (important).

You should be receiving **a periodic stream of info as you ride**; signs and map boards should **relay answers to your potential questions** and/or alert you to other dangers. This info **should require little effort to decipher**, based on the **average person's logical reasoning skills.**

When it works, it's a beautiful thing. Your afternoon spin is all the more enjoyable because **you never need to stop and question your whereabouts.** This should be a trail builder's goal, to **give you direction and confidence that you are headed the right way** and not towards a freeway onramp. **Consistent, predictable messaging** makes for a happy, safe, carefree cyclist.

If that objective is frequently not met, our blissful cruise can be interrupted often with **confusion and countless stops,** looking over maps, and swearing you will never return. (Or just swearing.)

Here in Ontario, signage is a mess.

It varies from **well done to a haphazard afterthought.** Too often on my way, I have noted **irregularities in trail signage** that had me unsure of where I was and where I was supposed to be going. Has this happened to you?

Earlier in the spring of 2023, I rode the **Rouge Valley Trail in Markham** to check on the status of the signage before I published this book. I wanted to check if they had improved their messaging since the last time I'd been there. They had actually **made it worse!** This is what finally prompted me to write about this topic. Now don't get me wrong, **I still enjoy every ride, no**

matter how confusingly it is laid out. Remember, I was into mountain biking back when we used a compass and luck to guide us.

But those of you buying this book may **have different, greater expectations.** You ride designated park paths and renovated rail trails, and you have the right to **expect that you won't get led astray.**

In reference to that Markham ride (or whatever it's called this week) and other inadequate locations, here are a few other sources of miscommunication I have encountered. Drum roll...

What's in a Name?

Unfortunately, many longer Rail Trail routes cross over numerous counties and communities, each of which wants to give **their portion of the trail a unique name.** This confuses riders when there's no visible change on the path. And it makes me **uncertain about what to call my reviews.**

So I wish that each trail would have **only one name, one I can remember to tell my friends about.** (Preferably a name that lasts and not a corporate sponsor or person who falls out of favour.) A descriptive name helps, and name the whole length of it the same.

Sign Installation and Maintenance

Sometimes, while riding along, I just know that a **landscape architect or the sign crew** installing the signposts and map boards **never tested their handiwork.** The signs fail to deliver.

You gotta wonder:

"Did anyone actually ride a bike the length of the route afterwards?"

The size of the sign, its placement, and how easy it is to read the messaging as you cycle past, are all important and **should be sorted on the trail, not on your office computer.**

On a trail that's short on signs, markers, and maps, riders may suffer from **gaps in the info flow** from one end to the other. Sometimes this is a **financing issue on a project that's not yet fully funded.** (On the other hand, I've also seen the opposite: **excessive signage,** which is **visual pollution and redundant.**)

Another potential problem is signs that have been vandalized, stolen, or sun-bleached or are simply outdated. These old or missing signs need replacing, but often there isn't the budget to carry this out. More gaps.

Here Is What Works

Nothing is perfect, but the **gold standard for bicycle trail design has to be Holland** (& Denmark). My trip there last year was an **eye-opener as to how well this can be done.** As you might guess, each country has **nationwide standards** for how bike signs are to look, and how they deliver their messages.

It's like everyone is working from the **same design manual** (because they are) when it comes to how different kinds of cycling messages are conveyed about **directions, current location, speed limits, traffic management, crossings, services, etc.**

Also consistent everywhere are the **size of the sign and maps, and what colours, fonts, and symbols are used.** Same with where signs are to be posted—**how high off the ground, how soon before a turn—and how often the messages are repeated, and so on.** It's been all tested and **worked out.**

As we were cycling in Holland, we soon learned that if we did not **see a waypoint sign as predicted,** we had most likely missed the last turnoff. And sure enough, that was the case, I might add not often and more our fault for looking elsewhere as tourists do.

That **commonality in what signs to look for** and **where they are expected to be** on the route, anywhere we went in the country, was key to enjoying our bike tour.

Weekend riders want to be lazy, **think less**, and ride on holiday mode. A ride should be a **getaway from life's busy schedule and hassles.** I get that: we all want to be guided down the path, **reassured that we are not lost,** and get prompted when to turn or watch out for something.

The solution can be **as simple as a painted line down the middle of the path.** This concept works so well for me and is **cheap to install.** You pedal away, carefree, following the line like a **trail of popcorn** until it stops, then you head back.

Uniform directional signs, with a simple message, easily understood with enough time to react, work. I think all trail junctures need a little map with **an arrow on it that states "You are Here."** This **confirms to riders the status of their current location** if in doubt and can help cyclists who wish to change plans.

Also nice to see are **small kilometre path markers** that tell you how far you have gone and how far you still have to go to get to the end.

Another example of efficiency (and fewer altercations) in Holland were **three separate designated routes.** One for cars, another for bikes and scooters, and the third for pedestrians.

Each has their own route and is not allowed to be on any other.

That way bikes don't slow down cars and walkers/hikers don't get in the way of bikes, and so forth. **It's organized, and it works.**

Yet in Ontario, when I see two paths in a park, there's **rarely a designated trail for each party.** Nope, they're just allowed to meander and use each other's lane.

QR code for the map

Walkers can be on the the boardwalk and bike path. Why both?

Silly Sign Syndrome

Adding just enough signage to do the job is a skill. **Humans are conditioned to read everything we see** in case it's important; it's a self-preservation thing. We live in a world where we **trust signs to be logical, consistent and give sound advice.**

And at the receiving end of a trail sign message, we have to **interpret the message correctly.** Yet some signs make me wonder,

"What were they thinking?"

I can't reason out the logic in why they exist. Could it be **liability, complaints, a make-work project** for the sign dept? LOL. Hmm, who knows. But I am starting to see **unnecessary, redundant signage I question.**

Signs stating the obvious are annoying. Are they really necessary? I wonder **how stupid some sign makers think cyclists are. (Apparently very.)** It is **insulting to the average bike rider** to have these signs pop up like weeds.

Here are a few favourites:

Slow Down!

Reading this suggests that we are all speeding, no matter at what speed. What my wife suggests is that the sign actually reads:

No Speeding! or Don't Speed!

See how that changes the tone and who this directive is meant for.

Cyclists Dismount

- I have seen this posted on hills, before bridges, and at intersections. Most of the time I, and other riders, carry on. We all have learned over the years **how to manage, thank you.** For me, sizing up the situation, I see **no reason to dismount.**

I have seen way more death-defying trails on my MTB. I am quite capable of riding down a steep, paved hill (that's the fun part!). Or crossing a bridge or an intersection with traffic.

I am not sure what **tiny percentage of beginner cyclists** need these signs. To the point, **if you can't handle the trail, then you're not ready.** You are welcome back when you can.

Yield to Pedestrians

- For the most part in my travels, I've encountered **very few cyclists who misbehave**. So the **abundance of signs** (again in Markham) **reminding us to play nice on the trail** with people walking is overdone, if not necessary.

Sure, there are riders who don't yield—but **would these signs change their ways?**

There is this concept of **Shared Use, Shared Responsibility.** Yet **the onus seems to be on cyclists to watch out** for free-roaming people: few signs tell **pedestrians to look out for themselves** and bicycles.

Walkers can have earbuds in, stare at their phones, and walk about without a care. More signs need to tell them to pay attention, **stay to the right so we can pass,** or to use the other path. Now that would **balance trail ownership** a bit more.

Overdone!

With that said, not all signs are by-laws. They could be "suggestions." You decide what is the appropriate action for your situation, for the traffic on the path, and for your own health. I**f a bridge is busy or a hill is slippery, then yes, it could be time to walk it.**

I'll leave you with **one more scenario.** I was humming along the **Millennium RT** near **Picton.** Out in the **middle of nowhere**, pedalling through a wooded swampy section all alone, with no traffic, no cross-roads. Suddenly I see a sign posted...

Maximum 10 KPH

What? I don't even know how slow that is on my bike and more importantly, **Why?** Later, I found out that turtles and snakes cross there and the sign is directed more to the ATV crowd.

This sign was just confusing, and **there was no follow-up to explain it.** You see, **we need to reason out a message** to decide if we are to **obey it or question** its statement. Going that slowly there seemed bizarre; there was **not enough information** posted for me to make an **educated choice.** (No critters got harmed, only mosquitoes.)

Carpooling Concepts

If you're not riding your bicycle to get to the trailhead, you will **need to plan another way to get there.** And since my books send riders off to all parts of Ontario, I hope you can **make your travels as eco-friendly as possible** to reduce pollution, the number of cars on the road, and the cost of expensive fuel.

Your choices are **buses** (city & regional), **trains** (& subway & GO trains) and **planes** (for those who can ;^). All are possibilities.

Buses and train service, sadly, has diminished for decades, but if you're able to use it, you can often **avoid traffic jams, relax,** and stare out the window while **some else does the driving.**

If you can make the connections work, they offer solutions. Use them both ways, or on the way out and ride back the other direction, if you are up to it.

LET'S GO GREEN

If you drive to the start of a point-to-point ride, you can also **use public transit to get back to the trailhead** before you get in your car to drive home. (A couple I know would ride to the airport, box their bikes, fly to Europe, and ride out from that airport, to start their bike tour. How cool!)

The customary means of transportation will be a **car/van/pickup truck** (either your own, or a **rental for the day**).

Let me offer you a few ideas on some **carpooling and shuttling scenarios.** We're going to assume that whatever vehicle you use can **carry your bike and a few others.** The more carrying capacity each vehicle has in these scenarios, the more open your options are.

1 Carpooling

- The most common scenario is for everyone to **meet at a carpool parking lot** by a highway interchange or other predetermined parking lot central to where everyone lives.

Here they all pile into one or two vehicles with their bikes and head off out of town to the trailhead. This works just fine if the bike ride for the day is a **loop.**

The problem with **linear Park or Rail trails is that they don't loop**. So how does one **see more landscape and not ride the same route twice?** You could hit the **sideroads** to find your way back, but this could make that kind of loop **too long or just is not appealing.**

2 Rider Double Backs

- Another concept is **each driver has to ride back before the halfway point** along the route to then **drive their car to the trail endpoint**. The rest of the cycling group continues on to the end and waits for their lift to arrive and then everyone heads home.

This scenario **enables most cyclists to continue one way along the full length** of the path with only the driver(s) having to double back at some timely moment on the trail. Drivers will need to factor in the **return time to their vehicles** and the **drive time to the endpoint.**

This could continue for a **multi-day trip**, where each day there is a **different driver to do the car shuttling;** that person only rides the first part of the trail that day.

3 Designated Driver

 - A variation of this is where the **driver(s) are not cyclists** and drive to the endpoint after **dropping rides off at the start**. They might be **friends/spouses joining the trip** who prefer to do other things during your ride and meet up with you later.

Again, for a multi-day trip, if your group does not have designated drivers for the trip, **cyclists can alternate who sacrifices a day off** or wants a rest day and does the driving.

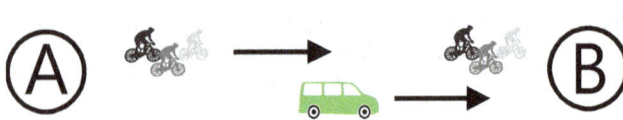

4 Vehicle Shuttling

- This last scenario is **a little convoluted but works. Best when there are just two riders**, or if **everyone** wants the luxury of **cycling together the whole length at once**. And there also are **cars/vans that can carry all the bikes and riders back.**

Vehicles meet at the closest end of the route, **point A.** Let's say **two cars and a van.** Two drivers head with their **car and van to endpoint B** while the rest of the riders have to wait (more coffee & muffins) or arrive later. Drivers should also **leave their bikes** back with the group waiting.

At **point B** the vehicle that can shuttle all the riders and bikes back is left there. That driver gets a **ride back to point A in the smaller car.** Once they return to A everything is set up for **everyone to enjoy the ride together, one way.**

When the ride group gets to **point B, they use the vehicle left there to shuttle them and their bikes back to A** and their cars. As you can tell, not the best scenario as it **adds extra time** to set up and **at least two vehicles burn gas for twice the length of the trail**. OK for a day ride, but over a few days, why bother? **Pick #2 or #3 as a better strategy.**

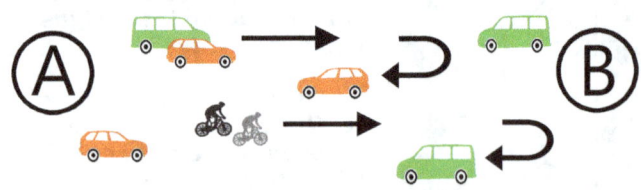

Or, as an upgrade, you could **hire a bike touring company** with a "sag wagon" as support to carry your group's gear and help with breakdowns (or with tired legs, sagging behind.) Now everyone gets to ride—at a price. This is the reason touring businesses exist: to lighten your load and take care of the logistics.

BTW you can apply these concepts for a hiking or Nordic ski group outing. And with less gear, it is easier to plan.

photo - Paulo LaBerge

Bikepacking Basics

Flipping through this book, you might be getting ideas to **expand your rides further.** Perhaps it is time to take on **more challenging quests** than a flat Rail Trail. You could add on a few dirt/gravel backroads and make it a loop, turning it into an overnight trek or longer. If that **urge to explore and rough it a bit is appealing** to you and your mates, read on.

The Bikepacking Concept

In the last decade **Bikepacking has emerged as another form of bike touring,** similar in concept, yet different in many ways. Unlike travelling busy highways on thin shoulders doing 80+ km a day, **bikepacking follows a less travelled route, at a slower pace.**

Similar to backpacking on a hiking trail, but done on a bicycle, it's a combination of **singletrack trails, dirt paths, gravel sideroads, and Rail Trails**—anything that allows you to keep moving while **avoiding busy highways**—with few worries about traffic mishaps. The journey will require a sturdy bike and more effort on slower terrain.

With little traffic or noise to distract, you enjoy **a more scenic, immersed experience** with your surroundings. Self-reliant, you carry the essentials on your bike as you **test your stamina and skills on ever-changing terrain.** You can take on the role of a **modern explorer.**

Travelling off the beaten path requires a different kind of bike and bags from traditional road touring. Let's look at what you should use.

Which Bike to Use

Since most bikepacking routes cover unpaved gravel and dirt roads, there will be loose grit, sand, potholes, and puddles. Some lonely backroads may have larger rocks, mud, washboarding, and steeper climbs than better-travelled roads. Singletrack trails in the woods can mean increased climbs, lumps, and bumps.

The bike you use needs to have **wide tires with ample tread** for the terrain and a solid bike frame that can take the knocks and hold on to your bags. Either a **gravel bike** or a **mountain bike** could work.

A hardtail MTB or hybrid bike with a **front shock might be ideal**; even an old rigid-framed MTB could work out. It depends **how much comfort you seek.** Just be sure, before you leave, that **your rig is all tuned up** with no known issues.

Whatever bike you use, it needs to have **low enough gears to take on the climbs,** fully loaded. Again, a mountain bike is well suited for the job, or a **fatbike,** if you dare to do a winter trek or, in summer, might wander into soft boggy/sandy areas.

How to Pack

Bags for bikepacking are configured a little differently than those for trippin'. Because the ride will be more bumpy, a bag hanging out from the seat post will **stay attached better** than saddlebags clipped on a rack. It also will not **catch onto branches** going down a narrow path. The other common choice is a **triangular tube bag** in the centre frame. **Heavier items** fare well here, near the **centre of gravity.**

photo - Paulo LaBerge

A water bottle on the frame and **water in a bladder in your backpack** is one way to configure it. Another bag **strapped to your handlebars** and even **smaller bags tied to your forks** are other ways bikepackers configure and carry their load.

There is no set way to do it—everyone is free to **do their own thing and customize.** Even making your own bags and attaching them on with tape, straps, or bungee cords is cool for an overnight. No need to spend lots of money; **it's a low tech, simple back-to-the-land vibe.**

What to Bring

Where you're going, and for how long, will set the tone for what you need to bring. (Not want, but need, as **weight is always a consideration on any bike trip.**)

You need to carry a **small bike repair kit** and pump, that's a given. Going further into the wilds of Ontario might prompt you to add a few extra items just in case—**quick link, derailleur hanger, spokes, brake cable**… A **first aid kit** is also advised. Then there are the core items you will always bring: **wallet, phone with battery pack, headlamp, sunglasses, sun and bug lotion, maybe a camera/GoPro.**

A simple overnight trek with plans to **eat out and sleep at a B&B/motel** could require just a change of clothes, rain gear, water, snacks, and your **credit card.** You will need to bring more supplies if you want to rough it or if you'll be riding through a place with few support services like convenience stores, food marts, and campgrounds.

The next decision is whether you will **cook meals but still sleep under a roof,** or bring a **tent and camp out,** too. Most bikepackers go this way, whether it's in keeping with the flavour of **riding off the grid** or because of tight budgets and remote locations.

If you're **bikepacking in the Ontario backcountry,** it's not like road touring. You may go hours between any chances to find provisions. If you are traveling solo, then **you need to carry everything:** stove, cookware, fuel, food, and first aid and bike repair kits.

If you're camping, a tent, sleeping bag, and mattress will add bulk; look for the **most compact and light items** you can afford, and make sure they're **rated for cold nights/wet days.** Do your research in finding what is best. Some campers bring an **ultralight folding chair** as a nice frill that feels luxurious after a long day.

Plan Your Trip

Here is where you and the buds have to **agree on the level of difficulty** you want to tackle. Much of **southern Ontario is laid out in a grid.** Country gravel roads tend to be flat and straight the more west you go. They're pretty easy to map out—and maybe a little dull.

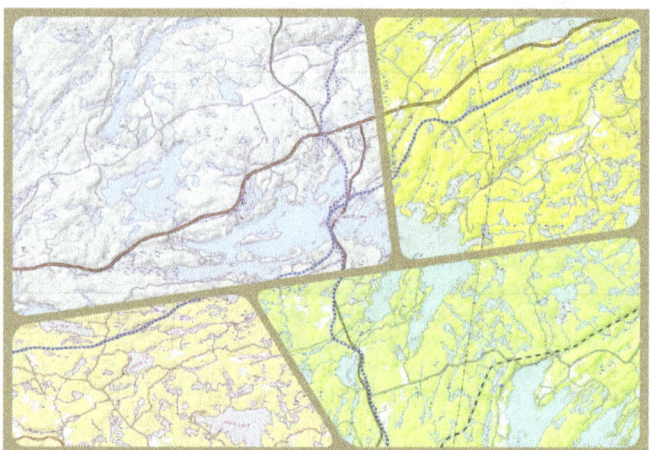

Closer to **Georgian Bay,** and north of **Peterborough or Kingston,** the terrain gets more hilly and roads start to wind and get more interesting. More adventurous riders (with good suspension) may find riding the **dirt logging roads** up by **Algonquin Park** and further north to your liking. If you look on detailed maps, they are everywhere—up in **North Bay, Timmins, all the way to Manitoba.**

Rail Trails are like **car-free cycling highways** that cover long distances. They're mostly flat, though some are rougher than others. There are a few MTB locations with cross-country type trails (**Kolapore, Oro, Haliburton, Larose, Ganaraska, Limerick**) that you perhaps could work into your ride, but not many, as most concentrate their loops in one tight area.

Perhaps hiking trails and logging roads could connect. **ATV trails** may be an option, but they can be noisy, dusty, rutted affairs. A **snowmobile path won't be suitable in summer:** these are often built on uneven ground that crosses marshes and frozen waterways in the winter, relying on snow to cover up problems.

I think **one reason bikepacking has taken off** is the multitude of **online resources, portable phones, and GPS devices** riders can use to plan and travel with. **This has opened up so many ways to find routes** and stay on them while travelling. And, most importantly, you can **check the weather,** as long as you've got a cell connection..

A few notable resources are bikepacking.com, gaia. com, trailforks.com, openstreetmaps.com, and windy. com.

One of the best ways of planning a trip is to **use a template from someone else's experience** so you're not the first one in. Then again, you might want to

break trail and be the first one to explore and make a claim to a new route you could **share online.**

A small problem with bikepacking is the question of **where to leave your car when you're gone for more than one day.** Most areas have **bylaws that prohibit you from parking overnight** without getting a fine or towed. It would be best to inquire with the **local town officials** where it may be possible to park for a few nights, maybe at a **community centre or a designated public lot.**

Your First Trip

Best you learn to swim in the shallow end: start with a simple, **short overnight trek to a nearby place** you are familiar with. You are more interested in **how well your setup performs and how the bike handles** than the scenery. Do the bags stay on the bike from all the vibrations? Tighten straps or buy better suited bags. Are you comfortable and in control of the bike? Shift around your bags (and what's in them) to **balance out the ride.**

Once you refine your setup and **work out the bugs,** you are set to take on grander plans and cycle further into the hinterland. I hope this piques your interest to look into the possibilities, as it has mine.

After riding and reviewing **every significant trail/ path in Ontario** (180), bikepacking seems to be **the next natural direction I am heading.** I just bought myself a hybrid gravel 1x10 bike with a front and seat shock. With my years of camping/canoeing experience and my new bags, **I am keen to see where I go** here in the province and elsewhere.

photo - Paulo LaBerge

photo - Paulo LaBerge

Bike Trails Elsewhere

As the book comes to a close, I think it's fitting to send you off **beyond Ontario**. My three books pretty much cover all the good trails that currently exist in the province; now, **let's look elsewhere.**

Curiosity and a sense of adventure may have you wondering **where in this world one can ride** some decent bicycle trails. Depending on whether you don't mind some gravel under your wheels or you prefer pavement, there's a lot out there to be found.

I've always dreamed of how intriguing it would be to **fly out every weekend to a new North American city.** You could bring your bike or rent one, ride the designated bike paths, and do the tourist thing. It has to be **the best way to see a place.**

On a bike, you can ride and park freely anywhere. It's **faster than walking** and you're not confined in a car. There's **never a traffic jam**, parking fee, or a need to fill up on gas. When you see a lookout, beach, cafe, patio… **you just pull over.** No better way to **be a carefree tourist.**

An extravagant and expensive thought this may be, yet occasionally it can be done. With a little **planning and research** on your chosen destination, you can plan a **weekend riding itinerary starting from your hotel** (which might rent bikes), and fan out to a few favourite sights. Most tourist spots have bike paths leading to them. This is not a coincidence.

Holland - The best bike network in the world!

Research Sources

Look up **city and regional tourism websites** to find suggestions for **self-guided, signposted official bike paths** and itineraries. Scrutinizing **Google Maps** or **OpenStreetMap** with the **bike trail layer turned** on can reveal some good rides. And of course, what **cycling mates, bike clubs**, and online **route tracking sites** suggest are good leads too.

Bike route guide books and websites exist for provinces, states, and whole countries, if you are up for that large a tour. You can buy specialized field guides for bike touring in specific places; there are whole books each for the **Rhine, Loire**, and **Danube**

Rivers, as they tend to have few hills and lots of towns along them. For more hills and incredible scenery, you can get guides for regions like **Tuscany, Provence**, and **the Swiss Alps.**

Even **bike touring sites** can give you clues, but now you are getting away from self-guided thinking. This may happen if you find **you have more money than time** to do the planning leg work. Then sign up and treat yourself to the real leg work … on your bike, in some fantastic place.

Last year I did a **Bike and Barge** tour of **southern Holland.** This is a cool concept where you ride every day and meet up every evening with your moving accommodation—a sleek riverboat—in a new town for dinner and a sleepover. This package is just one example of the many different ways cycling and tourism can blend; there could also be a **hiking, canoeing, or snorkelling** component to your travels. You can buy into this kind of package, or make up your own tour.

Doing Your Holidays

There is just **one key piece of advice** I want to state. It is far better to **use up your time at home sorting out your trip** in advance than to try to organize things once you've left home. This can be a real **vacation time waster** and downer. Don't wait until you're away in a foreign land to work out those loose ends.

Sure, you can sit in your hotel room using the free wi-fi to sort out your daily itinerary, looking up **where to go, how to get there, what to see, when it opens, and what it costs, then booking tickets.** But why would you leave this homework for the last minute, when you're already on "holiday time?" **Holidays are when you do things, not read about them.**

Here is a recent example that we didn't even realize would be a hassle: **public transit.** As tech keeps changing (and likely prompted by the recent pandemic), **you can no longer buy a paper ticket** to ride a train, or toss some change into the receptacle as you board the city bus. **You have to buy tickets with your phone.** On our last trip, every city we went required us to download a transit app, create an account, and confirm our email address before we could even **get a ticket for a day trip.**

Here is a short list of places I've been to or heard of that are **worthy of investigating** to get you started. These are bicycle trails/paths with the least amount of road riding involved (just how we like 'em).

For bicycle trails (not road riding; that is another list altogether), these **Ontario cities** are better and more bike friendly than most - Toronto, Mississauga, Ottawa, Kitchener, London, Guelph

Elsewhere in Canada, bike paths in **these cities rank favourably** for a visit - Montreal, Victoria, Vancouver, Saskatoon, Calgary, Halifax, Charlottetown, Fredericton, Moncton, St. John's

Listed by Province:

NFLD

The T'Railway is a very long (883 km) wilderness Rail trail that cuts across the middle of the island.

Nova Scotia

A very long Rail trail in various states of development circles the peninsula. Around **Halifax**, the **Annapolis Valley**, and **Cape Breton**, parts of the route are resurfaced for gravel bikes.

PEI

Confederation Trail - 449 km is an easy-going level rail trail that branches out in all directions across the island.

New Brunswick

Grand Manan Island - 70 km of shoreline on 18 bike trails

Quebec

Montreal has excellent waterfront trails and canals to explore, plenty there for a long weekend.
P'tit Train du Nord (The Little Train of the North) is a favourite 234 km Rail trail that heads north of Montreal into the Laurentians, with lots of amenities to support it.
Véloroute des Bleuets (Blueberry Route) 256 km bike path/road around Lac Saint-Jean
Petit-Témis 134 km Rail Trail from Rivière-du-Loup to Edmundston, NB

Ontario

Toronto GTA and **Ottawa** have the largest cycling networks, as you may know. **London** and **Kitchener** have enough for a few days' visit.

Saskatchewan

Saskatoon - 105 km Meewasin Valley river route

Alberta

Calgary - About 850 km of bike trails; try the Bow to the Elbow River on to Glenmore Reservoir.
Iron Horse Rail Trail - is a 300 km long, multi-use recreational gravel MTB route in NE Alberta; you can start from Edmonton
Banff National Park - Rocky Mountain Legacy paved 22 km and Goat Creek trail for a gravel/MTB outside of the town of Banff

BC

Vancouver - Stanley Park Seawall, Seaside Greenway, Central Valley Greenway and Jericho Beach to UBC - Pacific Spirit Regional Park
Port Coquitlam - Traboulay PoCo Trail

Vancouver Island - Cowichan Valley Trail, the Kinsol Trestle is one of the world's largest wooden bridges
Victoria - Galloping Goose Trail, E&N Rail Trail, Colquitz Creek, Lochside Regional Trail
Kettle Valley Rail Trail at 600 km is a spectacular ride full of tunnels and high trestle bridges
Northstar Rail Trail 25 km from Kimberly to Cranbrook

Kettle Valley trail Kelowna

USA:

American cities with good cycling networks - Portland, San Francisco, San Jose, Minneapolis, Philadelphia, Seattle, Denver, Boston, Sacramento, Washington DC, Salt Lake City, Pittsburgh, Austin

Empire State Trail - 1200 km from Buffalo to NYC, encompassing the Erie Canalway, Hudson Valley Greenway, and Champlain Valley trails.
Great Allegheny Passage RT - 240 km from Cumberland, MD, to Pittsburgh, PA
Little Miami Scenic Trail (Ohio) - 125 km Springfield to Newtown, OH
Greenbrier River Trail (West Virginia) - 123 km from Cass to Caldwell, WV
Katy Rail Trail (Missouri) - 385 km from Machens to Clinton, MO

If you want to see **how cities in the world rate** in terms of bike-friendliness, look up "Copenhagenize Index" and "People for Bikes City Ratings" online - fascinating!

I can tell you already that **Holland** and **Denmark** are consistently **top picks**, and my experience there agrees with the masses. A cycling holiday there is sure to please, if the weather behaves.

The Canadian - **Trans Canada Trail** and **BC Rail Trails** and the American - **Rail to Trails Conservancy** are good sources for Rail trail ideas.

There are so many! I could go on, but it's the end of the book. And it's time for us both to get a ride in...**may the weather be on your side and the wind at your back.**

About the Author

When **Dan Roitner** became a teen, he bought himself a 10-speed bicycle and began to ride farther than in his childhood days of going around the block. Now he could get to the schoolyard, the mall, and the movies (the Fox Theatre).

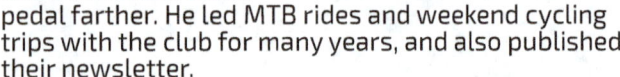

But it wasn't until he joined the Toronto Bicycling Network (TBN) cycling club in his mid-30s that he started to pedal farther. He led MTB rides and weekend cycling trips with the club for many years, and also published their newsletter.

In the last three decades, he has been expanding his cycling universe. He has ridden every major Park path, Rail bikeway, and MTB trail in the province, and on his vacations, he's travelled on bike paths in Vancouver, Calgary, Montreal, Boston, Denver, and San Francisco, and toured as far away as Holland, Denmark, and France.

With his background as a retired photographer and skills in graphic design, layout and mapping, he launched a website in 2013 - **ontariobiketrails.com.** From that humble beginning, he has shared over 150 new locations to ride and has published three guidebooks (including this most recent one) on Ontario bike trail destinations.

He started as a road rider, then fell for mountain biking (no major injuries, lol) and is now migrating to gravel rides and bikepacking treks farther afield.

Dan also manages a sister site, **ontarioskitrails.com,** to stay busy and fit in the winter with Nordic skiing and snowshoeing.

Dan is now retired and lives north of the Toronto Beaches area with his wife Teresa Lohan, his son Trevor, and their cat. Some of his other pastimes are gardening, baking, home handyman, photo & video editing, electronic music production, and board games.

Acknowledgements

Books, especially factual ones, are detailed, time-consuming monsters! What may seem like a few months of research and writing will stretch out to more in no time.

In publishing jargon, this is officially a **self-published** book, yet I didn't do this alone, and I should not overlook those around me who made the task easier. My thanks to:

My parents, long gone, who let me follow my own path. As uncertain as it may have seemed to them, it did lead to success. My Dad, a weekend writer himself, showed me the way.

At home, my wife **Teresa** and my son **Trevor** were willing to follow me for years on new bike trails (and be subjects in my photos). Many of our vacations were planned around scouting new trails; I think all of these were memorable times, and I hope Teresa and Trevor agree.

During the prolonged production of the book, they were supportive and patient. Their understanding on the homefront freed me to focus on all the book's moving parts. Teresa helped at the end to output the elevation graphs.

This is my second book with my **talented editor, Jen Groundwater**. She has been a perfect fit for this guide and **invaluable** in massaging (as I would describe it) my text to a finer standard.

I also wish to acknowledge the open-source community that enabled me to produce this volume with free software, without which the costs to publish a book on this niche topic would have been prohibitive.

I thank the Ontario government (MNR) mapping services and all the contributors on OpenStreetMap for sharing their mapping data. Sorting out the history of individual rail lines was made easier (not easy) with information found on Wikipedia, Charles Cooper's Rail Pages, and Old Time Trains.

I would also like to **thank all my cycling friends**, some who are in the pages of this book and others from my past. Your company and comments along the way have enriched my cycling life.

You can **contact Dan by email** at -staff@ontariobiketrails.com

My Other Two Books

If you liked this book, check out the two other trail guides in the series.

- They are available as **eBooks** on my website - ontariobiketrails.com
- You can purchase them in **paperback** from **Amazon.ca** or **Indigo/Chapters**, or order one through your local bookstore

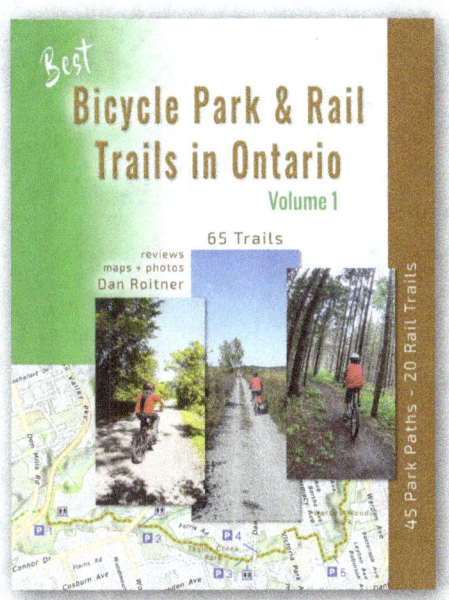

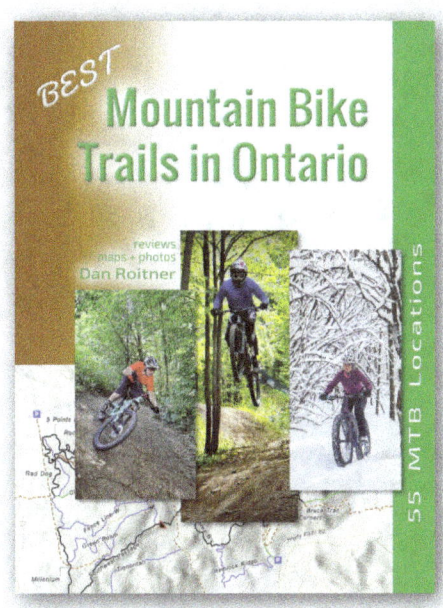

Bonus eBook Download

If you own a paperback copy of this book, you are welcome to **download a free PDF** version of this guide to take with you on your phone or tablet. Visit this web page - **ontariobiketrails.com/pr2** for the download link.

I ask that you respect the **enormous amount of work** spent creating this book and do not share the file around. Just because you can doesn't mean you should. **Please don't be a bike pirate!**

the end